The Asyut Project

Edited by
Jochem Kahl, Ursula Verhoeven
and Mahmoud El-Khadragy

Volume 2

2012
Harrassowitz Verlag · Wiesbaden

Seven Seasons at Asyut

First Results of the Egyptian-German Cooperation in Archaeological Fieldwork

Proceedings of an International Conference at the University of Sohag, 10th–11th of October, 2009

Edited by
Jochem Kahl, Mahmoud El-Khadragy,
Ursula Verhoeven and Andrea Kilian

2012
Harrassowitz Verlag · Wiesbaden

Publication of this volume has been made possible by the generous funding of the Deutsche Forschungsgemeinschaft (German Research Foundation).

Illustration on the cover (montage of a drawing with a photo): Ammar Abu Bakr.

Bibliografische Information der Deutschen Nationalbibliothek
Die Deutsche Nationalbibliothek verzeichnet diese Publikation in der Deutschen Nationalbibliografie; detaillierte bibliografische Daten sind im Internet über http://dnb.d-nb.de abrufbar.

Bibliographic information published by the Deutsche Nationalbibliothek
The Deutsche Nationalbibliothek lists this publication in the Deutsche Nationalbibliografie; detailed bibliographic data are available in the internet at http://dnb.d-nb.de.

For further information about our publishing program consult our website http://www.harrassowitz-verlag.de

Printed on permanent/durable paper.
Printing and binding: Memminger MedienCentrum AG
Printed in Germany

ISSN 1865-6250
ISBN 978-3-447-06529-0

Sohag University: Opening speech by Prof. Mahmoud El-Khadragy (left).

Participants of the excursion to Gebel Asyut al-gharbi.

Contents

Preface ... ix

JOCHEM KAHL
Asyut and The Asyut Project ... 1

MAHMOUD EL-KHADRAGY
The Nomarchs of Asyut During the First Intermediate Period and the Middle Kingdom ... 31

URSULA VERHOEVEN
The New Kingdom Graffiti in Tomb N13.1: An Overview ... 47

SAMEH SHAFIK
Epigraphic Work at Asyut ... 59

MEIKE BECKER
The Reconstruction of Tomb Siut II from the Middle Kingdom ... 69

MONIKA ZÖLLER-ENGELHARDT
Wooden Models from Asyut's First Intermediate Period Tombs ... 91

ANDREA KILIAN
Pottery Offering Trays: General Observations and New Material from Asyut ... 105

ABD EL-NASER YASIN
An Overview of Islamic Pottery ... 119

MAGDALENA PATOLLA
Human Bones from Tombs of the Old Kingdom ... 129

AHMED A. EL-KHATIB
Historic Plant Records from Tombs of Gebel Asyut al-gharbi ... 143

Plates ... 147

Preface

On the 10th of October 2009, at the University of Sohag, the members of The Asyut Project had the pleasure of presenting some of the aims and results of their long term Egyptian-German project on the ancient necropolis of Asyut during a conference entitled "The Asyut Project - Seven Seasons of Egyptian-German Cooperation in Archaeological Fieldwork". This international and interdisciplinary meeting could be realized only because of the fruitful cooperation between several persons and institutions:

Professor Mohamed Sayed Ibrahim overtook a memorandum between the Sohag University and the Johannes Gutenberg-University (JGU) of Mainz from 2008; he has been very interested in our work and has supported our team on several occasions, last but not least in form of this conference. He enabled us to use a wonderful congress hall for this event, and provided us with all the facilities that we needed. We enjoyed the benefits of perfect organization, and our thanks are due not only to him but also to the staff of the university who worked on the preparations for several weeks in the background.

Financial support for the conference was provided by the Egyptological department of the JGU Mainz.

The bulk of the work in arranging this conference in Sohag lay of course in the hands of Professor Mahmoud El-Khadragy and his team, namely Professor Ahmed A. El-Khatib. All of the participants have to thank them most deeply for their immense efforts.

The conference was accompagnied by two documentary films made by Ammar Abu Bakr M.A., artist at Luxor University, to whom we would like to express our gratitude for presenting our work and the Asyutian artefacts in such a fascinating and evocative manner.

On the second day of the conference there was an excursion to the Gebel Asyut al-gharbi to visit the site itself and to discuss various features of the tombs with the scientific community of guests and participants.

The preparation of this volume laid in the hands of Andrea Kilian and we would like to thank the publishers Otto Harrassowitz for their support. For advice regarding English the "Übersetzernetzwerk" (Jörn Schüler, Mannheim) deserves to be mentioned. Some of the results of the 2010 season have been incorporated in this volume, although the title of the book refers to only "Seven Seasons in Asyut" which are those of 2003-2009. We would like to list briefly the development of the project over this period, together with the people and institutions involved:

- 2003: Survey mission to Asyut by J. Kahl, M. El-Khadragy
- 2004: Fieldwork season financed by JGU Mainz and Westfälische Wilhelms-Universität Münster. J. Kahl, M. El-Khadragy, U. Verhoeven

- 2005-2007: Short term project at JGU Mainz financed by the German Research Foundation (DFG). Project Director: U. Verhoeven, Field Directors: J. Kahl, M. El-Khadragy
- Since 2008: Long term project at JGU Mainz financed by DFG. Project Director: U. Verhoeven, Field Directors: J. Kahl, M. El-Khadragy
- Since 2010: Long term project at Freie Universität Berlin and JGU Mainz financed by DFG. Project Directors: J. Kahl, U. Verhoeven; Field Directors: J. Kahl, M. El-Khadragy, M. Abdelrahiem.

We are very much indebted to these universities and especially to the German Research Foundation. Such extensive fieldwork would not have been possible without their financial backing.

During these first seven years of The Asyut Project the cooperation between the Egyptian, German and other international colleagues has been outstanding. We would like to thank all the researchers, assistants, students and specialists, as well as the workers and the other people involved, for their extensive contributions and their commitment. Every year the season in the gebel has started in the middle of August which has meant that the daily work has not been easy for both Egyptian and European team members.

This is also the occasion to thank all the people who have supported and enabled our work during these years. We are greatly indebted to the Ministry of Antiquity and the Supreme Council of Antiquities, particularly Dr. Zahi Hawass, Dr. Sabri Abd El-Aziz, Dr. Magdy El-Ghandour and Dr. Mohamed Ismail; the General Directors of Middle Egypt, the late Mr. Samir Anis Salib and Dr. Abdel-Rahman El-Aidi; the Director General of Asyut, Mr. Abd El-Satar Ahmed Mohamed, and his predecessors Mr. Ahmed El-Khatib, Mr. Hani Sadek Metri and the late Mr. Mohamed Abd El-Aziz; the inspector of the magazine at Shutb, Mrs. Nadja Naguib; the accompanying inspectors Emad Bostan Ata, Rageh Darwish Khalaf, Magdy Shaker, Mohamed Mustafa Al-Shafey, Ahmed Abd-Alrahim Abd-Almagid and Adly Garas Matta; the head of the restorers, Mr. Mohamed Salah, and the restorers Ahmed Abd El-Dayem Mohamed, Khalid Gomaa Sayed, Gamal Abd El-Malik Abd El-Moneam, Naglaa Abd El-Motty Fathy, Helal Qeli Attalaa, Mahmoud Hasan Mohamed Sallam, Abir Mohamed Ali Mosa and Nagla El-Rage.

Finally, our fieldwork would never have enjoyed any success without the efficacious support of the local ghafirs, especially the *Urgestein* Quraim (Mohamed Saad Moursi), or without that of the police and the military, of Reis Ahmed Atitou and Reis Zekry who supervised the numerous workmen, and of Sobhey and Salama, our drivers.

We simply cannot thank them enough and we hope that we will have the pleasure of continuing to work together for many years to come.

Mainz, May 2011

Jochem Kahl, Mahmoud El-Khadragy, Ursula Verhoeven, Andrea Kilian

List of participants of the Asyut Project 2003-2009 in chronological order:

Mahmoud El-Khadragy, Egyptologist (2003-2009)
Jochem Kahl, Egyptologist (2003-2009)
Mahmoud El-Hamrawi, Egyptologist (2003)
Sameh Shafik, epigrapher (2003, 2005-2009)
Eva-Maria Engel, archaeologist (2003-2005)
Ursula Verhoeven, Egyptologist (2004-2009)
Ulrike Fauerbach, surveyor (2004-2006)
Monika Zöller, Egyptologist (2004-2008)
Yasser Mahmoud Hussein, Egyptologist (2004-2008)
Omar Nour El-Din, Egyptologist (2004)
Meike Becker, Egyptologist (2005-2008)
Dietrich Klemm, geologist (2005)
Rosemarie Klemm, Egyptologist (2005)
Christiane Dorstewitz, student of Egyptology (2005)
Diana Kleiber, student of Egyptology (2005)
John Moussa Iskander, Egyptologist (2005, 2007)
Ilona Regulski, epigrapher (2006-2007)
Ammar Abu Bakr, draughtsman (2006-2009)
Fritz Barthel, photographer (2006, 2007)
Hazim Saleh Abdallah, Egyptologist (2006-2007)
Eva Gervers, student of Egyptology (2006-2009)
Andrea Kilian, Egyptologist (2006-2009)
Mohamed Naguib Reda, Egyptologist (2006-2007)
Laura Sanhueza-Pino, student of Egyptology (2006-2008)
Abd El-Naser Yasin, Islamic Studies (2007-2009)
Jan Moje, Egyptologist (2007)
Manja Maschke, surveyor (2007-2008)
Magdalena Patolla, anthropologist (2007-2009)
Ibrahim Kedees, Egyptologist (2007-2008)
Hytham Aly Madkour, Egyptologist (2007-2008)
Ahmed Ali El-Khatib, botanist (2008-2009)
Hesham Faheed Ahmed, Egyptologist (2008-2009)
Nadine Deppe, archaeologist (2008)
Chiori Kitagawa, zooarchaeologist (2008)
Mohamed Mustafa Al-Shafey, Egyptologist (2008-2009)
Mohamed Helmi, Egyptologist (2008-2009)
Veronika Wagner, student of Egyptology (2008)
Mohamed Abdelrahiem, Egyptologist (2009)
Ina Eichner, byzantine archaeologist (2009)
Thomas Beckh, Egyptologist (2009)
Silvia Prell, Egyptologist (2009)
Josuah Pinke, Egyptologist (2009)
Josephine Malur, Egyptologist (2009)

Corinna Garbert, architect (2009)
Cornelia Goerlich, student of architecture (2009)
Barbara Reichenbächer, student of Egyptology (2009)

Asyut and The Asyut Project

Jochem Kahl

1. Asyut: a city of culture, a border town and a wounded city

Museums all over the world display masterpieces of art which were found at Asyut. Especially worth mentioning are objects from the late First Intermediate Period/Period of Regions (for that term cf. MORENZ 2010: 35) and the Middle Kingdom, e.g. the wooden models of armed troops from the tomb of the nomarch Mesehti (Eleventh Dynasty; Egyptian Museum Cairo, CG 257, 258; GRÉBAUT 1890-1900, 30-36, Pls. 33-37; BIETAK 1985), the wooden statues (i.a. Paris, Louvre E 11937) from the tomb of Nakhti (CHASSINAT/PALANQUE 1911: 48-49, Pls. 11-12; KAHL 2007: 93-95) or the coffin of Wepwawet-em-hat with a diagonal star clock on its lid (Vienna, Kunsthistorisches Museum ÄS 10135; HÖLZL 2007: 64-65). But also high quality pieces of art from later periods are known, e.g. a double-statue representing Wepwawet and Hathor-Isis (New York, MMA 17.2.5; cf. recently DUQUESNE 2008: 2-3), the cult chamber of the tomb of Amen-hotep (Ägyptisches Museum Berlin, Inv. 31010/1; Cleveland, Museum of Art, Inv. 63.100; Toledo (Ohio), Museum of Art, Inv. 62/64, Zürich, Kunsthaus, Inv. 1963/36; KARIG 1968: 27-34; KAHL 2007: 97-99) and a Graeco-Roman statue of a dog (Paris, Louvre E 11657; KAHL 2007: 153-154).

Egyptology has claimed Asyuti workmanship to be one of the best in Ancient Egypt. William Stevenson Smith wrote in 1957:

> Toward the end of the First Intermediate Period the workmanship at Assiut was well ahead of anything else being produced at any other site except at Thebes.
> (SMITH 1957: 223).

William C. Hayes concluded two years later:

> During the early Nineteenth Dynasty the ancient Upper Egyptian town of Si'ut (modern Asyut) was the home not only of several well-to-do officials of the national administration, but also of an accomplished atelier of sculptors, to whose able hands we owe … admirable pieces of private tomb statuary.
> (HAYES 1959: 347-349).

In like manner Asyuti architecture is held in high esteem. Dietrich Wildung classed the tombs of Asyuti Middle Kingdom nomarchs to the most important monuments of their period (WILDUNG 1984: 34). Walther Wolf highlighted the architecture of Tomb I:

> In Asjut erreicht das Grab des Gaufürsten Djefai-hapi in seiner stützenlosen Felsenhalle eine Weite, die auch spätere Zeiten nicht übertroffen haben.
> (WOLF 1957: 312).

Today also Asyuti texts of the Twelfth Dynasty nomarch Djefai-Hapi I belong to the most classics: Alan Henderson Gardiner included 282 quotations from Djefai-Hapi's tomb inscriptions in his Middle Egyptian Grammar (GARDINER 1957). The tomb of Djefai-Hapi I (Siut I; Tomb I) is the most quoted textual source in Gardiner's Egyptian Grammar after Sinuhe, The Eloquent Peasant and the Teachings of Ptahhotep (Table 1).

Literary works	Number of quotations
Sinuhe B	569
Peasant B1	358
Ptahhotep	347
Siut I (= Tomb I; Djefai-Hapi I)	282
Shipwrecked Sailor	272
Beni Hasan I	199
Admonitions (pLeiden 344 rto.)	160
Dialogue of a Man with his Soul	157

Table 1: Quotations in GARDINER 1957.

Not only modern Egyptology, also the ancient Egyptians esteemed Asyuti products (KAHL 1999; KAHL 2007: 16-18). Texts from Asyuti First Intermediate Period/Period of Regions and Middle Kingdom tombs were copied on monuments and papyri throughout Egypt from the New Kingdom to the Roman Period, such as we see in the tombs of Senen-mut (TT 353; KAHL 1994: 41-42), Puy-em-re (TT 39; MONTET 1928: 68), Mont-em-hat (TT 34; KUHLMANN/SCHENKEL 1983: 73, note 254), Ibi (TT 36; KUENTZ 1934: 161) and others (cf. in detail KAHL 1999) as well as on Roman papyri from Tebtynis (OSING 1998a). Presumably via libraries (KAHL 1999: 283-355), these texts were frequently copied and recopied and thus constitute a continuous tradition. The Asyuti material circulated all over Egypt: in Thebes, Naga el-Hasaya (near Edfu), Memphis/Saqqara, Heliopolis, Sais, Roda(?), Athribis, Kom Abu Yasin, Tuna el-Gebel and Tebtynis (KAHL 1999: 302-17). Asyut formed part of Egypt's cultural memory, that is to say, the stored knowledge and memories of the past which are specific to a given culture and through which a culture creates its identity in an ongoing process (for the conception of the cultural memory cf. ASSMANN 1992).

And even ancient people abroad were interested in Asyuti workmanship. Presumably during the Second Intermediate Period statues of persons named Djefai-Hapi were deported to Sudan and the Near East (HELCK 1976: 101-115; VALBELLE 1998: 176-183). They were valued as prestige objects in the Sudan (KENDALL 1997: 24-27; REISNER 1931: 80; DUNHAM 1937-1938: 14, Fig. 7) and in Lebanon (CHÉHAB 1969: 22, Pl. 4.1).

These short introductory remarks might reveal the importance of ancient Asyut as a city of culture. But Asyut was also a border town and a wounded city (cf. KAHL 2007: 3-20 for more details).

Despite of its location in the center of Egypt and just for that very reason Asyut played the role of a border town on many occasions. The etymology of Asyut's ancient toponym – *S3ww.ti* "The Guardian" (OSING 1976: 320, 866, note 1377) – refers to her unique geographical position: Situated to the south of the Gebel Abu el-Feda, the most dangerous passage of the Nile to the north of the First Cataract (KAHL 2007: 14), and at the beginning of the desert road Darb al-Arbaᶜin ("The Forty Days Road"; KAHL 2007: 14-15), Asyut served as a crossroad along the Egyptian trade routes. Asyut was vulnerable and open to incursions, because it provided a direct link to the South. It was therefore a site of great strategic importance for the last five millennia and was involved in wars on numerous occasions.

A reflection of these times of war is represented by a dense attestation of weapons and soldiers in Asyut during Pharaonic Egypt. First Intermediate Period/Period of Regions and early Middle Kingdom nomarchs depicted themselves in their tombs with their troops – either as wall decoration as in Tomb IV (EL-KHADRAGY 2008), Tomb N13.1 (EL-KHADRAGY 2007a; KAHL 2007: 81, Fig. 60) and the Northern Soldiers-Tomb (H11.1; EL-KHADRAGY 2006a: 162, Fig. 6) or as models such as in the tomb of Mesehti (GRÉBAUT 1890-1900, 30-36, Pls. 33-37; BIETAK 1985), or they had weapons and models of weapons as grave goods (e.g. Tomb III; publication by Monika Zöller in preparation). Hitherto unique is a representation on the walls of Tomb III (KAHL 2007: 76, Fig. 53): Here, Egyptian soldiers are depicted fighting against each other. Bows and arrows (D'AMICONE/POZZI BATTAGLIA 2009a/2009b: 54) were used as grave goods for First Intermediate Period/Period of Regions burials. Soldiers are well attested by the so-called Salakhana stelae, votive stelae, which date from the New Kingdom to the Late Period (DUQUESNE 2009: 575-594). Also the census register Papyrus Oxyrhynchos 984 recto from 89/90 CE mentions several soldiers (cf. infra 5.9.1).

Several horizons of destruction are attested for Asyut – the earliest one at the end of the First Intermediate Period/Period of Regions, when a civil war between Herakleopolis in the north and Thebes in the south severely affected the country. Asyut was obviously the last bastion of the Herakleopolitan kingdom and the final theatre of war, since Asyuti local rulers were the closest allies of Herakleopolis. These events must have occurred between 2063 and 2045 BCE (KAHL 2007: 6).

Also during the Second Intermediate Period Asyut and its surrounding area marked the border of a divided Egypt (BIETAK 1994: 27). There is circumstantial evidence that either the Hyksos or the Kushites plundered the Asyuti necropolis and eventually even the city itself (KAHL 2007: 10).

During the Assyrian invasion of Egypt, in the first half of the seventh century BCE, the Assyrian ruler Assarhaddon installed a governor in Asyut, who was driven away by dissident Kushites or Egyptians. Assurbanipal subsequently reinstalled this governor, but the governor himself finally revolted against his protector (Prism A; ONASCH 1994: 36, 55, 118-121). Asyut was once again the center of a civil war.

From 196 to 195 BCE the Theban rival king Ankh-Wennefer seized Aswan in the south of Thebes and advanced to the region of Asyut in the north. He brought his fight for Egypt's independence from the Ptolemaic sovereigns to the Asyuti region: A village near Asyut was depopulated. Once again Asyut was the critical point of separation in a civil war: Since we have no information that Ankh-Wennefer was able to move further to the north, we may suppose that he was driven back by the Ptolemies after a battle near Asyut (MCGING 1997: 299-310; VEÏSSE 2004: 11-26; KAHL 2007: 12).

In Late Antiquity Asyut was threatened and plundered by Blemmyes and other Nubian invaders (cf. KAHL 2007: 12).

Asyut's function as a border town is also reflected in the double vizierate during the New Kingdom as well as in Ptolemaic and Roman provincial administration. Both times Asyut marked the northern border of the southern administrative districts (KAHL 2007: 13).

On many occasions Asyut played the role of a border town, which led to its being wounded, ransacked and destroyed: Asyut has been a wounded city. According to the American sociologists Jane Schneider and Ida Susser "wounded cities, like all cities, are dynamic entities, replete with the potential to recuperate loss and reconstruct anew for the future" (SUSSER/SCHNEIDER 2003: 1). It is exactly this fate which might have led to Asyut's cultural achievements. Periods of flourishing art and architecture as well as prosperity followed periods of destruction.

2. The aims of The Asyut Project

Asyut's special role as a wounded city, a border town and a city of culture is the reason for our fieldwork in the western mountains of Asyut, in the Gebel Asyut al-gharbi (Pls. 14-15). Asyut's material culture, her theology, her schools and traditions show differences to other Egyptian cities and are an outstanding study object for the regional diversity within Ancient Egypt.

The Gebel Asyut al-gharbi is the only site currently accessible to explore ancient Asyut. The ancient city and its temples have been almost completely buried and lost under the strata of the alluvial plain and especially the rapidly growing modern city. Archaeological fieldwork is not possible without removing parts of the modern settlement. Illicit excavations of house owners in Asyut (KAHL 2007: 44) provide us with some information about the location of the main temple of Asyut, the temple of the chief deity Wepwawet. It can be located 8 meters beneath the modern surface in the Old City of Asyut (KAHL 2007: 39-48).

Beside the temple of Wepwawet we have inscriptional evidence of the temples of Anubis, Osiris, Hathor and Thoth (KAHL 2007: 49-54; cf. the contribution of Ursula Verhoeven in this volume). But, unfortunately, their exact location within the city is still unknown. Further temples or cults also attested to Maat, Aten, Amun-Ra, Amun, Khonsu, Sekhmet, Neith, Isis, Isis-Hathor, Horus son of Isis and son of Osiris, Serapis, Pepy I, Ramesses Meryamun, the God in Asyut, and Djefai-Hapi (KAHL 2007: 50, 54-58).

Despite this difficult situation of the archaeological inaccessibility of the city itself, the exploration of the mountain situated to the west of Asyut provides plenty of information on Asyuti culture.

The mountain peak of Gebel Asyut al-gharbi rises to over two hundred meters above sea level. The human installations in the gebel extend over several kilometers along the cultivated land – the gebel has been mainly used as necropolis at least since the Old Kingdom (perhaps even the Early Dynastic Period) until now, but also as quarry from the Pharaonic Period to modern times, as a destination for school excursions during the early New Kingdom, as a dwelling place for Christian anachoretes, as a place of prayer and a cemetery during the Islamic Period as well as a camp for the military (in modern times and maybe as early as during the Third Persian Occupation of Egypt). The objectives of The Asyut Project's work in the western mountain at Asyut are:

- Mapping the Gebel Asyut al-gharbi.
- Documenting single architectural structures, as for example a single tomb, a single monastery etc., and all related objects. This is due to the missing or incomplete documentation (of architecture, decoration, inscriptions, objects) as well as the endangered state of the structures.
- Determining and reconstructing the specific function of certain parts of the Gebel Asyut al-gharbi at a certain time period, e.g. the changes from the Middle Kingdom usage as a necropolis to the New Kingdom usage as a quarry and to the Coptic usage as a monastic site.
- General reconstruction of the complexity of the Gebel Asyut al-gharbi, its changes and its continuity.
- Reconstructing the "histories" of Asyut, i.e. the social history, the cultural history, the political history etc.
- Pinpointing the Asyuti traditions and cultural achievements and thus contributing to the question of regional diversity in Ancient Egypt.

3. Gebel Asyut al-gharbi

According to Dietrich and Rosemarie Klemm (Klemm/Klemm 2006; Klemm/Klemm 2008: 112-115; Kahl/El-Khadragy/Verhoeven 2006: 242; Kahl 2007: 59-61), who undertook a geological survey for The Asyut Project in 2005, the mountain can be divided into eleven geological steps. Each step starts with a more massive limestone of 5-15 m thickness and grades at its top into marly and shaly beds of 0.5-3 m thickness. Climatic influences have shaped these beds into softly inclined slopes, while the more massive limestone, in comparison, form steep cuts. Thus, this rhythmic layering forms morphological steps, which can be easily followed over a stretch of a few kilometers due to their flat horizontal bedding. Nevertheless, in places the entire hill slope of the archaeological site of Gebel Asyut al-gharbi is so heavily covered with debris that it is hard to recognize these steps.

The geological division of the mountain also mirrors its use as necropolis. Thousands of rock tombs were hewn into the mountain and make it look like a honeycomb. Tomb builders respected the geological division of the mountain and built the tombs within one geological step, thus avoiding instability of their construction.

Several official larger excavations took place in Gebel Asyut al-gharbi (for details cf. the overviews given by RYAN 1988: 17-32; KAHL 2007: 21-33; ZITMAN 2010: 45-69):
- Mohammed Halfawee 1889
- Émile Gaston Chassinat and Charles Palanque 1903
- David George Hogarth 1906/07
- Ernesto Schiaparelli 1906-1913
- Ahmed Bey Kamal 1913/14.

All excavators succeeded in enlarging the museums of their countries (Paris, Louvre; London, British Museum; Turin, Egyptian Museum; Asyut, Khashaba Collection). However, all excavators neglected to publish a general map of Gebel Asyut al-gharbi or facsimiles of inscriptions and decoration or a plan of the architecture of the individual tombs. They also completely neglected to publish the results of their excavations. Only one, the French excavation, resulted in a monograph and an article (CHASSINAT/PALANQUE 1911; PALANQUE 1903). Kamal published a list of objects found during his fieldwork, but without adding drawings or photos of the objects (KAMAL 1916). Halfawee, Hogarth and Schiaparelli did not publish at all. Even notebooks from some of Schiaparelli's fieldwork seasons are missing. Some excavators used methods which do not correspond with the modern archaeological standard and which were already disputed during the beginning of the twentieth century: Hogarth used dynamite (RYAN 1988: 79), Chassinat and Palanque removed Coptic monuments (Deir el-Meitin) without recording them in order to reach First Intermediate Period/Period of Regions and/or Middle Kingdom tombs, which had been untouched at least since Coptic Period (CHASSINAT/PALANQUE 1911: 2-4).

4. The strategy of fieldwork

Fieldwork of The Asyut Project aims to generate a comprehensive picture of the function and changes of Gebel Asyut al-gharbi. Therefore different strategies of research are pursued, which complement each other.

4.1 Mapping Gebel Asyut al-gharbi

The complete lack of reliable maps and plans made mapping the Gebel Asyut al-gharbi one of the main tasks of The Asyut Project (before The Asyut Project started, only Hogarth's unpublished map of the necropolis existed, which is inaccurate or even faulty in several parts: e.g. there are tombs on the summit of the gebel contra Hogarth and ZITMAN 2010, who used Hogarth's map; the location of Stabl Antar (Tomb I) is wrong in Hogarth's map [or one may assume that Hogarth denoted Tomb II as Stabl Antar]).

Surveying and cleaning have been essential parts of every fieldwork season. This way more than 200 architectural structures could be mapped so far (Pls. 16-19). Some of them are large tombs, the cleaning of which took or will still take several seasons, others are small tombs, which were cleaned in only one day, still others are tombs of which the entrance is visible, but which have not yet been cleaned up. One can suppose that only a small percentage of the tombs cut into the rock are visible today. Destruction by quarrying activities, tomb robbers, rainfall and early excavators attributed to the ruinous state of Gebel Asyut al-gharbi. One can compare Gebel Asyut al-gharbi with a human body devoid of flesh and skin; just the skeleton is preserved. Due to quarrying about 10 to 15 meters rock surface is missing on each step of Gebel Asyut al-gharbi in direction of the modern city. For example, in front of Tomb I a complete roofed room was blown away at the end of the eighteenth century (cf. KAHL 2007: 86-92). And as a result of these activities, one can also see the steep front of the cliffs to the north and south of Tomb I. As a further result of quarrying, but also due to early archaeological fieldwork and landslide, most parts of the Gebel Asyut al-gharbi are covered by massive amounts of debris. Cleaning certain areas of the gebel often means removing a layer of debris more than six meters high (e.g. in front of the Tomb of the Dogs or in the inner hall of Tomb V).

The Asyut Project's map of the Gebel Asyut al-gharbi is arranged like a city map (Pl. 14). A grid system was laid over Gebel Asyut al-gharbi (FAUERBACH 2006). The grid system divides the map into 50 m x 50 m squares. These squares are labeled by a letter and a number (e.g. N13) and every single structure in this square is denoted in numerical order beginning with 1 (e.g. N13.1, N13.2 …). The advantage of this system is obvious: the structures on the map are easy to find. A system, however, such as that used by early Egyptologists is completely unclear as it gives just one number to tombs, which are spread all over the mountain (e.g. Tomb I, Tomb II etc.; it is regrettable that ZITMAN 2010 continued to use the old numbering system and even extended it: e.g. he gave Tomb N13.1 the number XVII. As a consequence, one has to search his map for the tombs: his Tomb XIII is in the northwest, his Tomb XVII in the northeast and his Tomb XVIII again in the northwest of the gebel). In addition, it is always possible to show parts of the map of Gebel Asyut al-gharbi in detail (Pl. 16) or to show only some prominent structures (Pls. 17-19).

4.2 Recording single structures

A thorough documentation of such individual architectural structures takes place, which promise to provide substantial information on Gebel Asyut al-gharbi and Asyut as well as on Egyptian history in general. This pertains particularly to the tombs of the nomarchs, which can be dated relatively precisely and are already well known in Egyptology, but have never been reliably documented. These tombs are Tomb I (P10.1; Djefai-Hapi I), Tomb III (N12.1; Iti-ibi), Tomb IV (N12.2; Khety II), Tomb V (M11.1; Khety I). The tombs are already mentioned in the publications of Griffith (GRIFFITH 1889a; GRIFFITH 1889b) and Montet (MONTET 1928; MONTET 1930-35; MONTET 1936), but these publications lack a complete description of the tombs: The architecture is not well recorded, mostly relying on the plans made by the French Expedition in 1799. Only parts of the inscriptions and decorations are reproduced in hand copy. These hand copies contain a number of mistakes; sometimes the inaccuracies and omissions in Griffith's copies are above 30% (e.g. in mortuary liturgy no. 7 on the northern wall of the first corridor). Other inscriptions and pictorial decoration were not recorded at all – probably due to the darkness in the tombs and the height of the tomb walls. It is obvious, for example, that ladders could not reach the upper parts of the inscribed wall in the first corridor of Tomb I. Therefore, the greatest number of mistakes in Griffith's hand copy were made in this corridor, or the inscriptions and the decoration were not copied at all. Also the finds from these tombs were never recorded at all. The objects found by The Asyut Project will be studied and published. Thus, for the first time, an archaeological documentation of Asyuti material including exactly recorded and dated locations is commenced. Even if this material comprises mostly fragments and is at first glance not as beautiful as the many objects from the early excavations, it will provide us with much more precise information concerning chronology and criteria for dating.

Other nomarchs' tombs will be recorded in the future subject to funding. Especially Tomb II (O13.1; Djefai-Hapi II, Pls. 30-31) and Tomb VII (Salakhana Tomb; Djefai-Hapi III) are candidates. Unfortunately the latter is used as a basecamp by the Egyptian military and is currently not accessible.

Other recently detected and hitherto unknown tombs will be studied completely: Tomb N13.1, which belonged to the nomarch Iti-ibi(-iqer), who lived during the very end of the First Intermediate Period/Period of Regions, when Mentu-hotep II had already conquered Asyut on his way to Herakleopolis (KAHL forthcoming), and the so called Northern Soldiers-Tomb (Tomb H11.1), which can approximately be dated to the end of the Eleventh Dynasty (EL-KHADRAGY 2006a; KAHL 2007: 83-84); this tomb was mentioned by MAGEE 1988: II, 36-38 for the first time.

In addition, nomarchs' tombs or possible nomarchs' tombs have been (re)located: P13.1 whose owner was a Hatia Djefai-Hapi (cf. VERHOEVEN 2011). Also the Tomb of Mesehti seems to have been relocated, but the final identification is still pending.

Although nomarchs' tombs provide plenty of information about ancient Asyut, they always reflect the highest social stratum of the Asyuti population. Therefore, also other smaller tombs were already recorded and will be recorded in future – especially on geological step 7 and also in the area of the Tomb of the Dogs. Already more than 80 tombs from the Old Kingdom to the early Middle Kingdom have been recorded on step 7.

Not only tombs for human beings, but also tombs for sacred animals are studied. Animal necropoleis are known from Asyut by written sources: necropoleis of canides, ibis, baboons, cattle, birds of prey (KAHL 2007: 66-68). The Asyut Project focuses on the so called Tomb of the Dogs area (O11), which could be located thanks to old travelogues, information of native people and a zooarchaeological survey (KAHL 2009: 117-121; KITAGAWA 2009: 122-129; KAHL/KITAGAWA 2010: 77-81).

4.3 Surveying certain parts of the Gebel Asyut al-gharbi

Several surveys conducted on the gebel shall provide new information about the mountain and the city. Up until now, the northernmost part of the necropolis (cf. KAHL 2008: 200; EICHNER/BECKH 2010: 208), the area around the Tomb of the Dogs (KITAGAWA 2009) and the areas around Deir el-Azzam and Deir el-Meitin (EICHNER/BECKH 2010) were surveyed. These surveys gave new insights especially into the Late Period and Coptic Period activities on Gebel Asyut al-gharbi.

Furthermore every year certain parts of the gebel have been surveyed by a surveyor or architect and visible tombs (i.e. not hidden by debris) have been entered into the map of the Gebel Asyut al-gharbi (cf. the preliminary reports in *Studien zur Altägyptischen Kultur* 2004-2011).

4.4 Tracing ways in the Gebel Asyut al-gharbi

There is textual evidence that causeways to tombs existed in the gebel. Part of the causeway to Tomb I was already found (ENGEL/KAHL 2009) and it is hoped to still detect causeways to other tombs.

On principle, there must have been routes into the gebel. Therefore geological step 7 has been chosen to be cleaned on a larger distance in order to find traces of eventual ways in that part of the necropolis.

4.5 Studying modern reports on the Gebel Asyut al-gharbi

Relatively recent information on the Gebel Asyut al-gharbi will also be recorded and compared with the current situation at the site: At the moment there is a focus on European and American travelogues from the eighteenth and nineteenth century on the one hand and on folk traditions about the gebel on the other hand, which are going to be gathered on the site.

4.6 Interdisciplinary research

Interdisciplinary research plays an important role in the fieldwork. Experts from the fields of Physical Anthropology, Zooarchaeology, Botany, Byzantine Archaeology, and Islamic Archaeology are constant partners in The Asyut Project.

4.7 Combining the different approaches

The combination of the results achieved from the different approaches of exploring Gebel Asyut al-gharbi will provide a dense picture of the mountain, its history, its functions and changes as well as of the regional diversity of the material and intellectual culture of Asyut from the Old Kingdom to the Mamluk Period. It is to be hoped that The Asyut Project will provide a much better understanding of the peculiarities of this Middle Egyptian metropolis.

5. Chronological outline of Asyut

5.1 Early Dynastic Period and Old Kingdom

5.1.1 General information about Asyut

Evidence for Asyut during the Early Dynastic Period and the Old Kingdom has been very scarce up until now. The earliest documented evidence for the Asyuti nome (13th Upper Egyptian nome) comes from the beginning of the Fourth Dynasty: King Sneferu established four domains there as shown in his Valley Temple (cf. JACQUET-GORDON 1962: 106, Fig. F, 132).

The earliest inscriptions (cf. KAHL 2007: 112) mentioning the town are the Fifth Dynasty sarcophagus of the vizier Min-nefer (Leiden, RMO AMT 106) and Pyramid Texts of the Sixth Dynasty (Pyr §§ 630a-c, 1634a-c).

5.1.2 Early Dynastic Period and Old Kingdom on Gebel Asyut al-gharbi

5.1.2.1 Early fieldwork

Gebel Asyut al-gharbi houses/housed some structures which can be dated to the Old Kingdom. Especially worth mentioning is an Old Kingdom tomb lost today, whose rear wall with nine standing rock cut statues was sketched by Bonaparte's Commission (PANCKOUCKE 1822: Pl. 46.9; WILKINSON 1843: 88; KAHL 2007: 69, 72).

Based on the dating of the inventory of tombs excavated by Hogarth in 1906/07, there are some late Old Kingdom tombs (Hogarth tombs 45, 49, 53-54 and 56-57) situated in the middle part of the mountain higher up the cliffs. However, their exact position is not certain due to the rough mapping by Hogarth (cf. RYAN 1988: 3; cf. also ZITMAN 2010: maps: 3, Map 1 [Hogarth's map without these tombs], 6, Map 3 [with approximate position of these tombs as assumed by Zitman], ZITMAN 2010: text: 71-91).

The coffin (BM EA 46629) of the Inspector of the Priests of the Ka-House of King Pepy, Hetep-nebi, was found in Hogarth Tomb 56 (DAVIES 1995: 146, Pl. 31.1; KAHL 2007: 57; ZITMAN 2010: maps: 112-113 [S8L]); the cartouche of Pepy might refer to Pepy I, who built several Ka-houses all over Egypt. Although it is tempting to suggest that Hetep-nebi lived during the Sixth Dynasty, there is no proof that he was a contemporary of King Pepy I. The cult for Pepy I in his Ka-House might have continued for some time after his death.

A cylinder seal (BM EA 47460-350; ZITMAN 2010: maps: 101, Fig. 27.2) of an official of King Pepy I was found in an unlabeled coffin in Hogarth's Tomb 53. But also this is no definite proof that the owner of the coffin was a contemporary of Pepy I. According to Magee it is unlikely that an official of Pepy I would be buried in an unlabeled coffin at Asyut. The seal may have been in the possession of the owner of this coffin after the death of Pepy I (MAGEE 1988: I, 62).

Finds from Schiaparelli's excavations point to a late Old Kingdom or early First Intermediate Period/Period of Regions burial in the lower cliffs in the northwest (ZITMAN 2010: text: 89-90), even if the exact locations of the Old Kingdom objects from Schiaparelli's excavations are not known due to missing digging diaries.

In addition, there are only few archaeological objects known from early excavations which could belong even to the Early Dynastic Period: The French excavations conducted in 1903 by Chassinat and Palanque brought to light some stone vessels, which are of Early Dynastic or early Old Kingdom date (CHASSINAT/PALANQUE 1911: 162, Pl. 31.2; KAHL 2007: 109, 114, Fig. 97). Schiaparelli excavated some vessels (pottery), which are called "archaic" in his inventory-list (1911-1913; ZITMAN 2010: text: 90, n. 589).

5.1.2.2 Fieldwork of The Asyut Project

On geological step 7, fieldwork conducted by The Asyut Project uncovered dozens of small shaft tombs in front and to the south of Tomb N13.1, originally covered with mud bricks. According to the pottery found in them, the tombs can be dated to the late Old Kingdom (Pls. 20-21). The finds still have to be studied in detail, but at the moment one can state that the burials were equipped with pottery, sometimes a headrest, a necklace, plants and a wooden coffin or a reed mat. The physical anthropological studies show that the buried people were mostly in relatively good physical condition (cf. the contribution by Magdalena Patolla in this volume).

Surveying Gebel Asyut al-gharbi also led to the discovery of Old Kingdom pottery at several locations between geological step 6 and step 9. The pottery was lying on the surface and might often have fallen down from the next higher step. This pottery can be dated from Third Dynasty to the late Old Kingdom (RZEUSKA 2011). Therefore one may conclude that the higher situated steps of Gebel Asyut al-gharbi were already used as a burial ground during the early Old Kingdom. Thus, for the first time the fieldwork of The Asyut Project brought to light evidence for an early occupation of the necropolis.

5.2 First Intermediate Period/Period of Regions

5.2.1 General information about Asyut

Asyut played a prominent role in Egypt during the end of the First Intermediate Period/Period of Regions. The city was the final stage of war between the aggressively expanding Theban troops and the northern Herakleopolitan Kingdom. The autobiographical inscriptions in the tombs of the nomarchs Iti-ibi (Tomb III) and Khety II (Tomb IV) report about this civil war, which affected Asyut for probably more than two generations (cf. KAHL 2007: 6-8; 74-79; BRUNNER 1937; SCHENKEL 1965: 74-89).

5.2.2 First Intermediate Period/Period of Regions on Gebel Asyut al-gharbi

5.2.2.1 Early fieldwork

According to the finds in museums, many burials from the First Intermediate Period/Period of Regions are known from Asyut, even if one cannot always clearly differentiate between late Old Kingdom and early First Intermediate Period/Period of Regions or late First Intermediate Period/Period of Regions and early Middle Kingdom. Unfortunately the exact origin of these finds was not recorded. Therefore determining an exact location of the finds and their tombs on the Gebel Asyut al-gharbi is difficult or impossible.[1]

Griffith's and Montet's copies (no facsimiles) of the inscriptions of Tomb III, IV, and V are still Egyptological standard (GRIFFITH 1889b; MONTET 1928; 1930-35; 1936).

5.2.2.2 Fieldwork of The Asyut Project

The Asyut Project focuses on the first systematic documentation of Asyut's First Intermediate Period/Period of Regions nomarchs' tombs. Tomb III, IV and V are/will be recorded for the first time in detail: their architecture, inscriptions, paintings and objects.

Fieldwork in Tomb V is still in progress. After removing debris more than six meters high from the collapsed roof and façade, two hitherto unknown shafts came to light (Pls.

1 Cf. Zitman's recent attempt (ZITMAN 2010) to map tombs in the gebel, of which objects are stored in the British Museum or in the Egyptian Museum in Turin. His maps are only tentative and his interpretation does not take into account the difficult situation in the gebel: Today, large areas of the Gebel Asyut al-gharbi are covered by debris caused by rainfall and the work of early excavators.

22-23). While one was unfinished, the other was completely hewn into the gebel and led to a burial chamber in the north. (The denomination of the directions corresponds to the religious conventions: The wall with the false door is called western wall according to the Egyptian idea of the Netherworld situated in the west. The exact geographical position of the false door is southwest). In addition to the known autobiographical inscriptions (KAHL 2007: 74; BRUNNER 1937: 11-16, 64-69; SCHENKEL 1965: 69-74; SCHENKEL 1978: 29-35; SPANEL 1989: 304-305), there are also traces of painted decorations in Tomb V, which show that the tomb was once completely decorated (EL-KHADRAGY/KAHL 2004: 241-243; KAHL 2007: 70).

Fieldwork in Tomb III (N12.1) is already finished. Tomb III seems to have been executed completely during the First Intermediate Period/Period of Regions (Pls. 24-25): In addition to the well-known autobiographical inscription on the eastern part of the northern wall, all walls of Tomb III were painted and/or inscribed (KAHL 2007: 76; EL-KHADRAGY/KAHL 2004: 236-239). There are also four vertical shafts hewn into the floor of the tomb's hall, each one leading to a burial chamber in the south. In front of the tomb are two small side chambers.

The decoration of Tomb IV (N12.2) was unfinished but, contrary to prevailing older Egyptological opinion, there were two completely executed shafts hewn into the floor of the tomb's inner hall (Pls. 26-27; EL-KHADRAGY 2006b).

The discovery of the tomb of Iti-ibi-iqer (N13.1, Pls. 28-29) in 2005, a nomarch who lived during the reign of Mentu-hotep II – who ruled at that time either over southern Egypt including Asyut or possibly already over the reunified Egypt – meant a substantial contribution to our knowledge about the end of the First Intermediate Period/Period of Regions. Inscriptions, decoration (EL-KHADRAGY 2007a) and the proportions of the figures (KAHL forthcoming) shed a new light on Asyut's history during the reunification of Egypt under King Mentu-hotep II.

In addition to these nomarchs' tombs, which will be studied completely, The Asyut Project revealed other tombs from that period providing new information about Asyut. Especially worth mentioning are some small tombs situated close to Tomb N13.1, which seem to be contemporary to this nomarch's tomb.

The relatively large Tomb N11.1 located on step 5 below Tomb V is also of a First Intermediate Period/Period of Regions or early Middle Kingdom date.[2]

5.3 Middle Kingdom

5.3.1 General information about Asyut

Middle Kingdom Asyut was a cultural center. As monumental tombs and wooden statues, high quality texts and coffins prove, Asyut housed a school of scribes, theologians, architects and sculptors during the First Intermediate Period/Period of Regions and the

2 It is to be hoped that a detailed study of the pottery by Andrea Kilian will clarify this point. A photo of this tomb is published in WILDUNG 1984: 154, Fig. 134, but there the tomb is erroneously attributed to the nomarch Iti-ibi.

Middle Kingdom (KAHL 1999: 17; KAHL 2007: 151-153).[3] They were able to produce high quality texts and works of art, simultaneously observing local types and styles. Presumably they worked at the nomarchs' court or at the temples and were in touch with artists and scholars from the residence (KAHL 2007: 153).

5.3.2 Middle Kingdom on Gebel Asyut al-gharbi

5.3.2.1 Early fieldwork

Early excavations revealed plenty of objects from Middle Kingdom Asyut: Probably most tombs of the French excavation conducted by Chassinat and Palanque in 1903 are of early Middle Kingdom date. These tombs are situated below Deir el-Meitin.

Hogarth's excavation discovered many objects, which are still waiting to be studied. Progress has been made by the recent publication of Middle Kingdom coffins and pottery by Marcel Zitman (ZITMAN 2010), although unfortunately there are no photos or drawings of the coffins included in the publication.

Also the Italian excavations conducted by Ernesto Schiaparelli focused on Middle Kingdom tombs. Statues and statuettes, parts of tomb walls, wooden models, coffins, headrests, pottery and other objects found their way to the Egyptian Museum in Turin without having been documented (cf. the exhibition Egitto Mai Visto, which gives an overview of the finds from the Italian excavations: D'AMICONE/POZZI BATTAGLIA 2009a and 2009b. The lack of basic documentation often reduces the possibility of substantial interpretation).

At present, Middle Kingdom objects from Kamal's fieldwork are widespread in collections all over the world (cf. the short report by KAMAL 1916 and the overview given by ZITMAN 2010: text: 64-68; maps: 281-282).

Inscriptions and decorations of Tomb I (Djefai-Hapi I; temp. Senwosret I) and Tomb II (Djefai-Hapi II) were copied several times (e.g. Hay [unpublished], GRIFFITH 1889b: Pls. 1-10; MONTET 1928: 54-68; 1930-35: 45-86), but never completely. The French Expedition recorded the architecture of Tomb I (PANCKOUCKE 1822: Pl. 44) and Tomb II (PANCKOUCKE 1822: Pls. 46.10, 47.1).

The Salakhana Tomb (Tomb VII; cf. KAHL 2007: 92-93) belongs to the nomarch Djefai-Hapi III (Twelfth Dynasty). Its architecture (PORTER/MOSS 1934: 264) is comparable to Tomb I and the large nomarchs' tombs at Qaw el-Kebir. Today, the tomb is inaccessible to researchers, because the Egyptian military is using it as a base.

Objects from the tomb of Mesehti (Eleventh Dynasty) appeared at the end of the nineteenth century and at the beginning of the twentieth century over several years and are for the most part today in the Petrie Museum, University College London and in the Egyptian Museum Cairo (cf. the useful list in ZITMAN 2010: maps: 210-212), but once again their original location within the tomb is not known. The state of documentation and publication of Middle Kingdom objects from early excavations is more than unsatisfactory.

3 ZITMAN 2010: text: 234 misinterpreted the statement in KAHL 1999: 17, when he claimed that there would be written that Siutian burials of the early MK would reflect the political or economic decline of the city. It is written, that the city did not gain the political importance of the First Intermediate Period/Period of Regions again, but that nevertheless the culture of the city was flourishing.

And it seems to be clear, that the original locations of most of the objects and the circumstances of their discovery will never be known.

5.3.2.2 Fieldwork of The Asyut Project

Several undertakings of The Asyut Project concern Middle Kingdom tombs in Gebel Asyut al-gharbi. Fieldwork has been conducted in Tomb N13.1 (nomarch Iti-ibi-iqer, temp. Mentu-hotep II, cf. 5.2.2.2; EL-KHADRAGY 2007a), in the Northern Soldiers-Tomb (Tomb H11.1, Eleventh Dynasty; EL-KHADRAGY 2006a), and in Tomb I (nomarch Djefai-Hapi I, temp. Senwosret I; KAHL 2007: 86-92; EL-KHADRAGY 2007b; EL-KHADRAGY 2007c; ENGEL/KAHL 2009). In addition, other Middle Kingdom tombs have been studied, e.g. Tomb II (nomarch Djefai-Hapi II, Twelfth Dynasty; cf. the contribution by Meike Becker in this volume), Tomb O11.15 (remains of a Middle Kingdom shaft with objects, among others a calcite statuette of a seated man; PRELL 2011), Tomb M10.1 (KAHL 2007: 95-96; VERHOEVEN forthcoming), Tomb I10.1 (KAHL 2007: 96-97).

Inscriptions and decorations on the walls of Tomb I have been recorded completely between 2004 and 2010 and are yet awaiting collation. Parts of this tomb escaped the attention of early researchers due to the tomb's height and darkness. Francis Llewellyn Griffith reported in 1889 that ladders and candles were his most important tools to transcribe hieroglyphs from the walls (GRIFFITH 1889a: 123). Today, we are able to use electricity and scaffoldings and receive full support from the restorers of the Supreme Council of Antiquities. Djefai-Hapi's tomb was cut into step 2, the lower stratum of the mountain. A sequence of rooms hewn into the mountain and measuring more than 55 meters in length is still standing today (Pl. 32). A further room was originally cut into the mountain. However, it was destroyed by quarrying at the end of the eighteenth century CE. Only a small part of the roof and some side walls are visible today (Pls. 33a-b). The original architecture of the monumental tomb could be reconstructed by archaeological remains, old travelogues and the famous ten contracts inscribed on one of the tomb walls (ENGEL/KAHL 2009). There were a shrine and a garden in the cultivated area as well as a causeway (Pl. 33a) leading to the today destroyed first room (Pl. 33b). The still preserved parts of the tomb consist of an eleven meters high first passage, a great

Fig. 1: Tomb I, Great Transverse Hall, eastern wall, northern part: ten contracts of Djefai-Hapi I (detail) (© Barthel 2010).

transverse hall, a second longitudinal passage and a second hall housing a large shrine cut from rock. The northern wall of the first passage originally showed the tomb owner and other pictorial decoration, but then the decoration program was changed and the quite unique mortuary liturgy no. 7 (cf. KAHL 1994, 1999: 53-186; ASSMANN 2002: 469-518) was written over the pictorial representations. The north-eastern wall of the great transverse hall is inscribed with the ten contracts, which Djefai-Hapi I made with the priests of the Wepwawet-temple and the Anubis-temple as well as with the workmen of the necropolis to guarantee his funerary cult (Fig. 1). The southeastern wall of the great transverse hall displays titles and epithets as well as a representation of Djefai-Hapi I in front of the names of King Senwosret I. The hall's ceiling (KAHL 2007: Pl. 8a) shows several different geometric patterns, some of them very similar to patterns from the Aegean. The second longitudinal passage is decorated with wall paintings which The Asyut Project detected in 2003 (EL-KHADRAGY 2007c). The innermost hall of the tomb houses a shrine, accessed by a small staircase and a double winged door (EL-KHADRAGY 2007b).

5.4. Second Intermediate Period

5.4.1 General information about Asyut

There is almost no information about Second Intermediate Period Asyut. Asyut seems to have once again marked the border line between a northern kingdom, ruled by the so called Hyksos, and scattered satellite states in the south. The find of Asyuti statues in Nubia may indicate looting of Asyut by the Hyksos or even by Kushite troops during the Second Intermediate Period (cf. KAHL 2007: 9-10).

5.4.2 Second Intermediate Period on Gebel Asyut al-gharbi

5.4.2.1 Early fieldwork

There is no information about Second Intermediate Period finds from earlier excavations, maybe due to the fact that objects from this period are in general insufficiently recognized and identified.

5.4.2.2 Fieldwork of The Asyut Project

The Asyut Project has also not yet found architecture or objects from the Second Intermediate Period.

5.5. New Kingdom

5.5.1 General information about Asyut

Asyut accommodated several temples in the New Kingdom (those of Wepwawet, Anubis, Osiris, Hathor) and also the cults of Amun-Ra, Isis, Khnum(?), Ramesses Meryamun, the God in Asyut, and Djefai-Hapi (KAHL 2007: 35-58). The temple of the chief deity

Wepwawet was probably the most important and largest in Asyut. During the reign of King Ramesses III it was surrounded by a more than 15 meters high wall (pHarris I, 59,2). Today, the temple is buried about 8 meters under the modern city of Asyut (GABRA 1931; KAHL 2007: 39-48).

New Kingdom Asyut is well known in Egyptology because of the "overseers of the double granary of Upper and Lower Egypt", the exceptional high standard of an atelier of sculptors at the end of the Eighteenth Dynasty and the beginning of the Nineteenth Dynasty, and the so called Salakhana Trove, a find of votive stelae and other objects.

The "overseers of the double granary of Upper and Lower Egypt" were the heads of the national grain administration and belonged to branches of a larger Asyuti family with close connections to the cult of Wepwawet (BOHLEKE 1993; KAHL 2007: 133-135). Statues and reliefs of the late Eighteenth and early Nineteenth Dynasty show a high cultural standard (HAYES 1959: 347-349; KAHL 2007: 153), some of them belong to the above mentioned high officials of the grain administration.

The Salakhana Trove comes from Tomb VII (the Salakhana Tomb, which owes its designation to its position behind the former slaughterhouse of Asyut) and presents a unique collection of votive stelae and other votive objects, which have a connection to the gods Wepwawet, Anubis, Osiris and Hathor. These objects are related to "popular religion" (DUQUESNE 2007; DUQUESNE 2009; BECKER 2007).

5.5.2 New Kingdom on Gebel Asyut al-gharbi

5.5.2.1 Early fieldwork

Excavations from the beginning of the twentieth century did not focus on New Kingdom Asyut. The First Intermediate Period/Period of Regions and the Middle Kingdom evoked more interest, even if there were also tombs and burials of the New Kingdom excavated as the cult chamber of Amen-hotep proves, the representations of which are now scattered over four collections in Berlin, Zürich, Cleveland and Toledo/Ohio (cf. KAHL 2007: 97-99). For the position of the New Kingdom tombs in Gebel Asyut al-gharbi cf. WILD 1971.

5.5.2.2 Fieldwork of The Asyut Project

The Asyut Project found substantial and exceptional evidence of the New Kingdom on Gebel Asyut al-gharbi. Next to hundreds of mostly fragmented ushebtis in Tomb III, which seem to have been left there by the early excavators, also some ushebti finds point to a New Kingdom date of Tombs N12.3 and N12.4. In addition, pottery and relief fragments were found during the last eight seasons. The most spectacular find, however, were the visitors' graffiti in Tomb N13.1 from the beginning of the Eighteenth until the end of the Twentieth Dynasty (KAHL 2006; VERHOEVEN 2007: 85-87; KAHL/VERHOEVEN 2008; VERHOEVEN 2008; VERHOEVEN 2009). They do not only transmit literary texts, they also inform about temples and cults in New Kingdom Asyut (cf. the contribution of Ursula Verhoeven in this volume).

5.6 Third Intermediate Period

5.6.1 General information about Asyut

There is only scarce information about Third Intermediate Period Asyut, even if the city seems to have been part of a small kingdom. At least for the Twenty-fifth Dynasty a local ruler called Pa-di-Nemti is attested, who seems to have reigned over Asyut (WEILL 1950: 57-65; LEAHY 1999: 230-232; KAHL 2007: 136). During the Assyrian invasion into Egypt, a man called Sikhâ (Djed-Hor) ruled Asyut (ONASCH 1994: 36, 55, 118-119).

5.6.2 Third Intermediate Period on Gebel Asyut al-gharbi

5.6.2.1 Early fieldwork

Early excavations brought some objects from the Third Intermediate Period to light, but they remained unpublished (e.g. ushebtis from Hogarth's excavation, which are now in the British Museum and will be published by Jan Moje). Not any single tomb of that period was attested by the early excavators.

5.6.2.2 Fieldwork of The Asyut Project

Third Intermediate Period objects, especially pottery and ushebtis, were found during the fieldwork conducted by The Asyut Project. These objects came from secondary interments and will give important information about regional styles during this period.

5.7 Late Period

5.7.1 General information about Asyut

Late Period Asyut housed temples to several cults and gods: Wepwawet, Anubis, Osiris, Hathor, Amun-Ra, Khonsu, Sakhmet, Neith, probably also Thoth (KAHL 2007: 35-58). Demotic papyri found in the Salakhana Tomb contain information on two Asyuti families and their priestly activities from the reign of King Amasis to the reign of King Cambyses (564-522 BCE; SOTTAS 1923: 34-46; SPIEGELBERG 1932: 39-52; SHORE 1988: 200-206; JOHNSON 1994: 113-132; KAHL 2007: 123-124).

A hoard of about 900 silver coins from Italy, Sicily, Macedonia, Thrace, Central Greece, Athens, Aegina, Corinth, the Greek Islands, Asia Minor, Caria, Sardes, Lycia, Cyprus and Cyrenaica attests connections with the Mediterranean. The hoard dates from the early fifth century BCE (PRICE/WAGGONER 1975).

5.7.2 Late Period on Gebel Asyut al-gharbi

5.7.2.1 Early fieldwork

Wainwright discovered the above mentioned Demotic papyri in the Salakhana Tomb in 1922. Other early excavators also found objects from the Late Period (e.g. a statuette of Ptah-Sokar-Osiris from Hogarth's excavations [BM EA 47577: TAYLOR/STRUDWICK 2005:

78]), but did not publish them in an adequate way, if at all. PALANQUE 1903: 121 noticed tombs from the Twenty-sixth Dynasty.

5.7.2.2 Fieldwork of The Asyut Project

Finds from the Late Period, e.g. pottery and ushebtis, occurred in the nomarchs' tombs of the First Intermediate Period/Period of Regions. These tombs seem to have been used for later burials. One of these finds, a golden earring (S05/073) found in Tomb III, once more provides archaeological evidence for connections with the Mediterranean or with the Achaemenids during the Late Period (KAHL 2007: 117, Pl. 9a).

One Late Period tomb is in the focus of The Asyut Project's research: the so called Tomb of the Dogs (Pls. 34-35; KAHL 2009: 117-121; KITAGAWA 2009: 122-129; KAHL 2010: 198-199; KAHL/KITAGAWA 2010; KITAGAWA 2011). This gallery tomb probably houses hundreds of thousands of mummified animal remains, which were deposited here from Late Period to Roman Period. The most frequently identified animal species was dog, followed by cat (*Felis* sp.), fox, and jackal (KITAGAWA 2011). The sizes of the dogs vary from small to large; their age at death ranges from neonatal to senior. Some of the dogs showed pathologies such as several fractured and incompletely healed bones or *Spondylosis deformans* (KITAGAWA 2011). The documentation and statistical analysis of the canine remains currently (2010) comprises 2378 entries (NISP: number of identified specimens) from the Tomb of the Dogs area and an additional 3690 entries from Deir el-Meitin area nearby. The analyzed osteological material may so far provide the most extensive database of Ancient Egyptian canines at all.

5.8 Ptolemaic Period

5.8.1 General information about Asyut

During Ptolemaic Period Asyut belonged to the large administrative district of Thebes, the Thebais. Asyut, at that time called Lykopolis, marked the beginning of the Thebais. The region of Asyut was once again the scene of a civil war. The Theban rival King Ankh-Wennefer (200-186 BCE) led a revolt against the Ptolemaic sovereigns. His expansion to the north ended near Asyut. In the following years he suffered serious setbacks and was driven back to the Theban area.

Temples are attested to Wepwawet, Anubis, and Thot/Hermes, cults are reported for Hathor (called "mistress of 16"), Maat, Amun-Ra-Ope, Isis, Horus son of Isis and son of Osiris (KAHL 2007: 39-58).

An archive of Demotic papyri from 181-169 BCE informs about family affairs between 208 and 169 BCE (THOMPSON 1934; SHORE/SMITH 1959: 52-60; VLEEMING 1989: 31-45; KAHL 2007: 124-127). The central figure of the archive is the lector-priest Tef-Hape, who worked in the necropolis of Asyut during the first half of the second century BCE. The documents concern a trial about the inheritance of Tef-Hape's father Pe-te-tum. The principal document (Papyrus BM EA 10591) is 2.85 m long and 32 cm wide. It is the longest preserved antique protocol of a judicial hearing at all (HOFFMANN 2000: 91).

5.8.2 Ptolemaic Period on Gebel Asyut al-gharbi

5.8.2.1 Early fieldwork

Early fieldwork produced some accidental finds of objects from the Ptolemaic Period, e.g. ushebtis.[4]

5.8.2.2 Fieldwork of The Asyut Project

Ptolemaic pottery and ushebtis were found in Tomb III and point to a reuse of that tomb during this period. Ostraca from the Ptolemaic Period come from the Tomb of the Dogs area.
For the Tomb of the Dogs cf. 5.7.2.2.

5.9 Roman to Byzantine Period

5.9.1 General information about Asyut

Temples are still attested to Wepwawet and Anubis, cults are attested to Serapis and Hathor (called "mistress of 16") (KAHL 2007: 39-58). Eventually, there were also cults installed for Ares (Onuris) and Apollo (Horus); this depends on the attribution of the census register Papyrus Oxyrhynchos 984 recto to Asyut or to Ptolemais. If one were to attribute the census register to Asyut, there would be more information about Asyut from 89/90 CE, for example personal names, indication of migration of people etc. (BAGNALL/FRIER/RUTHERFORD 1997; MONTEVECCHI 1998; SCHEIDEL 2001; CLARYSSE/THOMPSON 2006; cf. KAHL 2007: 128). In general, however, one can say that Asyut/Lykopolis is only sporadically attested in the papyrological documentation (MITTHOF 2001: I, 123).

A mythological manual from the second century CE found in Tebtynis records local myths, among others also from Asyut (OSING 1998b: 143-150). The manual reports about a temple, statues and an obelisk at Asyut. Charles Poncet observed the ruins of an ancient amphitheater and Roman mausolea in 1698 at Asyut (SAUNERON 1983: 90-94). Ägyptisches Museum Berlin houses two colossal statues which are reported to come from a temple at Asyut (FENDT 2009).

Roman Asyut is said to have been the hometown of the Graeco-Roman philosopher Plotinus (cf. CALDERINI 1922; MONTEVECCHI 2000).

Asyut was a center of Christianity in Byzantine Period (TIMM 1984: 235). Written sources provide information about Christian saints (well-known is John of Lykopolis, who lived in Gebel Asyut al-gharbi during the fourth century CE; cf. KAHL 2007: 138-140) and bishops (most famous are Melitius, bishop of Lykopolis/Asyut at the beginning of the fourth century CE, cf. KAHL 2007: 137-138; and Constantine, who was bishop of Asyut at the end of the sixth and the beginning of the seventh century CE, cf. KAHL 2007: 140) as well as about Coptic monasteries (cf. the general overview given by TIMM 1984).

4 Ushebtis from Hogarth's excavation were studied by Jan Moje and will be published within the series *The Asyut Project*.

5.9.2 Roman to Byzantine Period on Gebel Asyut al-gharbi

5.9.2.1 Early fieldwork

Early twentieth century archaeologists found burials and objects from early Roman Period, but omitted to publish them (for some objects from Schiaparelli's excavations cf. now D'AMICONE/POZZI BATTAGLIA 2009a/2009b: 74-83).

The ruins of two Coptic monasteries were mentioned by early excavators: Deir el-Meitin (DE BOCK 1901: 91; CHASSINAT/PALANQUE 1911: 3, Pl. 1), situated on geological step 5 of the mountain, and Deir el-Azzam on the mountain plateau (MASPERO 1900: 109-119; DE BOCK 1901: 88-90; GROSSMANN 1991: 809-810). Each monastery was surrounded by a cemetery, and these cemeteries were unprofessionally excavated. The monasteries were not comprehensively recorded and suffered further damage during the twentieth century (KAHL 2007: 99-103). In addition to these monasteries, early archaeologists recorded some tombs from the Pharaonic Period, which were reused as dwellings by Christian anachoretes (CLÉDAT 1908: 213-223; KAHL 2007: 103-106).

5.9.2.2 Fieldwork of The Asyut Project

With the exception of the Tomb of the Dogs (cf. 5.7.2.2.) there are only some traces of early Roman Period activities on Gebel Asyut al-gharbi. Late Roman pottery, however, is widespread over the mountain and attests busy activities during fourth to seventh centuries CE.

The results of surveys at Deir el-Azzam (Pl. 37) and Deir el-Meitin (Pl. 36) point to activities at Deir el-Azzam from the fifth to the thirteenth century CE or even later (EICHNER/BECKH 2010: 207) and to activities at Deir el-Meitin beginning latest with the fifth to seventh century CE (EICHNER/BECKH 2010: 208).

Another survey enabled The Asyut Project to date the mud brick building E11.1 (Pl. 16), the northwestern-most building on Gebel Asyut al-gharbi, into the fourth/fifth to eighth century CE (EICHNER/BECKH 2010: 208).

Finally, at the mountain plateau Kom el-Shuqafa, a concentration of amphora from the first to the fifth century CE (EICHNER/BECKH 2010: 208) as well as the finding of pottery used for cooking and storage attest that Kom el-Shuqafa was settled at that time.

5.10 Islamic Period

5.10.1 General information about Asyut

Up until now Gebel Asyut al-gharbi has been used as a necropolis for people from Asyut. Thus, it reveals a quite unique continuity of usage over more than 4500 years from the Old Kingdom (probably already from the Early Dynastic Period) to present. The modern cemetery covers ancient tombs cut into the mountain. Also Islamic saints are venerated there, cf. e.g. the mausoleum of Sheikh Abu-Tug (Pl. 38) and the tomb of Bint Sheikh el-Arab (Fig. 2).

Fig. 2: The tomb of Bint Sheikh el-Arab (© Kahl 2010).

5.10.2 Islamic Period on Gebel Asyut al-gharbi

5.10.2.1 Early fieldwork

There is no evidence of early fieldwork concerning the Islamic Period.

5.10.2.2 Fieldwork of The Asyut Project

Fieldwork of The Asyut Project revealed some ostraca and graffiti written in Arabic. Also two paintings showing a mihrab were found in Tomb N13.1 (KAHL/VERHOEVEN 2008: 68, Fig. 1), which gives evidence that the Eleventh Dynasty tomb changed its function from a pharaonic burial ground to a place of prayer in Islamic Period.

Numerous fragments of Mamluk glazed pottery were found in the tombs of the First Intermediate Period/Period of Regions and early Middle Kingdom nomarchs and attest that these tombs were either used as a dwelling or were at least visited during Islamic Period (YASIN 2008; cf. the contribution of Abd el-Naser Yasin in this volume). Glazed Islamic pottery was also found at Deir el-Azzam (EICHNER/BECKH 2010: 207).

In addition, there is some circumstantial evidence for archaeological activities on Gebel Asyut al-gharbi during the Mamluk Period: In Tomb V, The Asyut Project found a shaft from the First Intermediate Period/Period of Regions, which was unknown to modern Egyptology. Mamluk pottery and a hoe, which were found inside the shaft, a relatively thorough cleaning of the shaft and the fact that the ground floor of the tomb was still covered with a layer of filling material from Roman to Byzantine Period and only disturbed exactly at the opening of the shaft, point to Mamluk archaeological activities (cf. KAHL/MALUR 2011; for medieval Arab archaeological activities cf. EL DALY 2005: 31-55).

References:

ASSMANN 1992: J. Assmann, *Das kulturelle Gedächtnis: Schrift, Erinnerung und politische Identität in frühen Hochkulturen* (Munich 1992).

ASSMANN 2002: J. Assmann (unter Mitarbeit von Martin Bommas), *Altägyptische Totenliturgien. Band I: Totenliturgien in den Sargtexten des Mittleren Reiches* (Supplemente zu den Schriften der Heidelberger Akademie der Wissenschaften, Philosophisch-Historische Klasse 14, Heidelberg 2002).

BAGNALL/FRIER/RUTHERFORD 1997: R. S. Bagnall/B. W. Frier/I. C. Rutherford (eds.), *The Census Register P.Oxy. 984: The Reverse of Pindar's Paeans* (Papyrologica Bruxellensia 29, Brussels 1997).

BECKER 2007: M. Becker, Popular Religion in Asyut, in: J. Kahl, *Ancient Asyut. The First Synthesis after 300 Years of Research* (The Asyut Project 1, Wiesbaden 2007) 141-149.

BIETAK 1985: M. Bietak, Zu den nubischen Bogenschützen aus Assiut: ein Beitrag zur Geschichte der Ersten Zwischenzeit, in: P. Posener-Kriéger (ed.), *Mélanges Gamal Eddin Mokhtar* (Bibliothèque d'Étude 97/1, Cairo 1985) 87-97.

BIETAK 1994: M. Bietak (ed.), *Pharaonen und Fremde. Dynastien im Dunkel* (Vienna 1994).

BOHLEKE 1993: B. Bohleke, *The Overseers of Double Granaries of Upper and Lower Egypt in the Egyptian New Kingdom, 1570-1085 B.C.* (New Haven 1993).

BRUNNER 1937: H. Brunner, *Die Texte aus den Gräbern der Herakleopolitenzeit von Siut mit Übersetzungen und Erläuterungen* (Ägyptologische Forschungen 5, Glückstadt 1937).

CALDERINI 1922: A. Calderini, Nella Patria di Plotino, in: *Aegyptus. Rivista italiana di egittologia e di papirologia* 3, 1922, 255-274.

CHASSINAT/PALANQUE 1911: É. Chassinat/Ch. Palanque, *Une campagne des fouilles dans la nécropole d'Assiout* (Mémoires publiés par les membres de l'Institut Français d'Archéologie Orientale du Caire 24, Cairo 1911).

CHÉHAB 1969: M. Chéhab, Noms de personnalités égyptiennes découverts au Liban, in: *Bulletin du Musée de Beyrouth* 22, 1969, 1-47.

CLARYSSE/THOMPSON 2006: W. Clarysse/D. J. Thompson, *Counting the People in Hellenistic Egypt* (Cambridge 2006).

CLÉDAT 1908: J. Clédat, Notes d'archéologie copte, in: *Annales du Service des Antiquités de l'Égypte* 9, 1908, 213-230.

D'AMICONE/POZZI BATTAGLIA 2009a: E. D'Amicone/M. Pozzi Battaglia (eds.), *Egitto mai visto. La montagna dei morti: Assiut quattromila anni fa.* Trento, Castello del Buonconsiglio, monumenti e collezioni provincali, 30 maggio – 8 novembre 2009 (Trento: Castello del Buonconsiglio 2009).

D'AMICONE/POZZI BATTAGLIA 2009b: E. D'Amicone/M. Pozzi Battaglia (eds.), *Egitto mai visto. Le dimore eterne di Assiut e Gebelein.* Reggio Calabria, Villa Genoese Zerbi 21 febbraio – 20 giugno 2010 (Trento: Castello del Buonconsiglio 2009).

DAVIES 1995: W. V. Davies, Ancient Egyptian Timber Imports: An Analysis of Wooden Coffins in the British Museum, in: W. V. Davies/L. Schofield (eds.), *Egypt, the Aegean and the Levant. Interconnections in the Second Millennium BC* (London 1995) 146-156.

DE BOCK 1901: W. de Bock, *Matériaux pour servir à l'archéologie de l'Égypte Chrétienne.* Édition posthume (St. Petersburg 1901).

DUNHAM 1937-1938: D. Dunham, An Egyptian Statuette of the Middle Kingdom, in: *Worcester Art Museum Annual* 3, 1937-1938, 9-16.

DUQUESNE 2007: T. DuQuesne, *Anubis, Upwawet, and Other Deities. Personal worship and official religion in ancient Egypt.* Catalogue of the Exhibition at the Egyptian Museum, Cairo, March 2007 (Cairo 2007).

DUQUESNE 2008: T. DuQuesne, The Great Goddess and her Companions in Middle Egypt: new findings on Hathor of Medjed and the local deities of Asyut, in: B. Rothöhler/A. Manisali (eds.), *Mythos & Ritual. Festschrift für Jan Assmann zum 70. Geburtstag* (Religionswissenschaft: Forschung und Wissenschaft 5, Berlin 2008) 1-26.

DUQUESNE 2009: T. DuQuesne, The Salakhana Trove: Votive Steale and Other Objects from Asyut, in: *Oxfordshire Communications in Egyptology* 7, London 2009.

EICHNER/BECKH 2010: I. Eichner/Th. Beckh, The late antique and medieval monuments of the Gebel Asyut al-gharbi, in: J. Kahl/M. El-Khadragy/U. Verhoeven et al., The Asyut Project: Seventh Season of Fieldwork (2009), in: *Studien zur Altägyptischen Kultur* 39, 2010, 207-210.

EL DALY 2005: O. El Daly, *Egyptology: The Missing Millennium. Ancient Egypt in Medieval Arabic Writings* (London 2005).

EL-KHADRAGY 2006a: M. El-Khadragy, The Northern Soldiers-Tomb at Asyut, in: *Studien zur Altägyptischen Kultur* 35, 2006, 147-165.

EL-KHADRAGY 2006b: M. El-Khadragy, New Discoveries in the Tomb of Khety II at Asyut, in: *The Bulletin of the Australian Centre for Egyptology* 17, 2006, 79-95.

EL-KHADRAGY 2007a: M. El-Khadragy, Some Significant Features in the Decoration of the Chapel of Iti-ibi-iqer at Asyut, in: *Studien zur Altägyptischen Kultur* 36, 2007, 105-135.

EL-KHADRAGY 2007b: M. El-Khadragy, The Shrine of the Rock-cut Chapel of Djefaihapi I at Asyut, in: *Göttinger Miszellen. Beiträge zur ägyptologischen Diskussion* 212, 2007, 41-62.

EL-KHADRAGY 2007c: M. El-Khadragy, Fishing, Fowling and Animal-Handling in the Tomb of Djefaihapi I at Asyut, in: *The Bulletin of the Australian Centre for Egyptology* 18, 2007, 125-144.

EL-KHADRAGY 2008: M. El-Khadragy, The Decoration of the Rock-cut Chapel of Khety II at Asyut, in: *Studien zur Altägyptischen Kultur* 37, 2008, 219-241.

EL-KHADRAGY/KAHL 2004: M. El-Khadragy/J. Kahl, The First Intermediate Period Tombs at Asyut Revisited, in: *Studien zur Altägyptischen Kultur* 32, 2004, 233-243.

ENGEL/KAHL 2009: E.-M. Engel/J. Kahl, Die Grabanlage Djefaihapis I. in Assiut: ein Rekonstruktionsversuch, in: J. Popielska-Grzybowska/O. Białostocka/J. Iwaszczuk (eds.), *Proceedings of the Third European Conference of Young Egyptologists. Egypt 2004: Perspectives of Research. Warsaw 12-14 May 2004* (Acta Archaeologica Pultuskiensia 1, Pultusk 2009) 55-59.

FAUERBACH 2006: U. Fauerbach, The map of the necropolis, in: J. Kahl/M. El-Khadragy/U. Verhoeven, The Asyut Project: Third season of fieldwork, in: *Studien zur Altägyptischen Kultur* 34, 2006, 245.

FENDT 2009: A. Fendt, Helios und die Göttin. Zwei vergessene Kolossalstatuen aus dem römischen Ägypten in der Berliner Antikensammlung, in: *Jahrbuch der Berliner Museen, Neue Folge* 51, 2009, 47-61.

GABRA 1931: S. Gabra, Un temple d'Aménophis IV à Assiout, in: *Chronique d'Égypte* 6, 1931, 237-243.

GARDINER 1957: A. Gardiner, *Egyptian Grammar Being an Introduction to the Study of Hieroglyphs* (Oxford ³1957).

GRÉBAUT 1890-1900: E. Grébaut, *Le Musée Égyptien. Recueil de monuments et de notices sur les fouilles d'Égypte.* Tome premier (Cairo 1890-1900).

GRIFFITH 1889a: F. Ll. Griffith, The Inscriptions of Siût and Dêr Rîfeh, in: *The Babylonian and Oriental Record* 3, 1888-1889, 121-129, 164-168, 174-184, 244-252.

GRIFFITH 1889b: F. Ll. Griffith, *The Inscriptions of Siût and Dêr Rîfeh* (London 1889).

GROSSMANN 1991: P. Grossmann, Dayr al-Izam, in: A. S. Atya (ed.), *The Coptic Encyclopedia* 3 (New York 1991) 809-810.

HAYES 1959: W. C. Hayes, *The Scepter of Egypt. A Background for the Study of the Egyptian Antiquities in The Metropolitan Museum of Art. Part II: The Hyksos Period and the New Kingdom (1675-1080 B.C.)* (New York 1959).

HELCK 1976: W. Helck, Ägyptische Statuen im Ausland – ein chronologisches Problem, in: *Ugarit Forschungen* 8, 1976, 101-115.

HÖLZL 2007: R. Hölzl, *Meisterwerke der Ägyptisch-Orientalischen Sammlung*, Kurzführer durch das Kunsthistorische Museum 6 (Vienna 2007).

HOFFMANN 2000: F. Hoffmann, *Ägypten. Kultur und Lebenswelt in griechisch-römischer Zeit. Eine Darstellung nach den demotischen Quellen* (Berlin 2000).

JACQUET-GORDON 1962: H. K. Jacquet-Gordon, *Les noms des domaines funéraires sous l'Ancien Empire Égyptien* (Bibliothèque d'Étude 34, Cairo 1962).

JOHNSON 1994: J. H. Johnson, "Annuity Contracts" and Marriage, in: David P. Silverman (ed.), *For his Ka. Essays Offered in Memory of Klaus Baer* (Studies in Ancient Oriental Civilization 55, Chicago 1994) 113-132.

KAHL 1994: J. Kahl, S1S 380-418: Eine Textidentifizierung, in: *Göttinger Miszellen. Beiträge zur ägyptologischen Diskussion* 139, 1994, 41-42.

KAHL 1999: J. Kahl, *Siut – Theben. Zur Wertschätzung von Traditionen im alten Ägypten* (Probleme der Ägyptologie 13, Leiden – Boston – Cologne 1999).

KAHL 2006: J. Kahl, Ein Zeugnis altägyptischer Schulausflüge, in: *Göttinger Miszellen. Beiträge zur ägyptologischen Diskussion* 211, 2006, 25-29.

KAHL 2007: J. Kahl, *Ancient Asyut. The First Synthesis after 300 Years of Research* (The Asyut Project 1, Wiesbaden 2007).

KAHL 2008: J. Kahl, Mapping Gebel Asyut al-gharbi, in: J. Kahl/M. El-Khadragy/U. Verhoeven, The Asyut Project: Fifth Season of Fieldwork (2007), in: *Studien zur Altägyptischen Kultur* 37, 2008, 199-200.

KAHL 2009: J. Kahl, Tomb of the Dogs, in: J. Kahl/M. El-Khadragy/U. Verhoeven et al., The Asyut Project: Sixth Season of Fieldwork (2008), in: *Studien zur Altägyptischen Kultur* 38, 2009, 117-121.

KAHL 2010: J. Kahl, Tomb of the Dogs, in: J. Kahl/M. El-Khadragy/U. Verhoeven et al., The Asyut Project: Seventh Season of Fieldwork (2009), in: *Studien zur Altägyptischen Kultur* 39, 2010, 198-199.

KAHL forthcoming: J. Kahl unter Mitarbeit von A. Herzberg, Proportionen und Stile in den assiutischen Nomarchengräbern der Ersten Zwischenzeit und des Mittleren Reiches, in: E. Frood/A. McDonald/R. Parkinson (eds.), *Festschrift*.

KAHL/EL-KHADRAGY/VERHOEVEN 2006: J. Kahl/M. El-Khadragy/U. Verhoeven, The Asyut Project: Third season of fieldwork, in: *Studien zur Altägyptischen Kultur* 34, 2006, 241-249.

KAHL/KITAGAWA 2010: J. Kahl/Ch. Kitagawa, Ein wiederentdeckter Hundefriedhof in Assiut, in: *Sokar* 20, 2010, 77-81.

KAHL/MALUR 2011: J. Kahl/J. Malur, Tomb V, in: J. Kahl/M. El-Khadragy/U. Verhoeven et al., The Asyut Project: Eighth Season of Fieldwork (2010), in: *Studien zur Altägyptischen Kultur* 40, 2011 182-183.

KAHL/VERHOEVEN 2008: J. Kahl/U. Verhoeven, „Dornröschen" ist erwacht. Das neu entdeckte Grab N13.1 in Assiut, in: *Sokar* 16, 2008, 68-73.

KAMAL 1916: A. Bey Kamal, Fouilles à Deir Dronka et à Assiout (1913-1914), in: *Annales du Service des Antiquités de l'Égypte* 16, 1916, 65-114.

KARIG 1968: J. S. Karig, Die Kultkammer des Amenhotep aus Deir Durunka, in: *Zeitschrift für Ägyptische Sprache und Altertumskunde* 95, 1968, 27-34.

KENDALL 1997: T. Kendall, *Kerma and the Kingdom of Kush, 2500-1500 B.C.: The Archaeological Discovery of an Ancient Nubian Empire* (Washington 1997).

KITAGAWA 2009: Ch. Kitagawa, The fauna materials from the surface survey in the central part of the Gebel Asyut al-gharbi, in: J. Kahl/M. El-Khadragy/U. Verhoeven et al., The Asyut Project: Sixth Season of Fieldwork (2008), in: *Studien zur Altägyptischen Kultur* 38, 2009, 122-129.

KITAGAWA 2011: Ch. Kitagawa, Animal remains, in: J. Kahl/M. El-Khadragy/U. Verhoeven et al., The Asyut Project: Eighth Season of Fieldwork (2010), in: *Studien zur Altägyptischen Kultur* 40, 2011, 197-198.

KLEMM/KLEMM 2006: R. Klemm/D. D. Klemm, *Geological Report (on occasion of a visit at Gebel Asyut in 2005)* (January 2006; unpublished).

KLEMM/KLEMM 2008: R. Klemm/D. D. Klemm, *Stones and Quarries in Ancient Egypt* (London 2008).

KUENTZ 1934: Ch. Kuentz, Remarques sur les statues de Harwa, in: *Bulletin de l'Institut Français d'Archéologie Orientale* 34, 1934, 143-163.

KUHLMANN/SCHENKEL 1983: K. P. Kuhlmann/W. Schenkel, *Das Grab des Ibi, Obergutsverwalters der Gottesgemahlin des Amun (Thebanisches Grab Nr. 36). Band 1: Beschreibung der unterirdischen Kult- und Bestattungsanlage* (Archäologische Veröffentlichungen 15, Mainz 1983).

LEAHY 1999: A. Leahy, More fragments of the Book of the Dead of Padinemty, in: *Journal of Egyptian Archaeology* 85, 1999, 230-232.

MAGEE 1988: D. Magee, *Asyût to the End of the Middle Kingdom: A Historical and Cultural Study* (unpublished Ph.D. thesis, Oxford 1988).

MASPERO 1900: G. Maspero, Les fouilles de Deir el Aizam (Septembre 1897), in: *Annales du Service des Antiquités de l'Égypte* 1, 1900, 109-119.

MCGING 1997: B. C. McGing, Revolt Egyptian Style. Internal Opposition to Ptolemaic Rule, in: *Archiv für Papyrusforschung und verwandte Gebiete* 43, 1997, 273-314.

MITTHOF 2001: F. Mitthof, *Annona Militaris. Die Heeresversorgung im spätantiken Ägypten. Ein Beitrag zur Verwaltungs- und Heeresgeschichte des Römischen Reiches im 3. bis 6. Jh. n. Chr.*, 2 vols. (Papyrologica Florentina 31, Florence 2001).

MONTET 1928: P. Montet, Les tombeaux de Siout et de Deir Rifeh, in: *Kêmi. Revue de philologie et d'archéologie égyptiennes et coptes* 1, 1928, 53-68.

MONTET 1930-35: P. Montet, Les tombeaux de Siout et de Deir Rifeh (suite), in: *Kêmi. Revue de philologie et d'archéologie égyptiennes et coptes* 3, 1930-35, 45-111.

MONTET 1936: P. Montet, Les tombeaux de Siout et de Deir Rifeh (troisième article), in: *Kêmi. Revue de philologie et d'archéologie égyptiennes et coptes* 6, 1936, 131-163.

MONTEVECCHI 1998: O. Montevecchi, La provenienza di P. Oxy. 984, in: *Aegyptus. Rivista italiana di egittologia e di papirologia* 78, 1998, 49-76.

MONTEVECCHI 2000: O. Montevecchi, Ritorniamo a Licopoli e a Plotino, in: *Aegyptus. Rivista italiana di egittologia e di papirologia* 80, 2000, 139-143.

MORENZ 2010: L. Morenz, *Die Zeit der Regionen im Spiegel der Gebelein-Region. Kulturgeschichtliche Re-Konstruktionen* (Probleme der Ägyptologie 27, Leiden – Boston 2010).

ONASCH 1994: H.-U. Onasch, *Die assyrischen Eroberungen Ägyptens. Teil 1: Kommentare und Anmerkungen* (Ägypten und Altes Testament 27/1, Wiesbaden 1994).

OSING 1976: J. Osing, *Die Nominalbildung des Ägyptischen* (Mainz 1976).

OSING 1998a: J. Osing, PSI inv. I 3 + pCarlsberg 305 + pTebt. Tait Add. 2 e PSI inv. I 4 + pCarlsberg 306 + pTebt. Tait Add. 3. Copie delle iscrizioni nelle tombe di Assiut, in: J. Osing/G. Rosati (eds.), *Papiri geroglifici e ieratici da Tebtynis* (Florence 1998) 55-100.

OSING 1998b: J. Osing, PSI inv. I 72: Manuale mitologico per i nòmi VII – XVI dell'Alto Egitto, in: J. Osing/G. Rosati (eds.), *Papiri geroglifici e ieratici da Tebtynis* (Florence 1998) 129-188.

PALANQUE 1903: Ch. Palanque, Notes de fouilles dans la nécropole d'Assiout, in: *Bulletin de l'Institut Français d'Archéologie Orientale* 3, 1903, 119-128.
PANCKOUCKE 1822: C. L. F. Panckoucke, *Description de l'Égypte ou Recueil des observations et des recherches qui ont été faites en Égypte pendant l'expédition de l'armée française*. Ant. IV, Seconde édition (Paris 1822).
PORTER/MOSS 1934: B. Porter/R. L. B. Moss, *Topographical Bibliography of Ancient Egyptian Hieroglyphic Texts, Reliefs, and Paintings. IV. Lower and Middle Egypt* (Oxford 1934).
PRELL 2011: S. Prell, The Tomb of the Dogs Area, in: J. Kahl/M. El-Khadragy/U. Verhoeven et al., The Asyut Project: Eighth Season of Fieldwork (2010), in: *Studien zur Altägyptischen Kultur* 40, 2011, 194-197.
PRICE/WAGGONER 1975: M. Price/N. Waggoner, *Archaic Greek Coinage. The Asyut Hoard* (London 1975).
REISNER 1931: G. A. Reisner, Inscribed Monuments from Gebel Barkal, in: *Zeitschrift für Ägyptische Sprache und Altertumskunde* 66, 1931, 76-100.
RYAN 1988: D. P. Ryan, *The Archaeological Excavations of David George Hogarth at Asyut, Egypt* (Cincinnati 1988).
RZEUSKA 2011: T. Rzeuska, Pharaonic Pottery, Asyut 2010, in: J. Kahl/M. El-Khadragy/U. Verhoeven et al., The Asyut Project: Eighth Season of Fieldwork, in: *Studien zur Altägyptischen Kultur* 40, 2011, 199-209.
SAUNERON 1983: S. Sauneron, *Villes et légendes d'Égypte* (Bibliothèque d'Étude 90, Cairo ²1983).
SCHEIDEL 2001: W. Scheidel, (Review) Bagnall/Frier/Rutherford, The Census Register P. Oxy. 984: The Reverse of Pindar's Paeans (Brussels 1997), in: *Bulletin of the American Society of Papyrologists* 38, 2001, 147-151.
SCHENKEL 1965: W. Schenkel, *Memphis – Herakleopolis – Theben. Die epigraphischen Zeugnisse der 7.-11. Dynastie Ägyptens* (Ägyptologische Abhandlungen 12, Wiesbaden 1965).
SCHENKEL 1978: W. Schenkel, *Die Bewässerungsrevolution im Alten Ägypten* (Mainz 1978).
SHORE 1988: A. F. Shore, Swapping Property at Asyut in the Persian Period, in: J. Baines/T. G. H. James/A. Leahy/A. F. Shore (eds.), *Pyramid Studies and Other Essays Presented to I.E.S. Edwards* (The Egypt Exploration Society Occasional Publications 7, London 1988) 200-206.
SHORE/SMITH 1959: A. F. Shore/H. S. Smith, Two Unpublished Demotic Documents from the Asyut Archive, in: *Journal of Egyptian Archaeology* 45, 1959, 52-60.
SMITH 1957: W. S. Smith, A Painting in the Assiut Tomb of Hepzefa, in: *Mitteilungen des Deutschen Archäologischen Instituts Abteilung Kairo* 15, 1957, 221-224.
SOTTAS 1923: H. Sottas, Sur quelques papyrus démotiques provenant d'Assiout, in: *Annales du Service des Antiquités de l'Égypte* 23, 1923, 34-46.
SPANEL 1989: D. B. Spanel, The Herakleopolitan Tombs of Kheti I, *Jt(.j)jb(.j)*, and Kheti II at Asyut, in: *Orientalia* 58, 1989, 301-314.
SPIEGELBERG 1932: W. Spiegelberg, *Die demotischen Denkmäler. III. Demotische Inschriften und Papyri (CG 50023-50165)* (Catalogue Général des Antiquités Égyptiennes du Musée du Caire, Berlin 1932).
SUSSER/SCHNEIDER 2003: I. Susser/J. Schneider, Wounded Cities: Deconstruction and Reconstruction in a Globalized World, in: J. Schneider/I. Susser (eds.), *Wounded Cities. Destruction and Reconstruction in a Globalized World* (Oxford – New York 2003) 1-23.

TAYLOR/STRUDWICK 2005: J. H. Taylor/N. C. Strudwick, *Mummies. Death and the Afterlife in Ancient Egypt. Treasures from The British Museum presented by The Bowers Museum of Cultural Art* (Santa Ana, California 2005).

THOMPSON 1934: H. Thompson, *A Family Archive from Siut from Papyri in the British Museum* (Oxford 1934).

TIMM 1984: S. Timm, *Das christlich-koptische Ägypten in arabischer Zeit. Teil 1 (A-C)* (Beihefte zum Tübinger Atlas des Vorderen Orients, Reihe B (Geisteswissenschaften) 41/1, Wiesbaden 1984).

VALBELLE 1998: D. Valbelle, The Cultural Significance of Iconographic and Epigraphic Data Found in the Kingdom of Kerma, in: T. Kendall (ed.), *Nubian Studies 1998. Proceedings of the Ninth Conference of the International Society of Nubian Studies, August 21-26, 1998, Boston, Massachusetts* (Boston 2004) 176-183.

VEÏSSE 2004: A.-E. Veïsse, *Les « révoltes égyptiennes ». Recherches sur les troubles intérieurs en Égypte du règne de Ptolémée III à la conquète romaine* (Studia Hellenistica 41, Leuven – Paris – Dudley, MA 2004).

VERHOEVEN 2007: U. Verhoeven, Graffiti from the New Kingdom in Tomb N13.1, in: J. Kahl/M. El-Khadragy/U. Verhoeven, The Asyut Project: Fourth Season of Fieldwork (2006), in: *Studien zur Altägyptischen Kultur* 36, 2007, 85-87.

VERHOEVEN 2008: U. Verhoeven, Tomb N13.1: graffiti, in: J. Kahl/M. El-Khadragy/U. Verhoeven, The Asyut Project: Fifth Season of Fieldwork (2007), in: *Studien zur Altägyptischen Kultur* 37, 2008, 201-204.

VERHOEVEN 2009: U. Verhoeven, Die wie Kraniche balzen: Männerphantasien zur Zeit Amenhoteps III. in Assiut, in: D. Kessler/R. Schulz/M. Ullmann et al. (eds.), *Texte – Theben – Tonfragmente. Festschrift für Günter Burkard* (Ägypten und Altes Testament 76, Wiesbaden 2009) 434-441.

VERHOEVEN 2011: U. Verhoeven, Tomb P13.1, in: J. Kahl/M. El-Khadragy/U. Verhoeven et al., The Asyut Project: Eighth Season of Fieldwork (2010), in: *Studien zur Altägyptischen Kultur* 40, 2011, 186-191.

VERHOEVEN forthcoming: U. Verhoeven, "Der lebt nach dem Tod". Orthographisches und Biographisches in den Inschriftenfragmenten der Grabanlage M10.1 in Assiut, in: H.-W. Fischer-Elfert/R. B. Parkinson (eds.), *Middle Kingdom Studies in Memory of Detlef Franke* (Philippika, Marburg, in press).

VLEEMING 1989: S. P. Vleeming, Strijd om het erfdeel van Tefhapi, in: P. W. Pestman (ed.), *Familiearchieven uit het land van Pharao* (Zutphen 1989) 31-45.

WEILL 1950: R. Weill, Un nouveau pharaon de l'époque tardive en Moyenne Égypte et l'Horus de Deir el-Gebrâwi (XIIe nome), in: *Bulletin de l'Institut Français d'Archéologie Orientale* 49, 1950, 57-65.

WILD 1971: H. Wild, Note concernant des antiquités trouvées, non à Deir Dronka, mais dans la nécropole d'Assiout, in: *Bulletin de l'Institut Français d'Archéologie Orientale* 69, 1971, 307-309.

WILDUNG 1984: D. Wildung, *Sesostris und Amenemhet. Ägypten im Mittleren Reich* (Darmstadt 1984).

WILKINSON 1843: G. Wilkinson, *Modern Egypt and Thebes: being a description of Egypt; including the information required for travellers in that country* II (London 1843).

WOLF 1957: W. Wolf, *Die Kunst Aegyptens: Gestalt und Geschichte* (Stuttgart 1957).

YASIN 2008: Abd El-Naser Yasin, Islamic Pottery Findings, in: J. Kahl/M. El-Khadragy/U. Verhoeven, The Asyut Project: Fifth Season of Fieldwork (2007), in: *Studien zur Altägyptischen Kultur* 37, 2008, 206-207.

ZITMAN 2010: M. Zitman, *The Necropolis of Assiut. A Case Study of Local Egyptian Funerary Culture from the Old Kingdom to the End of the Middle Kingdom* I-II (Orientalia Lovaniensia Analecta 180, Leuven 2010).

The Nomarchs of Asyut During the First Intermediate Period and the Middle Kingdom

Mahmoud El-Khadragy

Reinvestigating the ancient necropolis of Asyut by the Egyptian-German joint mission of Sohag University and the Johannes Gutenberg-Universität Mainz for seven successive seasons (2003-2009) provided us with rich information concerning the administration of the nome during the latter part of the First Intermediate Period and the Middle Kingdom. Not only that much of the already known tombs were reinvestigated and properly documented, but the necropolis was surveyed for mapping purpose, which led to the discovery of an unknown tomb (N13.1; Pl. 28-29), adding much to our knowledge concerning the administration of Asyut at the time of the reunification of Egypt by Nebhepetre. Nonetheless, more relevant tombs are still in need of further investigation, especially the so-called Northern Soldiers-Tomb (H11.1; Pl. 16), the badly preserved Tomb O14.2 (Pl. 19), which is located near Deir el-Meitin, and the now undecorated Tomb M12.1, which is situated in the upper level of the mountain (Pl. 14). This might fill some of the still existing gaps in our knowledge concerning the administration of Asyut during the Eleventh Dynasty.

Siut Tombs III (N12.1), IV (N12.2), V (M11.1), N13.1 and Hogarth Tomb III belong to five successive generations of nomarchs of a noble family of ancient race (cf. GRIFFITH 1889b: Pls. 13 [1], 15 [33]; for *qrḥt* – "the serpent-spirit", the term used by both Khety I and Khety II to show the nobility of their line, see: GARDINER 1909: 55-56 [7,5]; EDEL 1984: 151-53), who governed Asyut during the latter part of the First Intermediate Period up to the reunification of Egypt by Nebhepetre. All of those governors had the high ranks of *jrj pˁt* – "hereditary prince" and *ḥ3tj-ˁ* – "count", and all of them headed the local cult of both Wepwawet and Anubis under the titles *jmj-r ḥmw-nṯr n Wp-w3wt nb Z3wtj* – "overseer of priests of Wepwawet, lord of Asyut" and *jmj-r ḥmw-nṯr Jnpw nb R-qrrt* – "overseer of priests of Anubis, lord of Ra-qereret", while each one of them had local troops of soldiers under his command (cf. EL-KHADRAGY 2008: 226-229).

Chronologically, Khety I, the owner of Siut Tomb V (M11.1; Pl. 22-23), is the earliest of those nomarchs, as generally accepted and confirmed by the newly discovered Tomb N13.1 (cf. EL-KHADRAGY 2007b: 105-135; KAHL 2006: 25-29; KAHL/El-KHADRAGY/VERHOEVEN 2007: 84-87).

According to his biography, Khety I took swimming lessons together with the royal children at the court in Herakleopolis (GRIFFITH 1889b: Pl. 15 [20-22]) and sought to improve the irrigation system in Asyut (GRIFFITH 1889b: Pl. 15 [3ff]). Such statements might reveal the outlines of a new strategy adopted by later Herakleopolitan kings, which aimed at making Asyut the southernmost defensive buffer-state responsible for warding off the attacks of the ambitious Theban rulers of the early Eleventh Dynasty. To achieve this strategy, the Herakleopolitan kings followed three significant principles in dealing with the Siutian nomarchs: (1) educating the future nomarchs in the royal court to guarantee their loyalty, (2) establishing Asyut as the most important military stronghold in the South by having effective military troops and a fleet, (3) improving the province's economy through active plans which ensured sufficient harvest also in barren years (EL-KHADRAGY 2008: 231, with n. 104).

Khety I was followed in the governorship of Asyut by Iti-ibi, the owner of Siut Tomb III (N12.1; Pl. 24-25). The relationship between the two nomarchs remains uncertain. In his biography, Iti-ibi reports two successful battles against the Southern Nomes, which had banded together from Elephantine to Thinis (GRIFFITH 1889b: Pl. 11 [16-37]). As has already been suggested elsewhere (FRANKE 1987: 52), Iti-ibi served under the father of the Tenth Dynasty king Merikare. Allied with the father of Merikare (for the possible identity of the father cf. SCHARFF 1936: 7-10; VOLTEN 1945: 82-84; BECKERATH 1966: 20; GOEDICKE 1969: 142; LOPEZ 1973: 190-91; QUACK 1992: 107), Iti-ibi was involved in the invasion of Thinis (for the only available source referring to this invasion cf. QUACK 1992: 42-43, 179 [73-74]), which corresponds to the "rebellion of Thinis" dated to the 14th year of Nebhepetre (for such rebellion cf. CLÈRE/VANDIER 1948: §23, 19; SCHENKEL 1965: §374, 226-28). During the next phase of this war (cf. FRANKE 1987: 52-53) Nebhepetre recaptured Thinis sometime after his 14th year and before his 39th year (for the suggested date of the reunification of Egypt by Nebhepetre cf. QUACK 1992: 106) and advanced north

Fig. 1: Siut III (N12.1), Tomb of Iti-ibi: north wall, biographical inscription (© Kahl).

toward the border between the Tenth and Eleventh Nomes of Upper Egypt, wherein lies the locality known as *Jnt Ḥzj* (for *Jnt Ḥzj* cf. GOMAÀ 1986: 243-44).

The fact that Iti-ibi substituted his originally incised biographical inscription with some ideal autobiography executed in paint (GRIFFITH 1889a: 127-29; GRIFFITH 1889b: Pl. 12 [41-56]) suggests that Nebhepetre later advanced towards Asyut, and that Iti-ibi, who was still alive at that time, realized the improbability of warding off the attack of Nebhepetre, thereupon deciding to hide his original text referring to his earlier successful actions against the Thebans (Fig. 1).

In his office as governor of Asyut Iti-ibi was followed by his son Khety II, the owner of the unfinished tomb Siut IV (N12.2; Pl. 26-27), who served under the Tenth Dynasty king Merikare (cf. GRIFFITH 1889b: Pl. 13 [3, 22]; EL-KHADRAGY 2008: 235, Fig. 3 [22]). Unlike all the other First Intermediate Period Siutian nomarchs, Khety II held the nomarchic title *ḥrj-tp ꜥꜣ n Nḏft* – "great overlord of the 13th Nome of Upper Egypt" (GRIFFITH 1889b: Pl. 13 [36]; EL-KHADRAGY 2008: 234, Fig. 2), and claimed authority over Upper Egypt through his title *ḥrj-tp ꜥꜣ Šmꜥw* – "great overlord of Upper Egypt" (GRIFFITH 1889b: Pl. 13 [23]; EL-KHADRAGY 2008: 235, Fig. 3 [23]).

Alluding to the attack of Nebhepetre on Asyut, the biography of Khety II (Pl. 27b) referred to Siutian refugees who were returned by Khety II (GRIFFITH 1889b: Pl. 13 [17-18]; EL-KHADRAGY 2008: 233, Fig. 1 [17-18]), a possible destruction of the temple of Wepwawet, which Khety II had to restore later (GRIFFITH 1889b: Pl. 13 [19-22]; EL-KHADRAGY 2008: 235, Fig. 3 [19-22]), a possible suspension of the funerary services in the cemetery (GRIFFITH 1889b: Pl. 13 [28]; EL-KHADRAGY 2008: 235, Fig. 3 [28]), fighting and shooting arrows within the city (GRIFFITH 1889b: Pl. 13 [33]; EL-KHADRAGY 2008: 234, Fig. 2 [33]), beating people, whether young or old (GRIFFITH 1889b: Pl. 13 [33]; EL-KHADRAGY 2008: 234, Fig. 2 [33]), plundering properties in the street (GRIFFITH 1889b: Pl. 13 [33-34]; EL-KHADRAGY 2008: 234, Fig. 2 [33-34]) and acts of vandalism against houses (GRIFFITH 1889b: Pl. 13 [34]; EL-KHADRAGY 2008: 234, Fig. 2 [34]). These conditions could only have occurred as a result of the capture of Asyut by the troops of Nebhepetre following the recapture of Thinis after the 14th year of Nebhepetre (FRANKE 1987: 52-53) and the death of Iti-ibi in this fight. The same inscription points out that Khety II managed to push back the Theban aggressors and once again restore his territory with the support of the Herakleopolitan king Merikare (Fig. 2) (GRIFFITH 1889b: Pl. 13 [9-19]; EL-KHADRAGY 2008: Fig. 1 [9-19]).

Consistent with such turbulent times of civil war is a motif of military implication, characterizing the decoration of Khety II and some other Herakleopolitan Period chapels at Asyut (cf. KAHL 2007: 76, Fig. 53; EL-KHADRAGY 2007b, 123, Fig. 3). The scene, which is executed in sunk-relief, depicts three rows of soldiers, the third row of which is unfinished (Fig. 3) (EL-KHADRAGY 2008: 236-37, Figs. 4-5).

The newly discovered tomb of Iti-ibi-iqer (N13.1; Pl. 28-29) introduces us to another member of the same family of nomarchs who ruled Asyut during the latter part of the First Intermediate Period (EL-KHADRAGY 2007b: 105-135).

A scene decorating the eastern end of the southern wall of Iti-ibi-iqer's chapel suggests that Iti-ibi-iqer was the son and direct successor of Khety II in the governorship of Asyut.

The scene depicts a face-to-face representation of the tomb owner accompanied by a woman and a man called Khety (Fig. 4). To the left stands Khety, facing right. The label identifying him reads: … *[ḥ3tj]-ˁ ẖtmtj-bjtj smr wˁ[tj jmj-r ḥm(w)-nṯr n Wp-w3wt nb Z3wtj] jm3ḫ[jjw]* … *mrj nb R-qrrt* … *[ḥz]jj n nṯr=f njwtj Ḫtjj-jqr m3ˁ-ḫrw* –"… the [count], the sealer of the king of Lower Egypt, the sole companion, [the overseer of priests of

Fig. 2: Siut IV (N12.2), Tomb of Khety II, north wall, biographical inscription (© Kahl).

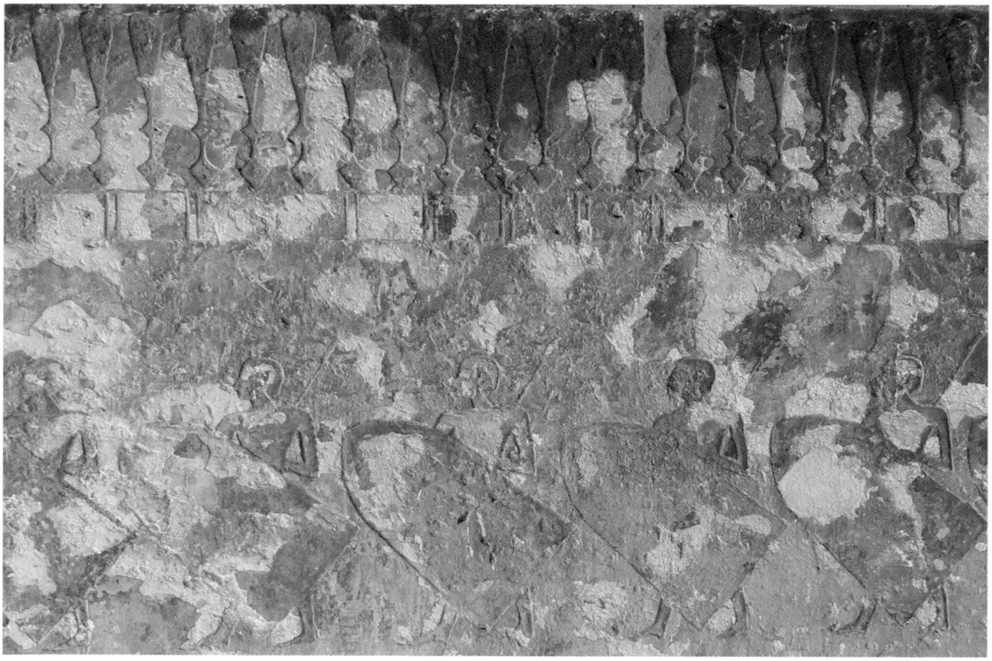

Fig. 3: Siut IV (N12.2), Tomb of Khety II, southern wall, marching soldiers (© Kahl).

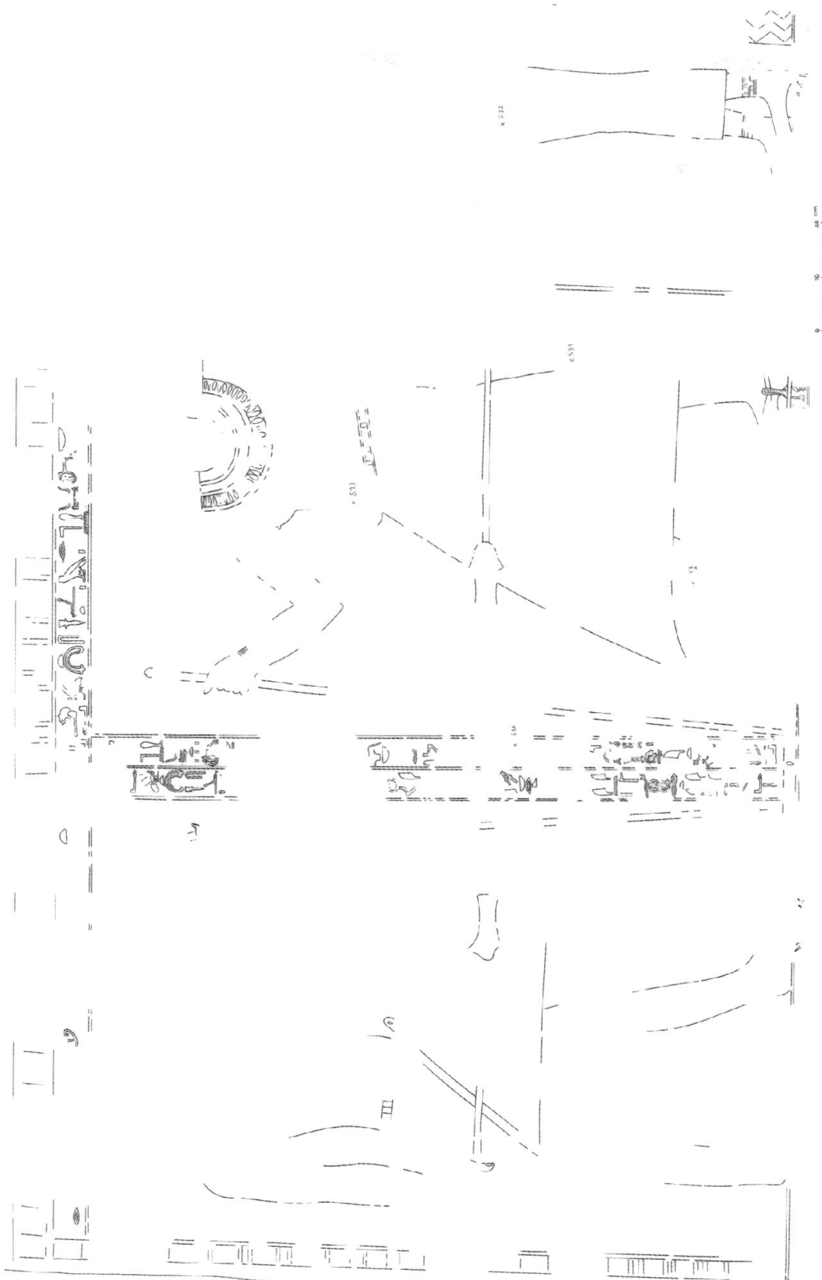

Fig. 4: N13.1, Tomb of Iti-ibi-iqer, south wall, eastern end, commemorating Khety II (© The Asyut Project; drawing: S. Shafik).

Wepwawet, lord of Asyut], the honored one, … beloved of the lord of Ra-qereret, … whom his local god [favours], Khety-iqer, true of voice", while the other figure is labeled: *[jrj] pʿt ḥ3tj-ʿ ḫtmtj-bjtj smr wʿtj jmj-r ḥm(w)-nṯr n Wp-w3wt nb [Z3wtj] … [jmj-r] ḥm(w)-nṯr n Wp-w3wt [nb Z3wtj] … Jnpw nb [R-qrr]t jm3ḫ[jjw] … j w3ḥ tpj t3 Jt(=j)-jb(=j)-[jqr] m3ʿ-ḫrw* – "[The hereditary] prince, the count, the sealer of the king of Lower Egypt, the sole companion, the overseer of priests of Wepwawet, lord of [Asyut], … [the overseer] of priests of Wepwawet, [lord of Asyut], … Anubis, lord of [Ra-qerere]t, the honored one … the one enduring on earth, Iti-ibi-[iqer], true of voice" (EL-KHADRAGY 2007b: 113-114, 128, Fig. 8).

Being *ḥ3tj-ʿ*, the most characteristic of nomarchs during the First Intermediate Period and the Eleventh Dynasty (HELCK 1958: 206-9), and a high priest of the local god Wepwawet, suggest that this Khety was a nomarch and that he is to be identified with one of the two well-known First Intermediate Period nomarchs of Asyut, Khety I (Siut V; M11.1) or Khety II (Siut IV; N12.2). Judging by the prominence given to the military scenes in the chapel of Iti-ibi-iqer (EL-KHADRAGY 2007b: 123-124, Figs. 3-4), his military title *jmj-r mšʿ n Nḏft ḫntt mj-qd=s* – "the overseer of the troops of the entire 13th Nome of Upper Egypt" (EL-KHADRAGY 2007b: 123, Fig. 3), which is not recorded for any other nomarch at Asyut during the First Intermediate Period, and his probably premature death suggested by his son Mesehti-iqer (EL-KHADRAGY 2007b: 107, 122, Fig. 2) preparing the tomb for him, Iti-ibi-iqer seems to have lived during the turbulent period of the civil war. Of the two men named Khety (Siut V and Siut IV), Khety I enjoyed a peaceful governorship (cf. GRIFFITH 1889b: Pl. 15 [1ff]; SCHENKEL 1965: 71-74 [§57]; regarding Khety I's efforts in developing the irrigation methods at Asyut, see: SCHENKEL 1978: 29sqq), in his biography Khety II refers to a military campaign against the Theban forces (GRIFFITH 1889b: Pl. 13 [9-19]; EL-KHADRAGY 2008: 233, Fig. 1 [9-19]), in which he allied with the Herakleopolitan king Merikare (cf. above).

One of the two table scenes flanking the central false door decorating the back wall of the chapel's niche of the tomb of Iti-ibi-iqer confirms this father-son relationship (Fig. 5) (EL-KHADRAGY 2007b: 114-115, 129, Fig. 9). Each scene is devoted to a woman; the left hand scene identifies the woman as *jm3ḫjjt mrjjt Ḥwt-ḥr Jt(=j)-jb(=j) m3ʿt-ḫrw* – "the honored one, beloved of Hathor, Iti-ibi, true of voice". Keeping in mind that a similarly named female relative accompanies Khety II in the decoration of the north wall of his chapel (cf. GRIFFITH 1889b: Pl. 13 [38-40]; EL-KHADRAGY 2008: 233, Fig. 2), and realizing that the wife of Iti-ibi-iqer is referred to once as *Snbtj-jqrt mst K3w=f* – "Senebti-iqeret, born of Kauef" (EL-KHADRAGY 2007b: 122, Fig. 2) on the north wall of his chapel, and that in each of the two well-preserved labels identifying the wife of Iti-ibi-iqer on the same wall she is introduced by the designation *ḥmt=f* – "his wife" (EL-KHADRAGY 2007 b: 122-23, Figs. 2-3), the lady represented here in the table scene is most probably Iti-ibi, the wife of Khety II, and the possible mother of Iti-ibi-iqer.

On the western end of the chapel's north wall is an inscription wherein Mesehti-iqer, the son of Iti-ibi-iqer, states that he prepared the tomb for his father. The inscription reads: *jrt.n=f m mnw=f m jz n jt=f ḥ3tj-ʿ jmj-r ḥm(w)-nṯr Jt(=j)-jb(=j) jn z3=f smsw mrjj=f jwʿw=f nb n jšt=f nbt ḥ3tj-ʿ jmj-r ḥm(w)-nṯr n Wp-w3wt nb Z3wtj Jnpw nb R-qrrt sḏm sḏmt wʿ m [jzt] [jmj]-r ḥm(w)-nṯr m3ʿ n Wp-w3wt Mzḥtj-jqr* "That what he did as his monument, namely a tomb for his father, the count, the overseer of priests, Iti-ibi. It is his eldest son, his beloved, his heir, the possessor of all his possessions, the count, the overseer of priests of Wepwawet, lord of Asyut, and Anubis, lord of Ra-qereret, the judge of that which one alone judges in the [palace], the true [overseer] of priests of Wepwawet, Mesehti-iqer" (EL-KHADRAGY 2007b: 107-108, 122, Fig. 2; for the interpretation, significance, grammatical analysis and variants of this dedicatory formula, see: TAUFIK 1971: 227-34; VITTMANN 1977: 21-32; EL-SAID 1985: 271-92; LEAHY 1987: 57-64; JANSEN-WINKELN 1990: 127-56; CASTLE 1993: 99-120; CASTLE 1994: 187-191).

The southern part of the east wall of Iti-ibi-iqer's chapel is decorated with a scene showing four registers of marching soldiers headed by a large figure of the troop-commander (Fig. 6) (EL-KHADRAGY 2007b: 124, Fig. 4). Looking at their weapons, some of the soldiers are armed with spears and large, pointed-top shields covered with cow hides

Fig. 5: N13.1, Tomb of Iti-ibi-iqer, niche, west wall, commemorating the mother Iti-ibi (© The Asyut Project; drawing: S. Shafik).

(register 4, nos. 2, 4) (for the Egyptian shields, see: NIBBI 2003: 170-81), while others are armed with bows and sheaves of arrows (register 4, nos. 3, 5).

The close resemblance of those marching soldiers to the two sets of wooden models of the well-known Siutian nomarch Mesehti (CG 257; CG 258) is striking. Firstly, the scene of marching soldiers of Iti-ibi-iqer shows a four-row arrangement of the represented troop of soldiers, the same arrangement is displayed in the two sets of wooden models of Mesehti. Secondly, the military scenes of Iti-ibi-iqer show a combination of Nubian archers and Egyptian spearmen holding shields, which are again represented in the two sets of wooden models of Mesehti. Keeping in mind Mesehti-iqer's statement that he prepared the tomb for his father (EL-KHADRAGY 2007b: 107, 122, Fig. 2) and the uniformity of the military troops in Tomb N13.1 and the models of Mesehti, in addition to the similarity of the names and most of the titles of both individuals, the identification of Mesehti-iqer of N13.1 with Mesehti of Hogarth's Tomb III is adopted here (Mesehti-iqer of N13.1 bore the titles *ḥ3tj-ʿ, jmj-r ḥmw-nṯr n Wp-w3wt nb Z3wtj, jmj-r ḥmw-nṯr Jnpw nb R-qrrt*; cf. EL-KHADRAGY 2007b: 107-108, 122, Fig. 2, while Mesehti of Hogarth's Tomb III held the titles *jrj-pʿt, ḥ3tj-ʿ, jmj-r ḥmw-nṯr n Wp-w3wt nb Z3wtj, jmj-r ḥmw-nṯr Jnpw nb R-qrrt*; cf. LACAU 1906: 101-33 [CG 28118, 28119]. If such identification of both Mesehti is

Fig. 6: N13.1, Tomb of Iti-ibi-iqer, east wall, south side, marching soldiers (© Kahl).

accepted, the lack of Mesehti's honorific title *jrj-pꜥt* from the father's tomb could be explained by a later promotion). However, it has already been suggested that Mesehti decorated the tomb of his father sometime after the 14th year of Nebhepetre and before his 39th year; i.e. before the reunification of Egypt by Nebhepetre (cf. EL-KHADRAGY 2007b: 116-118).

The unknown owner of the so-called Northern Soldiers-Tomb (H11.1; Pl. 16) is possibly a member of the Eleventh Dynasty; his tomb is dated to the Eleventh Dynasty, probably the reign of Nebhepetre Mentuhotep II, after the reunification of Egypt (EL-KHADRAGY 2006a: 154-55).

The decoration of the chapel's southern wall shows a fragmentary scene depicting four rows of marching soldiers armed with half-moon bladed battle-axes and holding large, full-length wooden shields with pointed tops covered by cow hide, cheetah skin and antelope skin (Fig. 7) (EL-KHADRAGY 2006a: 162, Fig. 6).

The same wall has a back-to-back representation of a jackal-headed god and goddess Hathor surmounted by a winged sun disc (Fig. 8). This jackal-headed god might be identified as Wepwawet, the local god of Asyut or, less likely, as Anubis, who was associated with its necropolis (for Asyut cemetery and the temple of Anubis, cf. GOMAÀ 1986: 269-73). Facing Hathor is a woman probably standing in a kiosk who is identified as *ḥm(t)-nṯr Ḥwt-[ḥr]* – "priestess of Hathor" (EL-KHADRAGY 2006a: 163, Fig. 7). The representation of marching soldiers suggests that the owner of this tomb might have been in

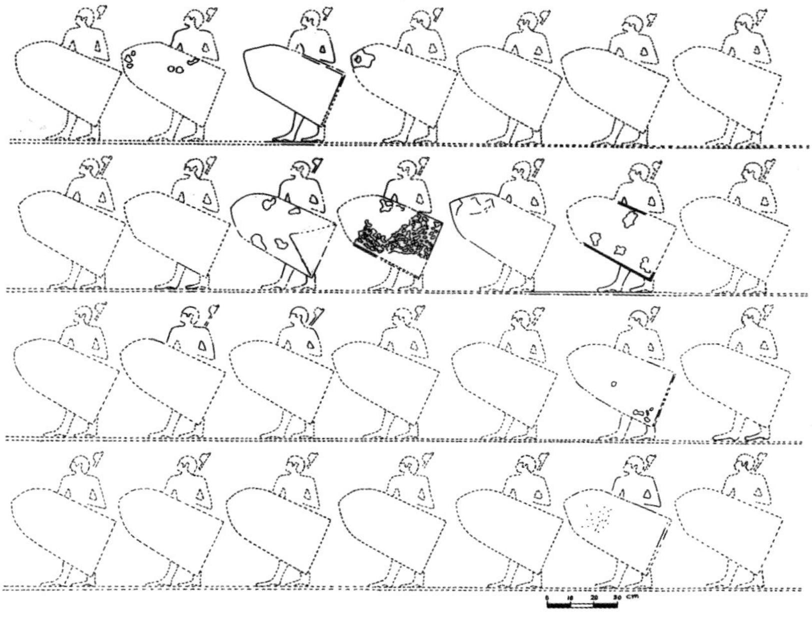

Fig. 7: H11.1, the Northern Soldiers-Tomb, chapel, south wall, marching soldiers, reconstruction (© The Asyut Project; drawing: S. Shafik).

charge of some local army, while the representation of a local jackal-headed god here might indicate that this unknown man was a high priest of that god. Considering that his probable wife represented in a relatively large scale in this tomb was a priestess of Hathor, which was a privilege of the royal court and the elite at that time (GILLAM 1995: 233), our tomb owner was probably a nomarch and overseer of the priests of either Wepwawet or Anubis.

The next known Siutian nomarch is ᶜAnu, who is known from some wall fragments kept now in the Turin museum (cf. ROCCATI 1972: 42-47). He was *ḥ3tj-ᶜ* – "count", and *jmj-r ḥmw-nṯr Wp-w3wt nb Z3wtj* - "overseer of priests of Wepwawet, lord of Asyut". His tomb is dated to the early Twelfth Dynasty (cf. ROCCATI 1972: 48).

Also belonging to the Early Twelfth Dynasty group of nomarchs is Djefai-Hapi II, the owner of Siut Tomb II (O13.1; Pl. 30-31). The tomb's date is suggested by its location on the geological step 6 of Gebel Asyut al-gharbi, in which the First Intermediate Period tombs Siut III-V and the Eleventh Dynasty Northern Soldiers-Tomb were cut, rather than step 2 used for the large Twelfth Dynasty tombs belonging to Djefai-Hapi I and Djefai-Hapi III (Salakhana Tomb). Confirming this date is the tomb's remaining interior part, the roof of which is supported by two pairs of pillars (Pls. 30, 31b), thereby belonging to the First Intermediate Period and early Middle Kingdom layout rather than the much complicated layout adopted for the large Twelfth Dynasty tombs in step 2, which consist of passages and transverse halls leading to one or more shrines (cf. GRIFFITH 1889b: Pls. 10, 20;

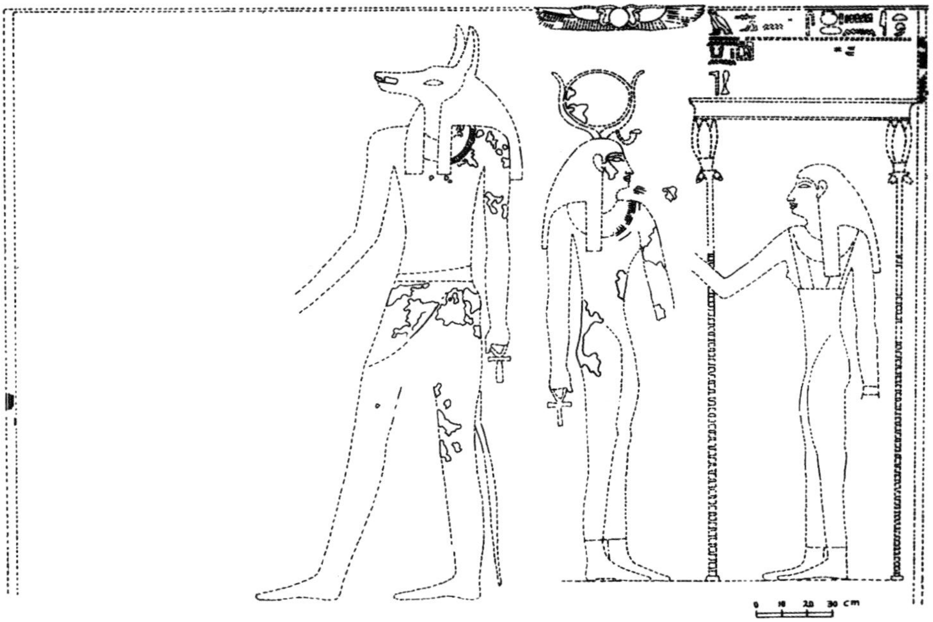

Fig. 8: H11.1, the Northern Soldiers-Tomb, south wall, priestess before Hathor and a jackal-headed god, reconstruction (© The Asyut Project; drawing: S. Shafik).

MONTET 1930-35: 86-89; MAGEE 1988: II, 12-13; EL-KHADRAGY 2006a: 156-57; KAHL 2007: 85-86).

Djefai-Hapi II held the nomarchic title *ḥrj-tp ꜥ3 n 3tf ḫntt mj qd=s* – "great overlord of the entire 13th Nome of Upper Egypt", in addition to the traditional responsibility in the local cult of Wepwawet as *jmj-r ḥmw-nṯr Wp-w3wt nb Z3wtj* - "overseer of priests of Wepwawet, lord of Asyut", and the usual honorific titles of the earlier Siutian nomarchs *jrj pꜥt* – "hereditary prince" and *ḥ3tj-ꜥ* – "count".

During the reign of Senwosret I Asyut was governed by Djefai-Hapi I, the owner of Siut Tomb I (P10.1; Pl. 32-33). The relationship between Djefai-Hapi I and his predecessor Djefai-Hapi II remains uncertain. The tomb of Djefai-Hapi I is one of the largest rock-cut private tombs in Egypt, the remaining part of which is more than 55 m long, with a maximum height of more than 11 m. In designing the tomb, Djefai-Hapi I adopted the main architectural features of a standardized Old Kingdom royal funerary complex; it has an east-west orientation with a gateway or a statue chapel on the level of the plain approached through a garden, a causeway and a higher leveled rock-cut chapel with the statue shrine on its east-west main axis (EL-KHADRAGY 2007a: 41-62; ENGEL/KAHL 2009: 55-59, Figs. 16-24).

The finely decorated tomb of Djefai-Hapi I (Fig. 9; cf. EL-KHADRAGY 2007c: 125-144) is famous for its ten contracts (Fig. 10; cf. the contribution of Jochem Kahl in this volume, p. 14, Fig. 1), which Djefai-Hapi I made with the priests of both Wepwawet and Anubis temples and the workmen of the necropolis, to guarantee his funerary cult (GRIFFITH 1889b: Pls. 6-8 [273-324]). According to the tomb inscriptions, Djefai-Hapi I received funerary equipment from the royal house (GRIFFITH 1889b: Pl. 3 [132]; EL-KHADRAGY 2007a: 47, 58, Fig. 3).

Djefai-Hapi I held the titles *jrj pꜥt* – "hereditary prince", *ḥ3tj-ꜥ* – "count", *ḥrj-tp ꜥ3 n 3tf ḫntt mj qd=s* – "great overlord of the entire 13th Nome of Upper Egypt", *jmj-r ḥmw-nṯr Wp-w3wt nb Z3wtj* - "overseer of priests of Wepwawet, lord of Asyut", *jmj-r ḥmw-nṯr Jnpw nb R-qrrt* – "overseer of priests of Anubis, lord of Ra-qereret", and *jmj-r ḥmw-nṯr n Wsjr nb jmntt* – "overseer of priests of Osiris, lord of the West".

Fig. 9: P10.1 (Siut I), Tomb of Djefai-Hapi I, Inner Passage, north wall, details of fishing scene (© Kahl).

The now inaccessible Tomb VII (Salakhana Tomb) belongs to Djefai-Hapi III, a possible descendent of Djefai-Hapi I (MONTET 1936: 134-135). The tomb is dated to the reign of Amenemhat II (MOSS 1933: 33). Djefai-Hapi III was *ḥ3tj-ʿ* – "count", and *jmj-r ḥmw-nṯr* – "overseer of priests". Although the nomarchic title *ḥrj-tp ʿ3 n 3tf ḫntt* – "great overlord of the 13th Nome of Upper Egypt" is not preserved, the large area of the tomb-chapel and the owner's responsibility as overseer of the priests of some unmentioned god are clear evidence that the tomb owner was a nomarch.

Situated on the open court of the tomb of Djefai-Hapi III is Tomb VI belonging to Djefai-Hapi IV, which is also inaccessible at present (MONTET 1936: 131-133). It dates to the reign of Amenemhat II or later (MAGEE 1988: II, 25). Being *jrj pʿt* – "hereditary prince", *ḥ3tj-ʿ* – "count", *jmj-r ḥmw-nṯr* – "overseer of priests" and *jmj-r mšʿ* – "overseer of the troops", Djefai-Hapi III was most probably also a nomarch.

As far as evidence shows, no resident governor for Asyut is known before Khety I (Siut V; M11.1) (cf. GOMAÀ 1980: 97-101; KANAWATI 1992: 170-173), who ruled Asyut two generations before the Tenth Dynasty Herakleopolitan king Merikare. From that time onwards we have much information about the administration of Asyut, introducing us to

Fig. 10: P10.1 (Siut I), Tomb of Djefai-Hapi I, Great Transverse Hall, east wall, north side, contracts (© Barthel 2006).

three distinctive groups/families of nomarchs who headed both the secular and religious administration of the province up to the middle of the Twelfth Dynasty.

Of the earliest family, five successive generations of Siutian governors are known, including Khety I (Siut V; M11.1), Iti-ibi (Siut III; N12.1), Khety II (Suit IV; N12.2), Iti-ibi-iqer (N13.1) and Mesehti (Hogarth Tomb III). Mesehti probably witnessed the final phase of the civil war between Herakleopolis and their Theban rivals which led to the reunification of Egypt sometime after the 14th year of Nebhepetre and before his 39th year; in any event, Khety I's family did not survive the Theban victory.

Little is known about the next line of Siutian rulers, who reigned over Asyut after the fall from power of Khety I's family due to the reunification of Egypt by Nebhepetre. Of those governors the earliest is probably the unknown owner of the so-called Northern Soldiers-Tomb (H11.1), while the latest known governor of this group is ᶜAnu, who was still in power during the early Twelfth Dynasty. However, large tombs with roofs supported by pillars and showing the projecting shoulders characteristic of the First Intermediate Period and the early Middle Kingdom tombs at Asyut (cf. MAGEE 1988: I, 9-13) might be attributed to nomarchs of this group. One of these tombs (O14.2), the owner of which is unknown, is situated near Deir el-Meitin and is decorated with wrestlers and some pastoral scenes. Another tomb (M12.1), now undecorated, is situated in the upper level of the mountain (cf. EL-KHADRAGY 2006b: 91).

Noteworthy, however, is that none of the abovementioned governors held the nomarchic title *ḥrj-tp ꜥꜣ n Nḏft* – "great overlord of the 13th Nome of Upper Egypt", except for Khety II, and hence *ḥꜣtj-ꜥ* – "count" is actually the most characteristic for the Siutian nomarchs during the First Intermediate Period as well as the Eleventh Dynasty (cf. HELCK 1958: 206-209).

During the first part of the Twelfth Dynasty Asyut was governed by a new line of nomarchs headed by Djefai-Hapi II (Siut II; O13.1). Most of them held the nomarchic title *ḥrj-tp ꜥꜣ n ꜣtf ḫntt* – "great overlord of the 13th Nome of Upper Egypt". Other members of this family are: Djefai-Hapi I (Siut I; P 10.1: reign of Senwosret I), Djefai-Hapi III (Salakhana Tomb: reign of Amenemhat II) and Djefai-Hapi IV (Tomb VI: reign of Amenemhat II or later).

References:

BECKERATH 1966: J. von Beckerath, Die Dynastie der Herakleopoliten (9./10. Dynastie), in: *Zeitschrift für Ägyptische Sprache und Altertumskunde* 93, 1966, 13-20.

CASTLE 1993: E. W. Castle, The Dedication Formula *ir.n.f m mnw.f*, in: *The Journal of Egyptian Archaeology* 79, 1993, 99-120.

CASTLE 1994: E. W. Castle, Further Observations on the Dedication Formula *ir.n.f m mnw.f*, in: *The Journal of Egyptian Archaeology* 80, 1994, 187-191.

CLÈRE/VANDIER 1948: J. J. Clère/J. Vandier, *Textes de la première période intermédiaire et de la XIème dynastie* (Bibliotheca Aegyptiaca 10, Brussels 1948).

EDEL 1984: E. Edel, *Die Inschriften der Grabfronten der Siut-Gräber in Mittelägypten aus der Herakleopolitenzeit. Eine Wiederherstellung nach den Zeichnungen der Description de l'Égypte* (Abhandlungen der Rheinisch-Westfälischen Akademie der Wissenschaften 71, Opladen 1984).

EL-KHADRAGY 2006a: M. El-Khadragy, The Northern Soldiers-Tomb at Asyut, in: *Studien zur Altägyptischen Kultur* 35, 2006, 147-164.

EL-KHADRAGY 2006b: M. El-Khadragy, New Discoveries in the Tomb of Khety II at Asyut, in: *The Bulletin of the Australian Centre for Egyptology* 17, 2006, 79-95.

EL-KHADRAGY 2007a: M. El-Khadragy, The Shrine of the Rock-cut Chapel of Djefaihapi I at Asyut, in: *Göttinger Miszellen. Beiträge zur ägyptologischen Diskussion* 212, 2007, 41-62.

EL-KHADRAGY 2007b: M. El-Khadragy, Some Significant Features in the Decoration of the Chapel of Iti-ibi-iqer at Asyut, in: *Studien zur Altägyptischen Kultur* 36, 2007, 105-135.

EL-KHADRAGY 2007c: M. El-Khadragy, Fishing, Fowling and Animal-handling in the Tomb of Djefaihapi I at Asyut, in: *The Bulletin of the Australian Centre for Egyptology* 18, 2007, 125-144.

EL-KHADRAGY 2008: M. El-Khadragy, The Decoration of the Rock-cut Chapel of Khety II at Asyut, in: *Studien zur Altägyptischen Kultur* 37, 2008, 219-241.

EL-SAID 1985: R. el-Said, Formules de piété filiale, in: P. Posener-Kriéger (ed.), *Mélanges Gamal Eddin Mokhtar* (Bibliothèque d'Étude 97/1, Cairo 1985) 271-292.

ENGEL/KAHL 2009: E.-M. Engel/J. Kahl, Die Grabanlage Djefaihapis I. in Assiut: ein Rekonstruktionsversuch, in: J. Popielska-Grzybowska/O. Białostocka/J. Iwaszczuk (eds.), *Proceedings of the Third European Conference of Young Egyptologists. Egypt 2004: Perspectives of Research. Warsaw 12-14 May 2004* (Acta Archaeologica Pultuskiensia 1, Pultusk 2009) 55-59, Figs. 16-24.

FRANKE 1987: D. Franke, Zwischen Herakleopolis und Theben: Neues zu den Gräbern von Assiut, in: *Studien zur Altägyptischen Kultur* 14, 1987, 49-60.

GARDINER 1909: A. H. Gardiner, *The Admonitions of an Egyptian Sage from a Hieratic Papyrus in Leiden (Pap. Leiden 344 Recto)* (Leipzig 1909).

GILLAM 1995: R. A Gillam, Priestesses of Hathor: Their Function, Decline and Disappearance, in: *Journal of the American Research Center in Egypt* 32, 1995, 211-237.

GOEDICKE 1969: H. Goedicke, Probleme der Herakleopolitenzeit, in: *Mitteilungen des Deutschen Archäologischen Instituts Abteilung Kairo* 24, 1969, 136-143.

GOMAÀ 1980: F. Gomaà, *Ägypten während der Ersten Zwischenzeit* (Beihefte zum Tübinger Atlas des Vorderen Orients. Reihe B (Geisteswissenschaften) 27, Wiesbaden 1980).

GOMAÀ 1986: F. Gomaà, *Die Besiedlung Ägyptens während des Mittleren Reiches. I. Oberägypten und das Fayyum* (Beihefte zum Tübinger Atlas des Vorderen Orients. Reihe B (Geisteswissenschaften) 66/1, Wiesbaden 1986).

GRIFFITH 1889a: F. Ll. Griffith, The Inscriptions of Siût and Dêr Rîfeh, in: *The Babylonian and Oriental Record* 3, 1888-1889, 121-129, 164-168, 174-184, 244-252.

GRIFFITH 1889b: F. Ll. Griffith, *The Inscriptions of Siût and Dêr Rîfeh* (London 1889).

HELCK 1958: W. Helck, *Zur Verwaltung des Mittleren und Neuen Reiches* (Probleme der Ägyptologie 3, Leiden – Cologne 1958).

JANSEN-WINKELN 1990: K. Jansen-Winkeln, Vermerke. Zum Verständnis kurzer und formelhafter Inschriften auf ägyptischen Denkmälern, in: *Mitteilungen des Deutschen Archäologischen Instituts Abteilung Kairo* 46, 1990, 127-156.

KAHL 2006: J. Kahl, Ein Zeugnis altägyptischer Schulausflüge, in: *Göttinger Miszellen. Beiträge zur ägyptologischen Diskussion* 211, 2006, 25-29.

KAHL 2007: J. Kahl, *Ancient Asyut: The First Synthesis after 300 Years of Research* (The Asyut Project 1, Wiesbaden 2007).

KAHL/EL-KHADRAGY/VERHOEVEN 2007: J. Kahl/M. El-Khadragy/U. Verhoeven, The Asyut Project: Fourth Season of Fieldwork (2006), in: *Studien zur Altägyptischen Kultur* 36, 2007, 81-103.

KANAWATI 1992: N. Kanawati, *Akhmim in the Old Kingdom I: Chronology and Administration* (The Australian Centre for Egyptology: Studies 2, Sydney 1992).

LACAU 1906: P. Lacau, *Sarcophages antérieurs au Nouvel Empire* II/2 (Cairo 1906).

LEAHY 1987: A. Leahy, Multiple Adverbial Predicates in Ancient Egyptian. (The Formula *ir.n.f m mnw.f*), in: J. D. Ray (ed.), *Lingua Sapientissima. A seminar in honour of H.J. Polotsky organised by the Fitzwilliam Museum, Cambridge and the Faculty of Oriental Studies in 1984* (Cambridge 1987) 57-64.

LOPEZ 1973: J. Lopez, L'auteur de l'Enseignement pour Mérikarê, in: *Revue d'Égyptologie* 25, 1973, 178-191.

MAGEE 1988: D. Magee, *Asyût to the End of the Middle Kingdom: A Historical and Cultural Study* (unpublished Ph.D. thesis, Oxford 1988).

MONTET 1930-35: P. Montet, Les tombeaux de Siout et de Deir Rifeh (suite), in: *Kêmi. Revue de philologie et d'archéologie égyptiennes et coptes* 1, 1928, 53-68.

MONTET 1936: P. Montet, Les tombeaux de Siout et de Deir Rifeh (troisième article), in: *Kêmi. Revue de philologie et d'archéologie égyptiennes et coptes* 6, 1936, 131-163.

MOSS 1933: R. Moss, An Unpublished Rock-Tomb at Asyût, in: *Journal of Egyptian Archaeology* 19, 1933, 33.

NIBBI 2003: A. Nibbi, Some Remarks on the Ancient Egyptian Shield, in: *Zeitschrift für Ägyptische Sprache und Altertumskunde* 130, 2003, 170-81.

QUACK 1992: J. F. Quack, *Studien zur Lehre für Merikare* (Göttinger Orientforschungen. IV. Reihe: Ägypten 23, Wiesbaden 1992).

ROCCATI 1972: A. Roccati, Una tomba dimenticata di Asiut, in: *Oriens Antiquus. Rivista del Centro per le Antichità e la Storia dell'Arte del Vicino Oriente* 11, 1972, 41-52.

SCHARFF 1936: A. Scharff, *Der historische Abschnitt der Lehre für König Merikarê* (Sitzungsberichte der Bayerischen Akademie der Wissenschaften, Philosophisch-Historische Abteilung 8, Munich 1936).

SCHENKEL 1965: W. Schenkel, *Memphis - Herakleopolis - Theben. Die epigraphischen Zeugnisse der 7.-11. Dynastie Ägyptens* (Ägyptologische Abhandlungen 12, Wiesbaden 1965).

SCHENKEL 1978: W. Schenkel, *Die Bewässerungsrevolution im alten Ägypten* (Mainz 1978).

TAUFIK 1971: S. Taufik, *ir.nf m mnw.f* als Weihformel. Gebrauch und Bedeutung, in: *Mitteilungen des Deutschen Archäologischen Instituts Abteilung Kairo* 27, 1971, 227-234.

VITTMANN 1977: G. Vittmann, Zum Verständnis der Weihformel *irjnf m mnwf*, in: *Wiener Zeitschrift für die Kunde des Morgenlandes* 69, 1977, 21-32.

VOLTEN 1945: A. Volten, *Zwei altägyptische politische Schriften: Die Lehre für König Merikarê (Pap. Carlsberg VI) und die Lehre des Königs Amenemhat* (Analecta Aegyptiaca 4, Copenhagen 1945).

The New Kingdom Graffiti in Tomb N13.1: An Overview

Ursula Verhoeven

§1 Position and date of Tomb N13.1

The general map B1 of the necropolis of Asyut (Pl. 17) shows the position of Tomb N13.1[1], located about 30 m above Tomb III (Siut III; N12.1). It was discovered by The Asyut Project in 2005 not having been described or mentioned by anyone before. With its tomb-owner, nomarch Iti-ibi-iqer, N13.1 can be dated to the very end of the First Intermediate Period/Period of Regions[2] (ca. 2030 BCE) ranging exactly between the other great tombs of nomarchs of this times (Siut V, III, IV) and those of the Twelfth Dynasty (Siut II, I) buried in this necropolis, as Mahmoud El-Khadragy has shown in his contribution (cf. also KAHL 2007: 17, Fig. 8; EL-KHADRAGY 2007: 116-118).

The tomb entrance leading into the rock chambers (Pl. 29a) is lying behind a narrow forecourt with approx. 90 small shaft tombs dating from the end of the Old Kingdom until the Middle Kingdom (Pl. 20-21). Inside, the tomb dimensions of 8.40 m length (plus 2.40 m for the western niche) x max. 9.25 m width are moderate in comparison with other tombs in the neighbourhood. The architecture with only a few indications of a room divider on the floor, the walls and the ceiling, and with two pillars and the western niche is impressively clear and unassuming (Pls. 28, 29b). The stuccoed walls have a fine and colourful decoration painted on a bright underground. The scenes contain many impressive images of the tomb owner and his family, soldiers, as well as interesting activities of sailing, hunting, agriculture, feeding cranes, bull fighting and woodworking (EL-KHADRAGY 2007: 105-135; KAHL/VERHOEVEN 2008: 68-73; cf. also M. El-Khadragy in this volume, p. 35-39).

§2 The graffiti inside the tomb

Apart from these features of the original configuration, the tomb has preserved a particular treasure from later centuries: a great amount of graffiti in black or red ink written or painted on the tomb walls, which can be dated into the New Kingdom. This shows that visitors regularly came to this tomb for several purposes from approximately 500 until 900 years after the burial of Iti-ibi-iqer, as we will see.

1 For preliminary information about the tomb see KAHL 2007: 79-82 and his contribution in this volume. In the recent publication of Zitman (ZITMAN 2010: 28sqq., 42), the author continued to use the old numbering system with Roman numerals and even extended it. According to that system he refers to Tomb N13.1 as "Tomb XVII", which is very much regrettable, cf. also J. Kahl in this volume.

2 For that term see MORENZ 2010: 35.

The graffiti are to be found on each wall and both pillars, often relating to the original decoration. Currently the total amount of the Pharaonic graffiti is 201, comprising 142 textual graffiti and 59 pictorial representations.[3] Most of the graffiti cover the South wall (62 items), slightly less on the West wall with its niche (57 items) and the North wall (53 items). Only two graffiti are preserved on the mostly damaged East wall. Pillar A was used for 18, Pillar B for only nine graffiti (cf. the ground plan Pl. 28). Besides the Hieratic graffiti, there are only much younger ones from Islamic times: two Mihrab niches and ten Arabic texts, mainly from the Qur'an, drawn with red, black or yellow ink. Late Hieratic, Demotic, Coptic or Greek texts are not to be found in this tomb.

§3 The steps of documentation

After the discovery of Tomb N13.1 at the very end of the season of 2005, the graffiti could only be examined for a few hours, but Jochem Kahl already recognized that the "tomb's importance for the history of Asyut cannot be overestimated" (KAHL/EL-KHADRAGY/VERHOEVEN 2006: 242). Afterwards the tomb had to be immediately protected with a huge iron door.

In the season of 2006, Jochem Kahl, with the help of Monika Zöller, prepared a first inventory list of all graffiti he could distinguish: he counted 148 single graffiti while part of the South wall was still covered with debris (Fig. 1). Beside this, they took true to scale photographs of every item, which had a very good quality in relation to the difficult circumstances. In the second half of that season the restorers of the SCA prepared and cleaned the walls in a quite careful way. Subsequently, Sameh Shafik made the facsimile drawings of the decoration and Ilona Regulski those of the hieroglyphic inscriptions. Afterwards I was able to draw the first facsimiles of all graffiti by hand using large transparencies. But I had to abandon recording all the traces of destruction and decided to concentrate in this first step only on the remains of ink because of the lack of time on one hand and the partly damaged condition of the walls on the other, and only after discussions with Jochem Kahl and the epigraphers.[4] The facsimile sheets were photocopied on paper in a reduced size in the city of Asyut to be taken to Germany for study purposes.

Fig. 1: N13.1: Situation in 2006, southeast corner (© Kahl).

3 It is to be mentioned that the author has published further preliminary papers about the graffiti which differ from the present description here because of the state of research increasing from season to season: VERHOEVEN 2007; 2008; 2009a; 2010; in press a; in press b.

4 Cf. the contribution of Sameh Shafik in this volume.

Ulrike Fauerbach, our architect during that season, started with the stadia surveying which was continued by her colleagues Manja Maschke and Cornelia Goerlich in the following years.

During 2006 and 2007 and also in the season of 2008, I began to ink some clear graffiti, calking enlarged copies of the photos and using additionally the copies of the facsimiles for comparison and verification. In summer 2007, Fritz Barthel, professional photographer, came to Asyut for taking large format photos of the tomb, the decoration and the graffiti. At that moment, it was possible to discover potential connections between the graffiti and the original decoration because the tomb was completely clean and empty for the first time (VERHOEVEN 2008). New details could be discovered during the necessary re-examinations of the original graffiti, the facsimiles and the ink copies. At home, Monika Zöller prepared computer-aided sketches of each wall which show the position of the graffiti based on the measuring points by Ulrike Fauerbach and the large-scale photographs.

During the season of 2008, we took more exact measurements of all the graffiti: height, width, as well as distances from the ceiling and the corners. Eva Gervers started to concentrate on the picture graffiti which show fine drawings of human beings and animals carried out in black or red ink. We were also able to again detect some new graffiti we didn't notice before, especially a nice head of Hathor in red ink painted under the thigh of a figure of the seated tomb-owner. Further pictures are also incised or picked into the plaster: they show some animals as well as boats with cabin or sails and seem to be dating from later periods. The complete number of documented text and picture graffiti in N13.1 ultimately increased to 211 including the ten Islamic ink drawings.

In 2009, Svenja Gülden started her cooperation with the project for the purpose of preparing printable copies of the graffiti. After some final hand drawings she decided to copy the texts from the photos in a digital way using Adobe Photoshop and Illustrator. Now these drawings are continuously compared with the photos, facsimiles, and on-site re-examinations. Transliterations in hieroglyphs, translations and commentaries are still in progress. Although a few graffiti are already published, a complete edition is in preparation for the serial of The Asyut Project.[5]

§4 The appearance and layout of the text graffiti

The script is over-all Hieratic from very different hands, only one graffito is painted in hieroglyphs. The colour of the text graffiti is generally black, but red ink was used for some signs and in one case for the entire text. Another graffito had first been written in black ink, afterwards the first line was carved.

The length of a line varies from only one or two words up to a width of 135 cm. A special text is written in two very long lines covering 10.88 m starting on the North wall and continuing through the corner on to the different walls in the western part of the tomb. The text columns of the graffiti differ of course in width and may have up to 23 or 35 lines. A spatium is used in the case of one of the copies of the Teaching of Amenemhat between § 1

5 Working title: Ursula Verhoeven et al., Die Graffiti in Grab N13.1 in Assiut/Mittelägypten. I: Besuchertexte und literarische Graffiti aus dem Neuen Reich; II: Tintenzeichnungen aus dem Neuen Reich.

and 2. Once a scribe himself eliminated his own error by using a diagonal slash (N10, see below Pl. 3).

§5 The datings in the text graffiti

The few dates mentioned in the texts as well as palaeographic evidence show that the time span of the graffiti covers the entire New Kingdom: they must have been written between the beginning of the Eighteenth and the end of the Twentieth Dynasty.

Six graffiti, mainly from the North wall, originated under Amenhotep III between his first (1388 BCE) and his thirtieth year (1359 BCE; cf. BECKERATH 1997: 190). As example, the graffito mentioning the first year of this king, and therefore the oldest one with a historical reference, should be published on this occasion. The text with the preliminary number N7 (Pl. 1a-b) is written on the western half of the North wall, 126 cm under the ceiling and over the bright apron of the tomb owner. Its measurements are 32 x 4.5 cm and the graffito consists of two lines:

1) *rnp.t-sp 1 ȝbd 4 šmw sw 19 ḫr ḥm n nsw bjt (Nb-mȝꜥ.t-Rꜥ) sȝ Rꜥ Jmn-ḥtp ḥḳȝ Wȝs.t)*
2) *jw s*[6] *pw jr.t.n sẖ Mn jj r mȝȝ <ḥw.t-nṯr> nfr(.t)*

1) "Year 1, fourth month of the Shemu season, day 19 under the majesty of the double king (Neb-ma'at-Ra), son of Ra <(>Amenhotep, ruler of Thebes):
2) Then the scribe Men came, having come to see the beautiful <temple>."

The graffito with the latest dating is to be found on the southern half of the East wall citing the first year of Ramesses XI (1102/1098 BCE; BECKERATH 1997: 190). It is the graffito with the preliminary no. O2 (Pl. 2a-b), its dimensions are 45 x 12 cm, 115 cm under the ceiling. The three lines are located over the painted original decoration of armed soldiers, more precisely over a soldier in the third row of the four rows of soldiers standing behind a large figure of the tomb owner.

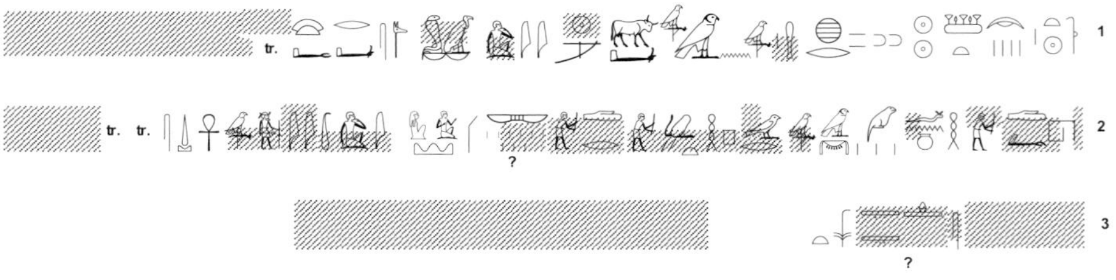

6 For this special construction, see below.

1) *rnp.t-sp 1 ꜣbd 4 ꜣḫ.t sw 22 ḫr ḥ[m] n Ḥrw kꜣ nḫt mry [Rꜥ] N[b.t]y wsr ḫꜥ[.w ///]*
2) *hd ḥfn.w Ḥrw nbw w[r p]ḥ.ty d[r] pḏ.wt [ps]ḏ.t] jt[y] ꜥnḫ wḏꜣ snb … (?) [hr jb (?)]*
3) *[mꜣꜥ (?)] sḥ[tp tꜣ.wy] nsw* […]

1) "Year 1, fourth month of the Akhet season, day 22 under the maje[sty] of Horus: the mighty bull, beloved by [Ra]; Two [La]dies: with strong weapons/ crown[s, …]
2) the one who attacks hundreds of thousands; Golden Horus: with gre[at po]wer, the one who drives [off] the N[ine] Bows, the soverei[gn], may he live, be prosperous and healthy … (?), [truly
3) contented (?)], the one who pa[cifies the two lands], the king." (*no further traces, rest of line destroyed*)

Commentary on O2:
Most of the epithets definitely belong to Ramesses XI (BECKERATH ²1999: 174-175), but two of them are not documented for this king as far as I know: The Nebty-name of Ramesses XI normally is *wsr ḫpš hd ḥfn.w*, here it is written *wsr ḫꜥ.w hd ḥfn.w* (maybe there was further text between these epithets at the end of line 1, which is now destroyed). In the very long Golden Horus name of this king, the scribe has written *dr psḏ.t pḏ.wt* instead of *sꜥnḫ tꜣ.wy* - an epithet which is common in several Ramesside titularies (cf. the Golden Horus name of Ramesses IX, Sethnakht, Merenptah, and Ramesses II; BECKERATH ²1999: 153-173). The following *hr jb mꜣꜥ* was maybe written there, but is now destroyed. The last epithet seems to have existed, but this is unsecure because of the few remains. After the two signs for *nsw* "the king" the surface doesn't show any more traces of ink, afterwards the surface is destroyed. Maybe the scribe was interrupted before he was able to finish the titulary and his visitor remarks. The script is full of verve and shows some nice ligatures. The first sign for the year (*rnp*) has a very special form because of the great line on the right side of the palm branch.

§6 The visitors' formulae

Most of the formulae of the visitors' graffiti are known also from other places, for instance from the Memphite necropolis, as Hana Navrátilová has shown recently (NAVRÁTILOVÁ 2007). One of the longest versions typically runs as follows (cf. for example NAVRÁTILOVÁ 2007: 49, 75):

jw.t pw jr.n sḫ NN
jj.t r mꜣꜣ ḥw.t-nṯr n.t NN
gm=f sy nfr.tj ḥr jb=f r ḥw.t-nṯr nb.t nfr.t
ꜥḥꜥ.n ḏd.n=f ḥwj p.t m ꜥn.tyw wꜣḏ
dfdf=s m snṯr m/ḥr tp-ḥr.t n s.t wr.t ntj NN jm=s
ꜥḥꜥ.n ḏd.n=f ḥtp-dj-nsw …

"Then the scribe NN came,
having come to see the temple of god NN.
He found it more beautiful in his heart than any other nice temple.

> Then he said: May the heaven rain with fresh myrrh and pour incense on top of the great place in which god NN is staying.
> Then he said: An offering that the king gives to …"

The opening phrase differs in some features of writing or spelling (*jw.t pw jr.n ..., jw.t pw jr.t.n …, jw pw jr.n ..., jj pw jr.n ..., jw s pw jr.n ..., jw sw pw jr.t.n ...*). Most of the texts forget the *t*-endings of the infinitive as it is common in Late Egyptian. An unusual but frequent form in the tomb shows a particle *s* or *sw* after the infinitive for which I know no parallel.

A very nice and completely preserved example for this kind of text was written by scribe Men on the North wall, now bearing the preliminary no. N10 (28 x 31 cm, 110 cm under the ceiling) (Pl. 3):

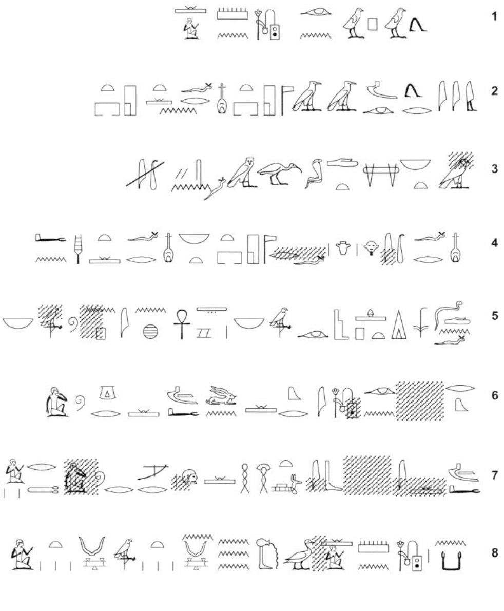

1) jw pw jr.n sẖ Mn
2) jj r mꜣꜣ ḥw.t-nṯr nfr.t n Ḥw.t-
3) Ḥrw nb.t Mḏd(n) gm.n=f sy ~~tj~~[7]
4) nfr.tj ḥr-jb=f [r] ḥw.t-nṯr nb.t nfr.t ꜥḥꜥ.n
5) ḏd.n=f dj-nsw-ḥtp Wsjr nb Tꜣ-ꜥnḫ Jnpw nb
6) Rꜣ-ḳ[rr.t] jr.n sẖ jḳr wn mꜣꜥ gr
7) mꜣꜥ [jḳr] bj.t wꜣḥ tp mrr rmṯ.w
8) n kꜣ sẖ Mn sꜣ wꜥb n Wp-wꜣ.wt Wp-wꜣ.wt
9) ms[.n] nb.t pr Nw.t sn=f Dwꜣw

7 Here the erroneously written *tj*-ending was eliminated by the scribe himself using a diagonal slash.

> “(1) Then the scribe Men came, (2) having come to see the beautiful temple of Hathor, (3) Lady of Medjeden. He found it (4) more beautiful in his heart [than] any other beautiful temple. Then (5) he said: May the king give an offering to Osiris, Lord of Ta-ankh, and Anubis, Lord of (6) Ra-qe[reret]. Made by the truly able scribe, the true (7) silent one, with [able] character, the humble one, beloved by the people (8) for the Ka of the scribe Men, son of the wab-priest of Wepwawet Wepwawet, (9) born by the lady of the house Nut. His brother (is) Duau.“

This kind of graffiti mentioning sites or temples might have been written, as is the case with the tombs of kings in Saqqara, “*out of a sense of curiosity and piety*, and with regard and respect for the *great monuments of a distant past*” and can be determined as “antiquarian” (Navrátilová 2007: 132, citing Peden). The temple of Hathor here in Asyut is of course not such a “great monument of a distant past”, but a recent and active temple, although it must certainly have had a long building tradition, as we can suppose. Therefore it seems difficult to refer to this type of graffiti in Asyut as “antiquarian”.

§7 Dedications to deceased ancestors

Very interesting are two graffiti with dedications of the offering *pr.t-ḫrw* for the able spirit of the Dead, the *ꜣḫ jḳr*, of two persons whose names correspond with the owners of Tomb Siut III (Iti-ibi: *Jt=j-jb=j*) and of Tombs Siut V or IV (Khety, here written: *H̱dj*). That would imply that the former nomarchs of the First Intermediate Period, whose tombs are lying directly underneath Tomb N13.1, were still well-known and considered to be powerful beings during the New Kingdom.

§8 Self representative texts and pictures

Another category contains graffiti with a kind of self-representative purpose (Navrátilová 2007: 134sqq.), for instance a small sketch of a seated man of rank at the end of a line which shows some less cursive Hieratic signs. In particular the sign for the scribal equipment is remarkable since it shows the details like in the hieroglyph. It is located very high on the South wall, only 14 cm under the ceiling, 20 x 6 cm, registered under the preliminary no. S24, and because of the tiny signs at the end of the text, the picture seems to have been drawn first (the depiction of the seated man differs from the original, cf. Pl. 4a-b):

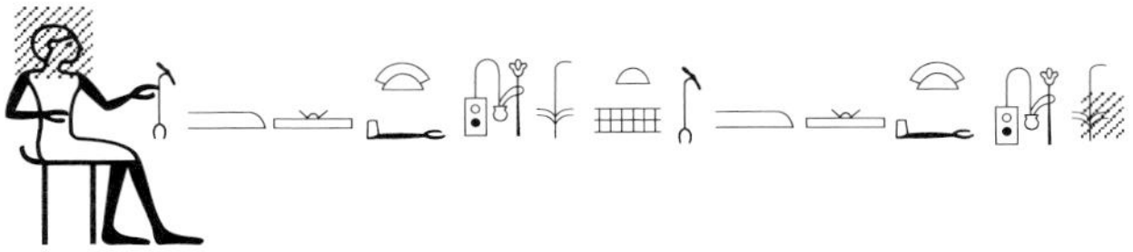
1

sẖ nsw Ḫꜥ-m-Wꜣs.t sẖ nsw Ḫꜥ-m-Wꜣs(.t)

“The Royal scribe Kha-em-waset, the Royal scribe Kha-em-waset”

§9 Signatures

"Signatures" (NAVRÁTILOVÁ 2007: 132) like "made by" occur at the beginning of short sentences as well as longer texts (also at their end), and also within or under animal drawings (KAHL 2007: 81, Fig. 62).

§10 Prayers or "piety-oriented" texts

Some graffiti asking gods for help on behalf of the writer seem to be dated to the Nineteenth Dynasty in comparison with the material in Saqqara (NAVRÁTILOVÁ 2007: 132-133). They start with *jrj nfr* (written once to three times) addressing the local gods Hathor and Wepwawet, while Amun is being present only in a small picture of a ram with turned horns under which the scribe has written *jrj nfr* with the same very black ink as used for the picture (Fig. 2).

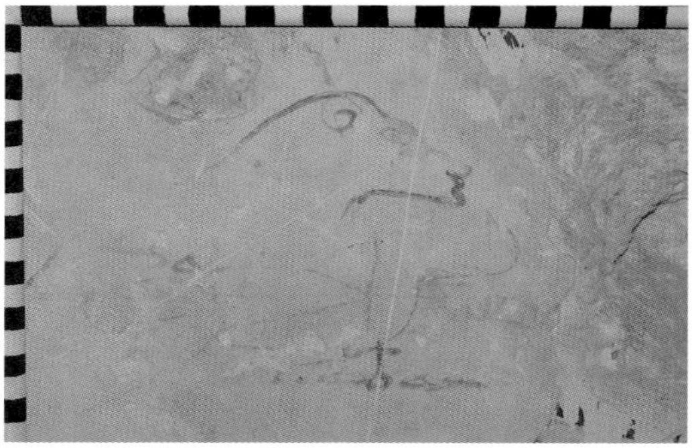

Fig. 2: Graffito N22-23: Ram head with text below (© Kahl).

§11 The mentioned temples and gods of Asyut

The texts in Tomb N13.1 mention five different temples of Asyut within the sort of graffiti called "antiquarian" or "descriptive" by Navrátilová (NAVRÁTILOVÁ 2007: 132):

1. the temple of Hathor, Lady of Medjeden (a place in the vicinity of Asyut),
2. the temple of Osiris, Lord of Ta-djeser (i.e. the necropolis in general),
3. the temple of Anubis, Lord of Ra-qereret (i.e. the necropolis in the Gebel Asyut al-gharbi),
4. the temple of Wepwawet, Lord of Asyut (i.e. the town),
5. the temple of Djefai-Hapi, which may be identical with its large rock tomb or possibly a separate temple for the deification of this nomarch as Jochem Kahl is presuming (Kahl 2007: 57-58).[8]

The scribes appeal to further gods in the offering formulae: Thot and Seshat without local epithets but chosen as responsible gods for words and writing (*Ḏḥwtj nb mdw.w-nṯr Sẖ3.t wr.t nb.t sẖ*), Osiris as "Lord of the Land of Living" (*nb t3 ꜥnḫ* – another denomination for the necropolis of Asyut), and Amun - without any specification.

Also the titles of priests, who are mentioned as writers or as fathers of writers, provide information about the cultic landscape of Asyut: many of them are wab-priests of Hathor and Wepwawet, in two cases we find scribes in the context of the local animal cult (*sẖ ḥw.t wnš* resp. *sẖ wnš n/m pr Wp-w3.wt nb S3w.yt* "scribe of the jackal house resp. of the jackals of the domain of Wepwawet": VERHOEVEN 2010: 197-198).

8 J. Kahl also presented a lecture at JGU Mainz on the 6th of Febr., 2006 about this question: "'Wie werde ich ein Heiliger?' oder Der Tempel des Djefai-Hapi".

§12 The creators of the graffiti

Apart from this simple religious agency of wab-priests and scribes, we can identify some special functions mostly with just one example: a prophet (*ḥm-nṯr*) and a first prophet of Wepwawet (*ḥm-nṯr tpj n Wp-wꜣ.wt*), two Royal scribes (*sẖ nsw*), one of them also chief of the bulls (*jmy-rꜣ kꜣ.w*), a shield bearer of pharaoh (*ḳr-ꜥ pr-ꜥꜣ*).

The texts don't mention many different personal names, which is surprising at first sight, but many graffiti are anonymous and some being of course destroyed. Particularly one individual seems to have been very productive and we actually know his family: the scribe Men, son of the wab-priest of Wepwawet Wepwawet, born by the lady of the house Nut, while his brother is named Duau. The names Men as well as Khaemwaset occur with and without a genealogy, therefore we have to examine the handwritings before we can identify them as associated with each other. Both names are also the subject of two very particular graffiti about their sexual behaviour with Libyan girls, maybe in sort of a joke (VERHOEVEN 2009c: 434-441). The name Iahmes, mentioned four times, seems to refer to three different persons. Further names occur only one or two times.

§13 The copies of literary resp. didactic texts

The most astonishing graffiti present passages from literary or didactic texts. This kind of literature is not found written on tomb walls elsewhere until now. The locations of these excerpts are marked by dots in the simplified ground plan (Fig. 3).

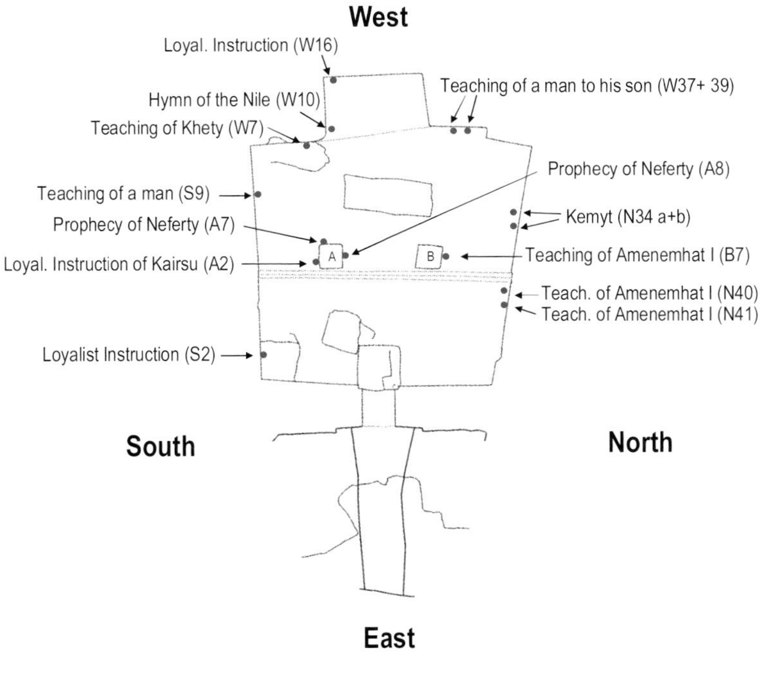

Fig. 3: Location of literary texts in Tomb N13.1

Beginning at the north-eastern corner, we find three text items with parts of the famous Teaching of King Amenemhat I, one being placed on the northern side of pillar B, two on the eastern half of the North wall, one of them written by the scribe Men, son of Wepwawet and Nut. Only two tiny and short citations from the beginning of the schoolbook Kemyt, which is also to be found on the South wall, follow on the North wall. The copies of the beginning of the Teaching of a man to his son on the West wall are also very short, but a longer one can be found on the South wall. In the niche of the West wall is an extensive part of the Loyalist Instruction, starting with §5, unfortunately not very well preserved. Long graffiti with the first paragraphs of this instruction can be found on the South wall and on pillar A. The last one partly preserved the name of the author of this Teaching for the first time, which could be identified as that of the well-known vizier Kaïrsu (VERHOEVEN 2009b). A very nice graffito in the niche made by scribe Iahmes is the next on the tour around the tomb. It presents some paragraphs of the famous Hymn to the Inundation. Around the corner the largest graffito, the Teaching of Khety, follows, again with a signature by scribe Men, son of Wepwawet and Nut. Concerning the reading of the name of the author (Khety vs. Dua-Khety), this text presents an interesting word order which must be read "Khety, son of Duauf" (VERHOEVEN 2010: 196). At the end two graffiti with parts of the Prophecy of Neferty, both on pillar A, are to be mentioned. The following list provides an overview which is updated in comparison to former publications of the author (VERHOEVEN 2010: 196; VERHOEVEN in press b):

No.	Title of literary opus	Copied paragraphs	Preliminary graffiti no.
1a	Teaching of King Amenemhat I	§(1a?-)3a-10c	North 40
1b	Teaching of King Amenemhat I	§1a-3d	North 41
1c	Teaching of King Amenemhat I	§1a-2e	Pillar B7
2	Hymn to the Inundation	§I,1-V,8	West 10
3	Teaching of Khety, Son of Duauf	ch. 1-6	West 7
4a	Teaching of a Man to His Son	§1,1-1,5	South 9
4b	Teaching of a Man to His Son	§1,1sqq., fragmentary	West 37
4c	Teaching of a Man to His Son	§1,1sqq., fragmentary	West 39
5a	'Loyalist' Teaching	§1,1-4,9	South 2 and 4
5b	'Loyalist' Teaching of the "Vizier Kaïrsu"	§1,1-2,7 and fragments	Pillar A2
5c	'Loyalist' Teaching	§5,1-10,9 and fragments of §11,1	West 16a
6a	Prophecy of Neferty	§Ia-IIIe, fragmentary	Pillar A7

6b	Prophecy of Neferty	§6a sqq., fragmentary	Pillar A8a (b-c?)
7a	Schoolbook Kemyt	Introduction and §1,1	North 34a
7b	Schoolbook Kemyt	§1,1	North 34b
7c	Schoolbook Kemyt	§1,1	South 25
8	"Beginning of the teaching", "Beginning of the teaching made by"		South 36, West 30, North 19 (7x), North 25 (?)

Nearly all of these copies of didactic literature in N13.1 start with the first paragraph, only two present subsequent parts, the first one in this list (1a) is too destroyed in the beginning to decide if it starts also with the introduction. Furthermore we can find short exercises, maybe of pupils, who only tried or started to write *ḥꜣ.t-ꜥ m* or *ḥꜣ.t-ꜥ m sbꜣ.yt* "beginning" or "beginning of the teaching", being found at various places on the walls. Apart from these headings there are also some singular *jw*-legs which seem to stand for the beginning of the visiting formula *jw pw jr.n=f*.

§14 Purpose of the graffiti

In summary we have to reflect on the purpose of all these texts, notes, pictures and "postcards" nearly on top of the hill of the Gebel Asyut al-gharbi. Tomb N13.1 offers a very nice view, shelter from the wind and the sun, is not too large and not too small for a comfortable rest and the walls are painted in light colours leaving enough space and a suitable surface for secondary texts. The writers of the graffiti display a certain piety to the local gods, praying for offerings or any good deeds and praising their temples in the city and the vicinity of Asyut. Dedications of offerings are addressed to the able spirits of the ancient tomb owners of the past. On the other hand the graffiti bear witness to the education and cultural knowledge of the scribes, while the didactic texts may have to be seen within the context of school training. We also find some short texts such as exercises by pupils or jokes which may indicate that the writing atmosphere was not always serious or pious. Dated visits of higher officials and the citation of Royal titularies demonstrate historical awareness and the singularity of members of the elite going on excursion to Asyut. Considering all these aspects I would like to state that Tomb N13.1 was a multifunctional place for commemoration performed by the intellectual elite during the New Kingdom, more precisely between ca. 1550[9] and 1102[10] BCE, while it was situated in an agreeable location of the distant past belonging to the western cemetery of the important city of Asyut.

9 This date is reconstructed as a result of palaeographic studies (cf. also VERHOEVEN in press b).
10 This date is based on the graffito with the latest dating under Ramesses XI (see above: O2).

References:

BECKERATH 1997: J. von Beckerath, *Chronologie des pharaonischen Ägypten* (Münchner Ägyptologische Studien 46, Mainz 1997).

BECKERATH ²1999: J. von Beckerath, *Handbuch der ägyptischen Königsnamen* (Münchner Ägyptologische Studien 49, Mainz ²1999).

EL-KHADRAGY 2007: M. El-Khadragy, Some Significant Features in the Decoration of the Chapel of Iti-ibi-iqer at Asyut, in: *Studien zur Altägyptischen Kultur* 36, 2007, 105-135.

KAHL 2007: J. Kahl, *Ancient Asyut. The First Synthesis after 300 Years of Research* (The Asyut Project 1, Wiesbaden 2007).

KAHL/EL-KHADRAGY/VERHOEVEN 2006: J. Kahl/M. El-Khadragy/U. Verhoeven, The Asyut Project: Third Season of Fieldwork, in: *Studien zur Altägyptischen Kultur* 34, 2006, 241-249, with Pl. 20-21.

KAHL/VERHOEVEN 2008: J. Kahl/U. Verhoeven, „Dornröschen" ist erwacht. Das neu entdeckte Grab N13.1 in Assiut, in: *Sokar* 16, 2008, 68-73.

MORENZ 2010: L. Morenz, *Die Zeit der Regionen im Spiegel der Gebelein-Region: Kulturgeschichtliche Re-Konstruktionen* (Probleme der Ägyptologie 27, Leiden 2010).

NAVRÁTILOVÁ 2007: H. Navrátilová, *The Visitors' Graffiti of Dynasties XVIII and XIX in Abusir and Northern Saqqara* (The Visitors' Graffiti I, Prague 2007).

VERHOEVEN 2007: U. Verhoeven, Graffiti from the New Kingdom in Tomb N13.1, in: J. Kahl/M. El-Khadragy/U. Verhoeven, The Asyut Project: Fourth Season of Fieldwork, in: *Studien zur Altägyptischen Kultur* 36, 2007, 85-87.

VERHOEVEN 2008: U. Verhoeven, Tomb N13.1: graffiti, in: J. Kahl/M. El-Khadragy/U. Verhoeven, The Asyut Project: Fifth Season of Fieldwork (2007), in: *Studien zur Altägyptischen Kultur* 37, 2008, 201-204.

VERHOEVEN 2009a: U. Verhoeven, Tomb N13.1: graffiti, in: J. Kahl/M. El-Khadragy/U. Verhoeven et al., The Asyut Project: Sixth Season of Fieldwork (2008), in: *Studien zur Altägyptischen Kultur* 38, 2009, 117.

VERHOEVEN 2009b: U. Verhoeven, Von der „Loyalistischen Lehre" zur „Lehre des Kaïrsu" – Eine neue Textquelle aus Assiut und deren Auswirkungen, in: *Zeitschrift für Ägyptische Sprache und Altertumskunde* 136/1, 87-98 with Pl. 12.

VERHOEVEN 2009c: U. Verhoeven, Die wie Kraniche balzen. Männerphantasien zur Zeit Amenhoteps III. in Assiut, in: D. Kessler et al. (eds.), *Texte - Theben - Tonfragmente. Festschrift für Günter Burkard* (Ägypten und Altes Testament 76, Wiesbaden 2009) 434-441.

VERHOEVEN 2010: U. Verhoeven, Tomb N13.1: More literary graffiti and the title "scribe of the estate of jackals", in: J. Kahl/M. El-Khadragy/U. Verhoeven et al., The Asyut Project: Seventh Season of Fieldwork (2009), in: *Studien zur Altägyptischen Kultur* 39, 2010, 196-198.

VERHOEVEN in press a: U. Verhoeven, Literarische Graffiti in Grab N13.1 in Assiut/Mittelägypten, in: P. Kousoulis (ed.), *Proceedings of the Tenth International Congress of Egyptologists, Rhodes 22-29 May 2008* (Orientalia Lovaniensia Analecta, Leuven).

VERHOEVEN in press b: U. Verhoeven, Literatur im Grab – der Sonderfall Assiut, in: G. Moers (ed.), *Dating Egyptian Literary Texts* (Lingua Aegyptia – Studia monographica, Göttingen).

ZITMAN 2010: M. Zitman, *The Necropolis of Assiut. A Case Study of Local Egyptian Funerary Culture from the Old Kingdom to the End of the Middle Kingdom* I-II (Orientalia Lovaniensia Analecta 180, Leuven 2010).

Epigraphic Work at Asyut

Sameh Shafik

History of the epigraphic work at Asyut

In the last three centuries a number of expeditions have worked in the cemetery west of Asyut, spending many years of fieldwork but finding great difficulties mostly due to the conditions of the scenes and inscriptions in the tombs of this cemetery (MAGEE 1988: 2-3; KAHL 2007: 21). Some of these expeditions are e.g:

- The French Expedition in 1799 (Fig. 1) (PANCKOUCKE 1822: pls 44-46),
- Robert Hay about 1825-1830,
- Francis Llewellyn Griffith about 1888 (Fig. 2) (GRIFFITH 1889b),
- Pierre Montet in 1911 and 1914 (MONTET 1928: 54),
- The Asyut Project since 2003 (Fig. 3) (EL-KHADRAGY/KAHL 2004; KAHL/EL-KHADRAGY/VERHOEVEN 2011 with further literature; cf. Jochem Kahl above).

The following comments describe the difficulties of the epigraphic work:

The French antiquary, artist and savant Dominique Vivant Denon wrote in 1798 that it would take years to copy and read the inscriptions (VATIN 1989: 1, 96-98, Pls. 30.2, 33.2; KAHL 2007: 25).

Adolf Erman wrote in his autobiography that he was always angry about the bad quality of copies made from the ten contracts in the tomb of Djefai-Hapi I (Siut I; P10.1). But when he saw the original inscription, he realized how difficult the work in the field on the original is. And then, he admitted that he understood the often problematic copies (ERMAN 1929: 216).

The difficult working conditions are the result of different circumstances:

a. The tombs of the western mountain of Asyut have been cut in an area with a limestone formation partially full of cracks and fissures. Evidence suggests that, for preparing a smooth surface for the decoration, the ancient Egyptians have dealt with the problem by using a layer of plaster with varying thicknesses from one place to the other. This layer has also collapsed in some spots (KAHL 2007: 76).
b. The wall surface is not smooth with lots of elevations and depressions (Fig. 4).
c. The enormous size of the tombs and of the decorated wall surfaces as well as the height of the walls represents a considerable difficulty. The height of the walls in the first passage of the tomb of Djefai-Hapi I (P10.1) is approximately 11 meters (KAHL 2007: 90).
d. The wall surfaces have suffered greatly from the effect of bats, bird droppings, soot and dust, resulting in the fading of many scenes.

e. Most of the entrances to these tombs and their façades are damaged, and as they all face east the sunlight hits the wall surfaces directly causing problems in controlling the direction of the light for any recording or photography.
f. The many additions, alterations and modifications of the recorded information, whether in the same era or at a later period, create great difficulty in establishing a coherent record. Examples to that may be seen in the tomb of Iti-ibi-iqer (N13.1) (EL-KHADRAGY 2007b: 134-135, Pls. 4-5).
g. Many travellers and visitors of the site have left numerous graffiti, prayers and dates on the walls (Fig. 5) (KAHL 2007: 72, 79sq., Pls. 5a-b; GRIFFITH 1889a: 177).
h. Where the limestone was of good quality, it was subjected to quarrying, often by using dynamite, which resulted in the loss of a great deal of scenes and inscriptions.

The technique used

The decision to use a specific technique in recording certainly depends on the characteristics and conditions of the wall surface. In the past scholars used a bleaching technique in which they took a photograph, then drew with a special ink over the outline and immersed the photograph in a liquid removing the photographic material leaving the inked outline only. Others rubbed the scenes with carbon paper over tracing paper then inking it, while again others directly traced on tracing paper etc. Nowadays, there is a preference for using digital epigraphy and we will come to that later. Until now, only handcopies have been made at Asyut.

From the beginning of the Asyut Project it was clear that before any work could be done the wall surfaces had to be cleaned and preserved. This was done by the Egyptian conservation team who should receive all our appreciation for the excellent results obtained. They started with mechanical cleaning followed by the chemical treatment for removing soot and dust, finally conserving the scenes by strengthening the colours and treating natural cracks and human vandalism.

As some of the scenes and inscriptions were at a considerable height we had to use a very high scaffolding for both conservation and recording. Two methods were used in recording:

1. Drawing from photographs. This was used in difficult or dangerous areas such as ceilings and fragile areas.
2. Recording on transparent plastic sheets which were fixed to undecorated spots on the surface. Scenes and inscriptions were copied using special gentle felt pens and with the help of cool lamps which we were able to move at different angles to obtain a full record of a faded scene or multiple texts recorded on top of each other. The drawings on plastic were reduced photographically, and then inked on calque paper.

In a next stage we are planning to use modern computer techniques like AutoCAD, photo plan, Photoshop, then comparing the results obtained by the two methods in order to reach a complete and reliable record. It should be mentioned, however, that digital epigraphy at the tombs of Asyut West would be extremely difficult and although we would endeavour to obtain reliable results, there are many factors against us. Digital epigraphy is as good as the photographs one can obtain. The height of some scenes, the uncontrollable lighting, the near impossibility of positioning the camera at a consistent distance from the wall at different heights and angles can easily produce distortions and make the joining of the photographs a very difficult, if not impossible task. In our line drawings we recorded the outlines of all scenes and inscriptions, leaving any damaged area as missing. Many expeditions tried either to hatch or to reconstruct the missing parts. We thought both methods to be unsatisfactory. The hatching will draw the attention of the viewer/reader's eyes to the missing part more than to the details of the scene itself, and the reconstruction of a scene would be imposing our interpretation of the scene's contents on the reader. As these records are meant to be for the specialist, we think it best to deliver to the reader only an accurate record of what is seen on the walls.

The results

1. A complete record in line drawings has been made for the first time for all the tombs in the western mountain at Asyut (cf. Figs. 6-7).
2. Some hitherto unknown sections have been recorded after cleaning them from the soot, others, thus, could be documented in greater detail. Examples for that are the inner passage of the tomb of Djefai-Hapi I (P10.1), the scenes and inscriptions of the north wall of the Great Transverse Hall, the shrine, the ceiling and the animal herding scene (Fig. 8) (EL-KHADRAGY 2007a: pp.44-45, Figs 3-6; compare e.g. SMITH 1957: 222, Fig. 1 to EL-KHADRAGY 2007c: 144, Fig. 12, 13).
3. A record has been made of all the preserved original scenes and inscriptions, as well as additions belonging to successive periods, beginning with the First Intermediate Period through the Middle Kingdom and many graffiti from the New Kingdom to the Islamic Period (KAHL 2007: 79-82, Figs. 61-62; VERHOEVEN 2009: 434-441).
4. The Asyut Project copied names and dates of visitors to the site who left inscriptions on the walls from 1799 (Fig. 5) until 1953.
5. Some fragmentary remains of colour were used to reconstruct certain scenes, for example in Tomb I (P10.1, Fig. 9), or those in the Northern Soldiers-Tomb. These played an important role in our reconsideration of the history of this period (EL-KHADRAGY 2006: 150-157. 161-164, Figs. 5-8; see also the contribution of Mahmoud El-Khadragy in this volume, p. 39, Fig. 7, p. 40, Fig. 8).
6. We were able to correct some of the previously copied scenes and inscriptions despite the fact that their present condition is probably much worse than when they were first recorded (EL-KHADRAGY 2007a: 44-51, VERHOEVEN in press).

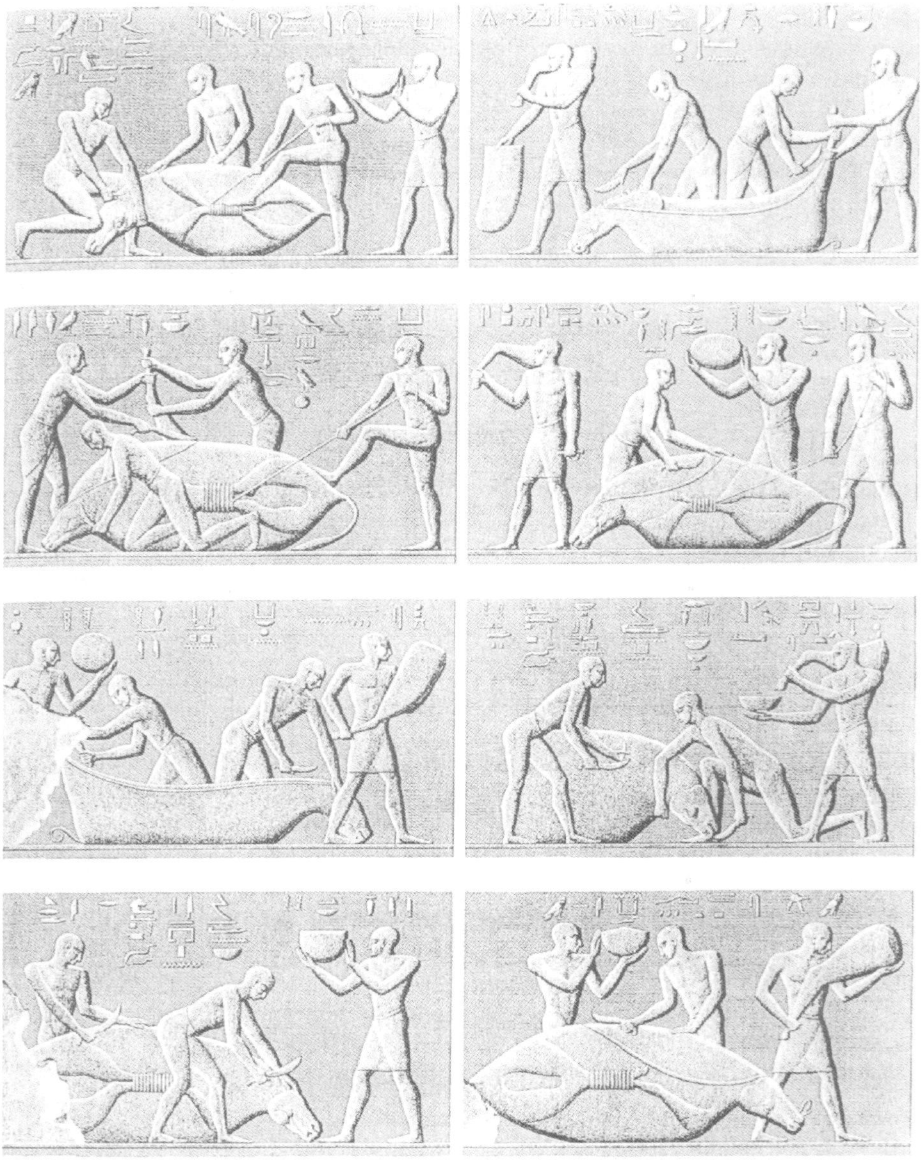

Fig. 1: P10.1 (Tomb I), shrine, after PANCKOUCKE 1822: Pl. 45.

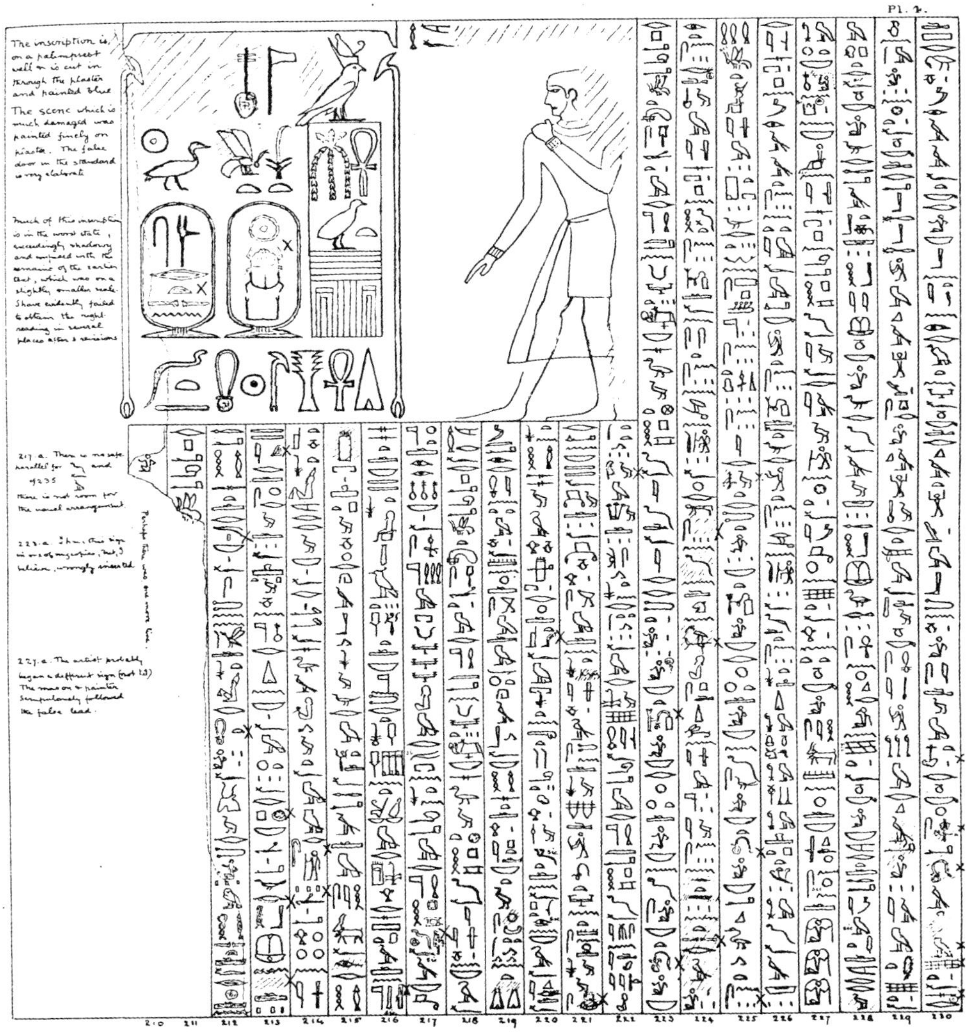

Fig. 2: P10.1 (Tomb I), Great Transverse Hall, east wall, after GRIFFITH 1889b: Pl. 4.

Fig. 3: P10.1 (Tomb I), Great Transverse Hall, east wall, not yet collated (© The Asyut Project 2005).

Fig. 4: N12.1 (Tomb III), north wall, layer of plaster collapsed in some spots (© Kahl 2005).

Fig. 5: P10.1 (Tomb I), passage between First Passage and Great Transverse Hall, south wall, traveller's graffito (© The Asyut Project 2005).

Fig. 6: N12.2 (Tomb IV), north wall (© The Asyut Project 2005).

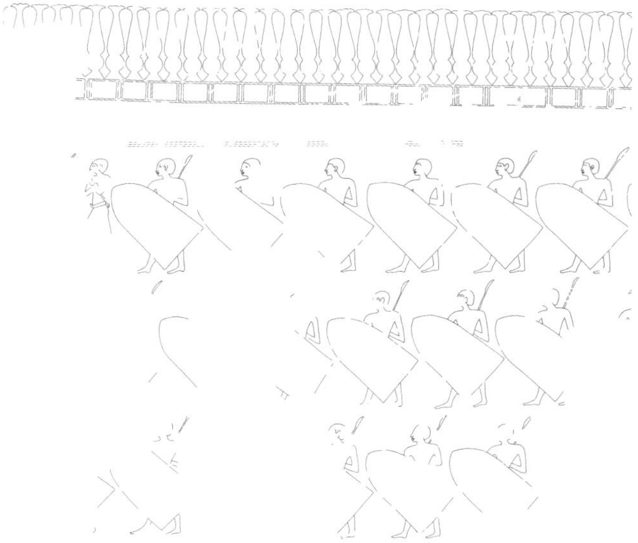

Fig. 7: N12.2 (Tomb IV), south wall
(© The Asyut Project 2005).

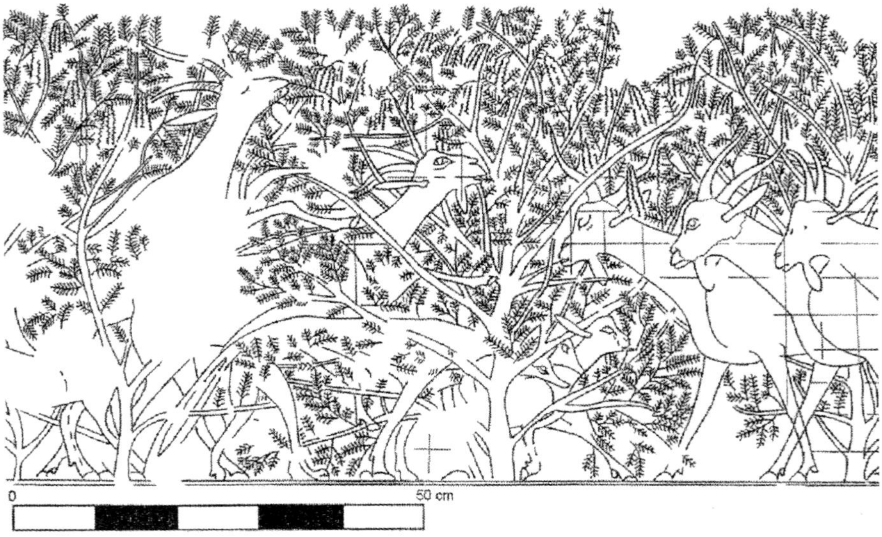

Fig. 8: P10.1 (Tomb I), Great Transverse Hall, north wall
(© The Asyut Project 2005).

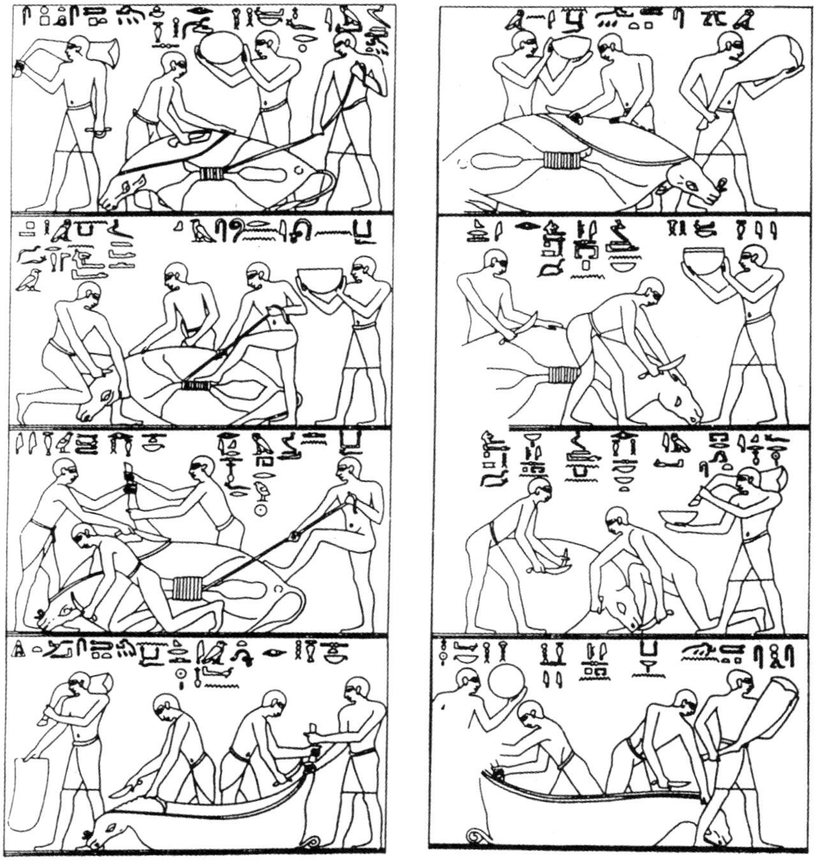

Fig. 9: P10.1 (Tomb I), shrine, reconstruction;
after EL-KHADRAGY 2007a, Fig. 7.

References:

El-Khadragy 2006: M. El-Khadragy, The Northern Soldiers-Tomb at Asyut, in: *Studien zur Altägyptischen Kultur* 35, 2006, 147-165.

El-Khadragy 2007a: M. El-Khadragy, The Shrine of the Rock-cut Chapel of Djefaihapi I at Asyut, in: *Göttinger Miszellen. Beiträge zur ägyptologischen Diskussion* 212, 2007, 41-62.

El-Khadragy 2007b: M. El-Khadragy, Some Significant Features in the Decoration of the Chapel of Iti-ibi-iqer at Asyut, in: *Studien zur Altägyptischen Kultur* 36, 2007, 105-136.

El-Khadragy 2007c: M. El-Khadragy, Fishing, Fowling and Animal-handling in the Tomb of Djefaihapi I at Asyut, in: *The Bulletin of the Australian Centre for Egyptology* 18, 2007, 125-144.

El-Khadragy/Kahl 2004: M. El-Khadragy/J. Kahl, The First Intermediate Period Tombs at Asyut Revisited, in: *Studien zur Altägyptischen Kultur* 32, 2004, 233-243.

Erman 1929: A. Erman, *Mein Werden und Mein Wirken. Erinnerungen eines alten Berliner Gelehrten* (Leipzig 1929).

Griffith 1889a: F. Ll. Griffith, The Inscriptions of Siût and Dêr Rîfeh, in: *The Babylonian and Oriental Record* 3, 1888-1889, 121-129, 164-168, 174-184, 244-252.

Griffith 1889b: F. Ll. Griffith, *The Inscriptions of Siût and Dêr Rîfeh* (London 1889).

Kahl 2007: J. Kahl, *Ancient Asyut. The First Synthesis after 300 Years of Research* (The Asyut Project 1, Wiesbaden 2007).

Kahl/El-Khadragy/Verhoeven 2011: J. Kahl/M. El-Khadragy/U. Verhoeven et al., The Asyut Project: Eighth Season of Fieldwork (2010), in: *Studien zur Altägyptischen Kultur* 40, 2011, 181-209.

Magee 1988: D. Magee, *Asyut at the end of the Middle Kingdom: a historical and cultural study* (unpublished Ph.D. thesis, Oxford 1988).

Montet 1928: P. Montet, Les tombeaux de Siout et de Deir Rifeh, in: *Kêmi. Revue de philologie et d'archéologie égyptiennes et coptes* 1, 1928, 53-68.

Panckoucke 1822: C. L. F. Panckoucke, *Description de l'Égypte ou recueil des observations et des recherches qui ont été faites en Égypte pendant l'Expédition de l'armée française*, Ant. IV, Seconde édition (Paris 1822).

Smith 1957: W. St. Smith, A Painting in the Assiut Tomb of Hepzefa, in: *Mitteilungen des Deutschen Archäologischen Instituts Abteilung Kairo* 15, 1957, 221-224.

Vatin 1989: *Vivant Denon, Voyage dans la Basse et la Haute Égypte.* Présentation de Jean-Claude Vatin (Cairo 1989).

Verhoeven 2009: U. Verhoeven, Die wie Kraniche balzen. Männerphantasien zur Zeit Amenhoteps III. in Assiut, in: D. Kessler et al. (eds.), *Texte – Theben – Tonfragmente. Festschrift für Günter Burkard* (Ägypten und Altes Testament 76, Wiesbaden 2009), 434-441.

Verhoeven in press: "Der lebt nach dem Tod". Orthographisches und Biographisches in den Inschriftenfragmenten der Grabanlage M10.1 in Assiut, in: H. W: Fischer-Elfert, R. B. Parkinson (eds.), *Middle Kingdom Studies, Gedenkschrift Detlef Franke* (Philippika, Marburg, in press).

The Reconstruction of Tomb Siut II from the Middle Kingdom*

Meike Becker

Introduction

The necropolis of Asyut holds some of the largest examples of ancient Egyptian private tomb architecture. In contrast to the long known and well described tombs of the local nomarchs Khety I, Iti-ibi and Khety II from the First Intermediate Period and the tomb of Twelfth Dynasty nomarch Djefai-Hapi I, the tomb of Djefai-Hapi II (O13.1; Pl. 30-31), commonly known as Siut II, has often been neglected. This is probably due to the poor state of preservation of the surviving inscriptions. Even at the beginning of the nineteenth century CE, the members of the Napoleonic Expedition were able to document no more than fragments of the decoration of the entrance (PANCKOUCKE 1822: Pl. 46.10; 47.1-2.10-11; 49.5). Since then only few publications refer to Tomb Siut II.

It is mentioned, for example, in compilations by Lepsius (LEPSIUS 1904: 15g; 156a-b), Brugsch (BRUGSCH 1891: 1512 [a-c]) and Mariette (MARIETTE 1889: Pl. 68c). Its inscriptions were subsequently copied by Griffith in 1888-1889 (GRIFFITH 1889a: Pl. 10, 20) as well as Montet in 1911-1914 (MONTET 1930-35: 86-89).

Based on recent research on the remaining inscriptions and the architecture I will present a reconstruction of the tomb.

According to a geological survey by Dietrich and Rosemarie Klemm, Tomb Siut II (O13.1, Fig. 1) is located at the same geologic step as those of the nomarchs from the First Intermediate Period Khety I, Iti-ibi, and Khety II (step 6; KAHL 2007: 60, Fig. 33; see general map B2, Pl. 18). Jochem Kahl therefore supposes a date for Djefai-Hapi II at the beginning of the Twelfth Dynasty. His second argument supporting this theory is the square cut layout of Siut II, which is much more similar to the tombs of the First Intermediate Period (KAHL 2007: 85).

Thus the tomb owner, Djefai-Hapi II, might in fact have lived earlier than his namesake Djefai-Hapi I, to whom the largest tomb in the necropolis of Asyut belongs: Siut I (P10.1).

* I would like to express my gratitude to Manja Maschke and Ulrike Fauerbach who shared their valuable thoughts during the research process and produced the layout and the reconstruction. Furthermore I owe thanks to Martin Ehlker for his advice regarding my English.

Fig. 1: Siut II (O13.1) in 2003 (© Kahl).

Fig. 2: Siut II in 1799 (after PANCKOUCKE 1822: Pl. 46.10).

According to the inscriptions, Djefai-Hapi II was nomarch of the 13th Upper Egyptian nome and belonged to the highest social level in the administrative and religious area. His titles show that *inter alia* he was Iripat and Hatia, sealer of the king of Lower Egypt, sole companion (of the king), true overseer of the priests of Wepwawet, councillor in Nekhen and overlord of Nekheb, herdsman of Apis, spokesman of every resident of Pe, splendid Ba, chief lector priest, master of the secrets of Osiris at his place, pupil of Horus, foremost of the sky, greatest of the tens of Upper Egypt, mouth of Nekhen, priest of Maat, and juridical provincial administrator.

After they had visited Asyut in 1799, the Napoleonic Expedition published a layout and several drawings in the Description de l'Égypte (PANCKOUCKE 1822: Pls. 46.10; 47.1-2.10-11; 49.5). These drawings convey an idea of the tomb's façade, which is partially destroyed today (Fig. 2).

According to Griffith, who visited Asyut in 1888, the façade was probably destroyed in 1885 or 1886 (GRIFFITH 1889b: 174). A photograph taken by W. M. F. Petrie in 1881 shows that large sections of the façade still existed at that time (photograph no. 154). Lepsius notes between 1842-1845: "Noch weiter südlich ist ein kolossales Grab mit einer Thüre, an 31 ½ Fuß hoch und 8 Fuß breit, nicht vollendet." (LEPSIUS 1904: 156).

Architectural description

In 2006 and 2008 Ulrike Fauerbach and Manja Maschke took the measurements of the tomb and produced a layout of the square-cut (ca. 16 x 16 m) tomb. In contrast to the layout made by the French scientists in 1799 (Fig. 3) the modern layout shows the destruction of the tomb's façade.

The ceiling of the tomb was supported by four pillars, of which today only truncated fragments at the floor and the ceiling are preserved (Pl. 31b). The south-western pillar is missing entirely (see Fig. 5). Worked edges are visible directly in front of both rows of pillars (Fig. 4). In the north-western corner is a large stone jut, which is located approximately in the middle of the wall (Fig. 4). The jut indicates that the stonecutting in the interior of the tomb has probably never been completely finished. In the necropolis of Asyut unfinished stone-cutting is frequent because of the sometimes difficult constitution of the material.

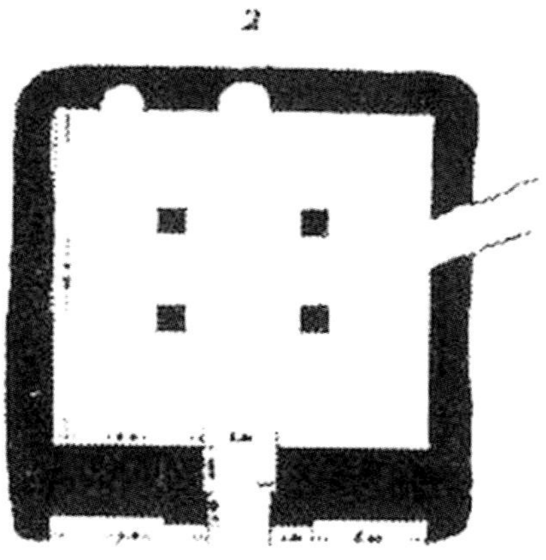

Fig. 3: Layout of Siut II (after PANCKOUCKE 1822: Pl. 47.2).

In the New Kingdom and afterwards there was considerable quarry activity both in the northern and in the southern part of the tomb. The northern quarry is a corridor that connects Siut II with the tomb of Iti-ibi (Siut III (N12.1) cf. Pl. 18). This quarry can be dated to the New Kingdom (KAHL 2007: 86).

In the southern half of the western wall of the tomb there are two false doors with niches (Fig. 6). They probably belong to the original conception of the tomb.

The southern niche is about 1.20 m in square and the carved upper edges at the ceiling (in a 90° angle to the west wall) are still visible (Fig. 7). In the northern edge of this niche is a door hinge that suggests a single-leaf wooden door (Fig. 8). Above the niche there are three rows of green hieroglyphs on yellow plaster (Pl. 5b). Two of them were already described by Griffith in 1888. For further details of the inscription see below.

The second niche is about 1.40 m wide and has a smaller door hinge in the northern edge. The actual depth of the original niche is indeterminate due to the extensive destruction. At the ceiling of this niche are remains of plaster painted in blue, white and red (Pl. 5a).

The south-eastern wall of the tomb displays a sloping passage that is probably leading to the burial chamber (Fig. 9).

Inscriptions

During the last 200 years inscriptions were found

- at the door limbs of the entrance,
- at the southern false door, and
- at the façade.

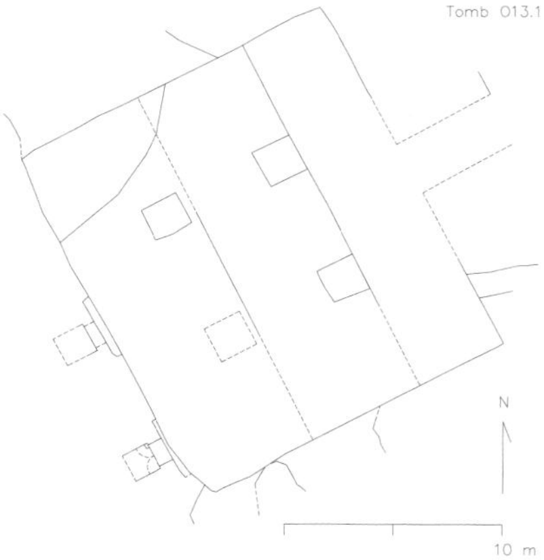

Fig. 5: Layout of Siut II (© The Asyut Project).

Fig. 4: Siut II: stone jut and worked edges in front of the pillars (© Kahl 2003).

Fig. 6: Siut II: false doors and niches; west wall
(© The Asyut Project; Becker 2008).

Fig. 7: Siut II: south niche, ceiling (© The Asyut Project; Becker 2008).

Fig. 8: Siut II: south niche, door hinge (© The Asyut Project; Becker 2008).

Fig. 9: Siut II: sloping passage
(© The Asyut Project; Becker 2008).

First of all I will discuss the inscriptions that are still visible today. Then follows a translation of those inscriptions on the façade and the entrance which are destroyed today and conveyed only by hand-copies of earlier scholars.

I already mentioned the fragmentary inscription at the lintel of the southern inner false door (Pl. 5b). While Griffith only noted two lines of inscription the recent facsimile (Fig. 10) shows that the inscription in fact consists of at least three lines. The text names the owner of the tomb – Djefai-Hapi II – and several of his titles.

Fig. 10: Siut II: remains of inscription above south niche (© The Asyut Project; drawing: M. Becker).

Inscription on the lintel of the southern false door

1	*[jr(j)-p]ʿ.[t] ḥꜣtj-ʿ ḫtm.tj bjtj smr wʿ.tj Ḥr.w(?) mnḫ ḥr.j-sštꜣ [ẖkr nzw?] jmj-rʾ ḥm.w nṯr [Ḏfꜣ=j]- Ḥ [ʿpj ms n Jdy]*	Iripat and Hatia, sealer of the king of Lower Egypt, sole companion of the Horus[1], one who is efficient, master of the secrets[2] [of the royal insignia[3]], overseer of the priests, [Djefai]-H[api, born by Idy[4]]
2	[////] *ẖrj-ḥꜣb.t* [////]	[///] lector priest [///]
3	[////] *ḥm* [////]	[///] servant / priest [///]

Another interesting inscription can be found at the southern side of the façade. Remains of 13 columns of inscription are still visible today (Figs. 11, 12). This inscription suffered severely from the destruction of the façade and is in a very bad condition.

1 Otherwise unknown combination. It could also be the phrase … *smr wʿ.tj bꜣ mnḫ* … - "… sole companion, splendid Ba …". But the hieroglyphic sign of the bird strongly resembles a falcon (Gardiner Sign-list G5) and not a stork (Gardiner Sign-list G29).

2 The unusual spelling of this title would consist of the crouching jackal and the phonetic complement *t* and the pottery kiln (Gardiner Sign-list U30) as determinative.

3 The only title that could fit to the oblong and upright sign (cf. WARD 1982: no. 1037).

4 Addition by MONTET 1930-35: 87.

Fig. 11: Siut II: view from southeast, inscription at the façade (© The Asyut Project; Gervers 2006).

Fig. 12: Siut II: inscription at the façade (© The Asyut Project; Becker 2008).

In 2005 Monika Zöller and I made a facsimile, which I collated in 2007 and 2008. The result of this work can be seen in Fig. 20. In addition to the hieroglyphic inscription one can see also the lines that separate the columns from each other. In several cases such a line crosses the inscription. This points to a later revision of the inscription.
The next two photographs (Figs. 13, 14) give an impression of the actual condition of the inscription.

Fig. 13: Siut II, façade, inscription detail; column x+1-x+3 (© The Asyut Project; Becker 2007).

Fig. 14: Siut II, façade, inscription detail; column x+9 (© The Asyut Project; Becker 2007).

Upon examining all publications concerning Siut II (see Tab. 1) in order to ascertain if any of the earlier scholars ever referred to this inscription and to find out about the former condition and dimensions of the inscription, we soon concluded that none of these publications mentions the inscription. That means it is likely that nobody has ever seen this part of the wall. At this point one particular question arises: Why? There are three explanations:

The first is that this part of the wall could have been hidden by debris, limestone chips and gravel. Because when Petrie visited Asyut in 1881 this part of the wall was covered with debris.

A second suggestion would be that the lighting conditions in front of Siut II are often not at their very best. During most of the day the inscription is completely in the sun. The ideal time to work on the inscription would be in the very small hours of the morning or at night under artificial light.

The last explanation is that some scholars only refer to older publications and photographs. Griffith for example refers to Nestor l'Hôte and photos of Arundale and

Petrie. That could perhaps mean that he didn't have the time to come to Siut II several times a day to check if some new hieroglyphic signs were visible.

To locate the position of the inscription in relation to the whole façade I combined the facsimile, a drawing of the Description de l'Égypte and a current photo of Siut II (Fig. 15).

façade	entrance
▪ PANCKOUCKE 1822: Pl. 46 [10]; 47 [1]; 49 [5] ▪ GRIFFITH 1889a: Pl. 20 ▪ BRUGSCH 1891: 1512 [b] ▪ LEPSIUS 1904: 15 g • ROBERT HAY MSS 29814, 87; 29847, 68 (London, British Library) • NESTOR L'HÔTE MSS 20396, 140 (Paris, Bibliothèque Nationale) • W. M. F. PETRIE photo no. 154	▪ PANCKOUCKE 1822: Pl. 47 [10] ▪ GRIFFITH 1889a: Pl. 10 [1-18] ▪ DE ROUGÉ 1877: Pl. 285-87 ▪ MARIETTE 1889: Pl. 68 [c] ▪ BRUGSCH 1891: 1512 [a+c] ▪ LEPSIUS 1904: 156 a+b ▪ MONTET 1930-35: 86-89 ▪ WILKINSON MSS X.52 (Oxford, Bodleian Library)

Tab. 1: Publications concerning Siut II (after PM IV, 262).

Fig. 15: Siut II: combination of several pictures.

The inscription must have been on the left bottom of the wall, below the tomb owner and maybe even next to the tomb owner. The elevation established by Manja Maschke confirms this assumption (Figs. 21, 22). That means only a small passage is preserved today and long passages between the columns are missing.

My main goal was to achieve a translation of the remaining text and to hopefully find textual parallels enabling a reconstruction of the text and its lacunae.

Very soon it became clear that comparing our inscription to other typical inscriptions of Middle Kingdom tomb entrances would not be successful. The remaining fragments in no case resemble biographical phrases, epithets, threat-formulae or other texts that address the living visitors of the necropolis.

The next step in identifying the text was to ascertain to which genre the remaining fragments can be allocated. The vocabulary (mentioning of the goddess Nut or an opening of heaven), indicates that it might be a religious text. So the next step was an extensive search for parallels within the corpora of Pyramid Texts and Coffin Texts (cf. VAN DER MOLEN 2000; SPELEERS n.d.); the results are presented in the following:

In column x+1 to x+4 we find the fragments:

[////n]*ḏ ḥr=ṯn ḫnt.jw* [///]	… Hail to you, who are the foremost …
[///].*w m ḫnt sḫ.t* ꜥ[///]	… from out of the field of …
[////]*Ḏf*-[*Ḥꜥpj*] *m zp n* [*sr*///]	… Djefai-[Hapi] …
[////*f*] *mj wp šn* [*wj*//*w*//]	… like him, whose hair is parted…

All these fragments belong to Coffin Text Spell 180, which is bequeathed on coffins from El-Bershe and Thebes (B2L [BM EA 30839], B3Bo [MFA 21.962-63], T1L [BM EA 6654], T2C [CG 28024]) and derives from chapter 473 of the Pyramid Texts (q.v. Pyr. 1059 a+b – 1061). The entire passage reads (FAULKNER 1973: 152):

> Hail to you who preside over abundance and who watch over provisions from out of the field (or: the field of standing).
> Give bread to NN that NN may eat of grain, that NN may become Khepri like him whose hair is parted, that NN may live again among the celestial kine; that NN may eat with his mouth like him whose hair is parted; and NN may be loosed in his hinder parts like Selket.
> May breath be in NN's nose and seed in his phallus like him who is invisible of shape.
> Not falling into the lake of *šnwnw*.

On the basis of this knowledge now one can amend this passage and complete the columns x+1 to x+4:

x+1 [////*n*]*ḏ ḥr=ṯn ḫnt.jw* [*bꜥḥ*]

x+2 [*zꜣꜣ.w ḏfꜣ*].*w m ḫnt sḫ.t* ꜥ[*ḥꜥ.t ḏ(j)=ṯn*]

x+3 [*t'.w n Ḏf-Ḥ*ʿ*pj wnm*] *Ḏf*-[*Ḥ*ʿ*pj*] *m npr* [*ḫpr Ḏf-Ḥ*ʿ*pj m Ḫprj*]

x+4 [*mj wḥm rn ḫnt m Mḥ.t-wr.t* (T1L) / *m whm m Mḥ.t-wr.t* (B2L) *wnm NN pn m*] *r'=f mj wp šn*. [*wj* //*w*//]

The only problem is the passage *Ḏf*-[*Ḥ*ʿ*pj*]- *m zp n* [*sr* …] in column x+3, which does not fit exactly. Perhaps one can assume a wrong spelling for *npr* – grain, and the standing man would then be a determinative for Nepri, the god of grain. The coffin T1L also has this version, but spells Nepri correctly.

Column x+5 is not all preserved and one can speculate if CT 180 continues until there.

In column x+6 the passage *wn* [*p.t*////*tꜣ?*] is comparable to a phrase of CT 225. The beginning of this spell is: *wn=k p.t tꜣ*… But in this case a suffix pronoun would be missing and columns x+7 and x+8 do not resemble CT 225.

In column x+7 there is also only a very small part left. It is not easy to find an equivalent for the passage [////]*f jpw njw ꜣḫ f?*// *nb* [////].

The following list (Tab. 2) represents the research results in Pyramid Texts and Coffin Texts, but none of the suggestions are a perfect match.

Phrase	**Source**
…4 ꜣḫ.w	PT 879?, 339, 467, 1092
…4 nṯr.w	evtl. PT 316, 348, 1141, 1385, 1284, 1483, 1510, 1548
…f jpw ḫnt	PT 1225, 1828, 2078
…nṯr.w 4 jpw…	CT 1145 (B1P; B1Be; B5C)
…4 jpw ꜣḫ.w…	CT 768 (T1L)
…nṯr.w jpw ꜣḫ.w…	CT 694 (B1P)
…4 jpw jmj jmnt.t…	CT 553 (B1Bo; B2Bo; B4C)
…4 ꜣḫ.w jpw…	CT 343 (B15C)
…ꜣḫ.w pw…	CT 335 (M8C; M7C)
…ꜣḫ.w jpw…	CT 335 (T1C; B9C; B3C; Sq4Sq; B1P; B5C; B1Y; Sq1C; Sq7C; M4C; M8C; M7C; M54C; L1NY; T1Be; L3Li; T2Be; M57C; M1Ny; BH1Br)
…m pr(j).w=f jpw njw wrr.t…	CT 78 (G1T; A1C)
…4 jpw nṯr.w…	CT 1 (B3Bo; B2Bo; B4Bo; B1P; B15C; B6C; B4C; MC105a; Y1C; S10C; ThT319)

Tab. 2: Possible parallels to column x+7.

The only remarkable observation is that the coffin T1L, which also conveys a solution in column x+3, has the phrase *jpw ꜣḫ.w* as well. It is in CT 768, in the sentence: *jn(j).n=sn n=f jfdw jpw ꜣḫ.w* – "they bring to him these four spirits". But to assume a connection at this point would be very speculative.

In column x+8 there is a reference to the goddess Nut, but otherwise it is not possible to allocate this phrase to a specific template.

In contrast, column x+9 shows a strong analogy with CT 225, which stems from chapter 17 of the Pyramid Texts and evolves to chapter 68 of the Book of the Dead. The phrase *sḫm=k m [ꜥ.wj]=k m rd.wj=k* – "May you have power in your arms and in your legs" matches this paragraph from the Coffin Texts. However, the following *pr(j).n=k* poses a problem, because it does not belong to CT 225.

Column x+10 *nb m r'=k ḥr md.wt=k ḥr šm.wt=k////] nb mnḫ?* – "in your mouth with your words and with your strides" has got a parallel structure, but this phrase is not part of CT 225 either. The basket could be read as *nb* and then the phrase would be "in every mouth, with all words and with every stride". But also for this alternative it is impossible to find a parallel.

Lastly, column x+13 mentions the tomb owner Djefai-Hapi, the overseer of the priests.

In summary, we may reconstruct the whole text as follows:

x+1	*[////n]ḏ ḥr=ṯn ḫnt.jw [bꜥḥ]*	[…] Hail to you, who are the foremost […]
x+2	*[zꜣꜣ.w ḏfꜣ].w m ḫnt sḫ.t* ꜥ*[ḥꜥ.t ḏ(j)=ṯn]*	[who watch over provisions] from out of the field of [standing. You may give]
x+3	*[t'.w n Ḏf-Ḥꜥpj wnm] Ḏf-[Ḥꜥpj] m npr [ḫpr Ḏf-Ḥꜥpj m Ḫprj]*	[bread to Djefai-Hapi, that] Djefai-[Hapi may eat] of grain, [that Djefai-Hapi may become Khepri]
x+4	*[mj wḥm rn ḫnt m Mḥ.t-wr.t* (T1L) / *m whm m Mḥ.t-wr.t* (B2L) *wnm NN pn m] r'=f mj wp šn. [wj //w//]*	[like one who repeats the name in front of the Great Flood (T1L) / that NN may repeat with/in the Great Flood (B2L); that NN may eat with] his mouth like him whose hair is parted […]
x+5	[…]	[…]
x+6	*[////] ḥr // w /// w s.t=sn wn [p.t///tꜣ?]*	[…] their places, the opening [of heaven …]
x+7	*[////]=f jpw njw ꜣḫ //// nb [////]*	[…] these four spirits […]
x+8	*[////].w Nw.t rḏ(j).n=j[////]*	[…] Nut, I gave […]
x+9	*[////] =k m? sḫm=k m [ꜥ.wj]=k m rd.wj=k pr(j).n=k? r [////]*	[…] may you have power in your [arms] and in your legs […]
x+10	*[////] nb/=k m r' nb/=k ḥr md.wt? nb/=k ḥr šm.wt [nb/=k////] nb mnḫ? [////]*	[…] in your mouth with your words and with your strides […]

x+11	*[////] nb //// nb mn ? s.t /// nb //// jmꜣ/ḥr // nb //t [////]*	[…] ? […]
x+12	*[////] nb //// p / nb snṯr // t n /r// nb/=k [////]*	[…] ? […]
x+13	*[////] (j)m(j)-r' ḥm(.w) nṯr [Ḏf]-Ḥꜥpj [////]*	[…] the overseer of the priests [Djefai]-Hapi […]

On the northern side of the façade are also some remains of decoration and inscription. The hieroglyphic remains are too fragmentary to be interpreted.

One interesting fragment is located directly on the northern part of the entrance. It is the lower fragment of a chair or a piece of furniture that could belong to a depiction of the seated tomb owner (Figs. 16, 17).

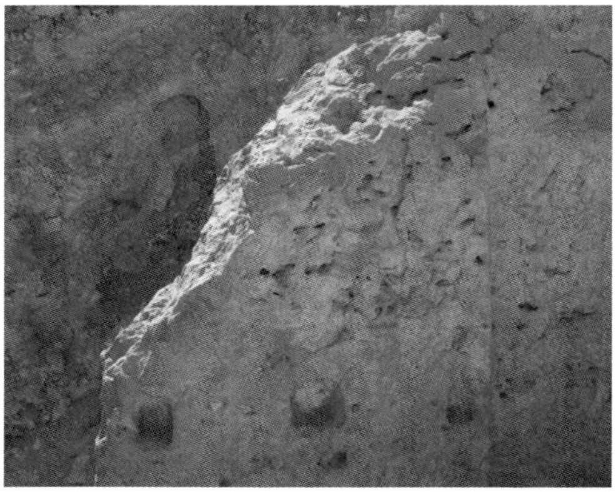

Fig. 16: Siut II: detail of northern entrance (© The Asyut Project; Becker 2007).

Fig. 17: Siut II: detail of northern entrance (© The Asyut Project; drawing: M. Becker).

Today the entrance of the tomb and the door limbs are nearly completely destroyed. However, the copies made in the nineteenth century submit several inscriptions which are translated in the following. The numbering follows GRIFFITH 1889a.

Southern door limb

3	*(j)r(j)-pꜥ.t ḥꜣtj-ꜥ ḫtmw bjtj smr wꜥ.tj (j)m(j)-r' ḥm(.w) nṯr n wn mꜣꜥ n Wp(j)-wꜣ.wt nb Zꜣwt Ḏf=j-Ḥꜥpj ms(j) n Jdy wr*	Iripat and Hatia, sealer of the king of Lower Egypt, sole companion (of the king), true overseer of the priests of Wepwawet, Lord of Asyut, Djefai-Hapi, born by Idy. One great[5]

5 Cf. LEPSIUS 1904: 156, α.

4	*m jꜣw.t=f ꜥꜣ m sꜥḥ=f mḥ jb n nzw ẖntj tꜣ.wj=f ꜥq jb=f ẖntj jdb.wj wr n nzw ꜥꜣ n bjtj sr m ḥꜣ.t rẖy.t*	in his office, great in his rank. Favorite of the king before the two lands[6]; his confidant before the two banks; great one of the king of Upper Egypt; great one of the king of Lower Egypt; official before the Rekhyt-people.
5	*ꜥꜣ ḥs.t r gs nb=f sẖnt n*	One great of favour at his lord's side; who is promoted by
6	*nzw r mj.tw=f wr wr.w*	the king more than his equals; greatest of the great ones,
7	*sꜥḥ smr.w jrr ḥzz.t*	nobles and officials; one who does what the one who favours him
8	*ḥz sw mnẖ jb jqr ṯz.w*	favours, virtuous one, excellent of speech;
9	*jr(j) mn.w m n'.t nj.t db ḥr pꜣw.t*	one who built monuments in the township of the hippopotamus (?) since the primeval times,
10	[//]*nj.t n'.t* [//] *ḥꜣtj-ꜥ Ḏf-Ḥꜥpj* [*mꜣꜥ ẖrw*]	[//][7] of the town [///][8] Hatia Djefai-Hapi [justified][9].

Northern door limb

11	*(j)r(j)-pꜥ.t ḥꜣtj-ꜥ ẖtmw bjtj smr wꜥ.tj (j)m(j)-r' ḥm.w nṯr n Wsjr nb jmnt.t Ḏf=j-Ḥꜥpj ms n Jdy ḥrj-tp ꜥꜣ n Nḏfy.t-*	Iripat, Hatia, sealer of the king of Lower Egypt, sole companion (of the king), true overseer of the priests of Osiris, Lord of the West, Djefai-Hapi, born of Idy, nomarch of the whole pomegranate nome[10] (13th Upper Egyptian nome),

6 MONTET 1930-35, BRUGSCH 1891, and MARIETTE 1889 read *tꜣ.wj*. The reading of GRIFFITH 1889a: Pl. 10 is not completely intelligible. It could also be *ḥrj-š* but then the meaning would remain obscure.

7 Montet does not mention any destruction in this area.

8 MONTET adds a *t*.

9 MARIETTE 1889: Pl. 68, c is the southern door limb. However it is not in the original columns but dispersed on three columns. The addition of *mꜣꜥ ẖrw* at the end of column 10 is logical (cf. BRUGSCH 1891: 1512 a).

10 Cf. LEPSIUS 1904 156, β.

12	*ḫnt.t mj-qd=s jmj-jz Nḫn ḥrj-tp Nḫb mdw Ḥp.w r' P nb bꜣ mnḫ ḫrj-ḥꜣb.t ḥrj-tp ḥrj-sštꜣ n Wsjr m s.t=f sbꜣ Ḥr.w*	Councillor in Nekhen (Hierakonpolis),[11] overlord of Nekheb (Elkab),[12] herdsman of Apis,[13] spokesman of every Pe-ite, splendid Ba[14], chief lector priest, master of secrets of Osiris, at his place, pupil[15] of Horus,
13	*ḫntj p.t wr mḏ.w-šmꜥ.w r' Nḫn ḥm nṯr mꜣꜥ.t zꜣb ꜥḏ-mr*	foremost of the sky, greatest of the tens of Upper Egypt, mouth of Nekhen, priest of Maat, juridical provincial administrator
14	*Dp jmj ḥr m-m nṯr ꜥꜣ m* [///]	of Dep, being under the great god ...
15	*m Wp(j)-wꜣ.wt (j)m(j)-r' ḥw.t nṯr m*	with Wepwawet, overseer of the temple at
16	*s.t ḏsr.t ḫntj s.t r s.t* [///]	the holy place, foremost place...
17	*ḥr* [///]	
18	*r ḫrw* [///]	

Lintel of the door

1	[///]	[///]
2(19)	*ḥꜣtj[-ꜥ] šps.w jy* [///] *ḫꜣs.t nfr.t m*	Hati[a], noble one [////] the beautiful desert is coming in/as
3(20)	[///]*nh nb r wꜥr.t tn jr(j).n<=j> mn.w r s.t šps.t ꜥḥꜥ.t nṯr* [///]	[///] Everyone came[16] to this necropolis. <I> made monuments at the noble place, the tomb of the god [///]
4(21)	[///]*pr n Wnn-nfr ḫꜥ(j)=k [Ḥrw ?///j] wꜣ(j).wt n* [///]	[///] the house of Wennefer. You appear [///] paths of [///]
5(22)	[///] *t n mḥ jb ḏ(j) ḥm.w* [///]	[///] trusted one, who gives priests?[///]
6	[///]	[///]

11 JONES 2000: 248.
12 JONES 2000: 2374.
13 DOXEY 1998: 348, suggests *ḥrj-tp Ḥp.w*. This interpretation however is based on a wrong division of the title *mdw ḥp* and the preceding titles.
14 BRUGSCH 1891: 1512, c reads *ḫrp/sḫm*.
15 BRUGSCH 1891: 1512, c ends here.
16 The determinative of the "walking legs" indicates a verb of motion.

Façade, on the left side next to the tomb owner

23	[/// *pr ḥ3t ḥ3tjw* /// *Z3wtj*] *jm3ḫ* [*Ḏf=j*]-*Ḥpj*	[/// foremost of the foremost /// Siut][17] the revered one Djefai-Hapi

The following inscriptions are assigned to Siut II only by Brugsch (BRUGSCH 1891: 1513). However, they were already destroyed during his lifetime. Therefore, it is not clear if they belong to Siut II at all. The first one poses the problem with the name of the mother, because on the southern door limb she is named Idy and not Jy-jnet. The second inscription cannot be located within Siut II either. According to Griffith (GRIFFITH 1889a: Pl. 3.132) this phrase belongs to the north wall of the shrine within the tomb of Djefai-Hapi I (Siut I). Also DE ROUGÉ 1877: Pl. 285 mismatches an inscription to Siut II even though it is a part of the famous contracts (the end of the ninth and the tenth contract) of Djefai-Hapi I (Siut I).

Mentioned without location

(j)m(j)-r' ḥm(.w) nṯr Ḏf=j-Ḥʿpj ms(j) n Jy-jn-t	overseer of the priests Djefai-Hapi, born of Jy-jnet

Above a priest carrying the limb of an animal as an offering

ḫrj-ḥ3b.t zḫ3.w jz pn rḏ(j) m nzw Ḫty z3 Ptḥ-m-s3=f	Chief lector priest, scribe of this tomb, that is given by the king, Ptahemsaf son of Khety

Hypothesis

Summing up:

- We have a religious text on the southern wall of the façade that was already revised in antiquity.
- On the northern part of the entrance we probably have the tomb owner seated on a chair.

For a tomb façade this decoration pattern is odd. I would therefore like to suggest a solution to this problem: The layout must be different than previously assumed: Even the depictions from the Napoleonic Expedition do not show the original façade of the tomb but rather an interior wall. This now second but last room – which we have to reconstruct – was destroyed sometime before the eighteenth century. Its decoration contained religious texts that show at least one revision.

17 It seems suitable to amend this part to *Z3wtj* because of the following determinative: village with crossroads.

Upon arriving at this interesting conclusion, I started looking for other hints in the terrain that would back up my hypothesis. While walking in the former forecourt – and now second but last room – of Siut II, a worked rock edge (Fig. 18) was detected in the southern part that is almost directly in line with the southern corner of the former façade next to the inscription. The distance between these two points is about 18 meters. The reconstruction thus indicates a second hall with a wall length of a minimum of 18 meters (Figs. 21, 22).

On the northern part of the terrain is another interesting feature (Fig. 19). There are two large and broken fragments. One is still *in situ* and the upper one has fallen down. The position of these pieces suggests that they could perhaps belong to the northern wall. Analogue to other tombs of the necropolis of Asyut with more than one hall – as for example Siut I (P10.1, Pl. 32), I10.1 (Pl. 16) and O12.1 (Pl. 19), it is possible that Siut II has not only two rooms but rather a total of three halls.

If we go so far as to reconstruct more than one further room, we could also compare the ceiling. As in Siut I and I10.1 the second but last room could possess a tunnel vault.

Fig. 18: Siut II: worked rock edge in the "forecourt", south part (© The Asyut Project; Becker 2008).

The conclusion of all these considerations shows a complete new idea of Tomb Siut II. Its architecture resembles the tombs of the Middle Kingdom closer than previously assumed. It does not resemble the tombs of the First Intermediate Period.

This places Djefai-Hapi II at the beginning of the Twelfth Dynasty (that means before Djefai-Hapi I) purely on the basis of the location of the tomb, being on the same geological step as the First Intermediate Period Tombs.

Fig. 19: Siut II: „forecourt“, north part
(© The Asyut Project; Becker 2008).

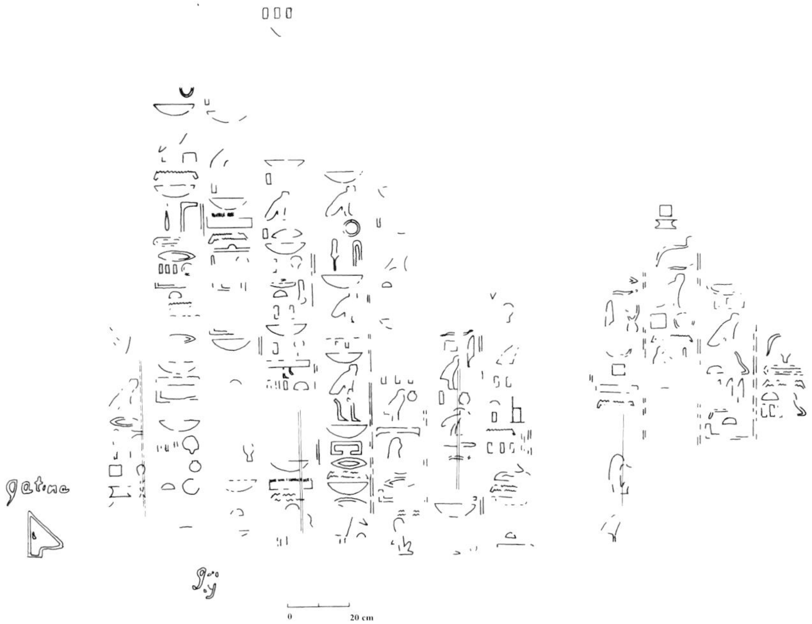

Fig. 20: Siut II: facsimile of the inscription at the façade
(© The Asyut Project; drawing: M. Becker 2009).

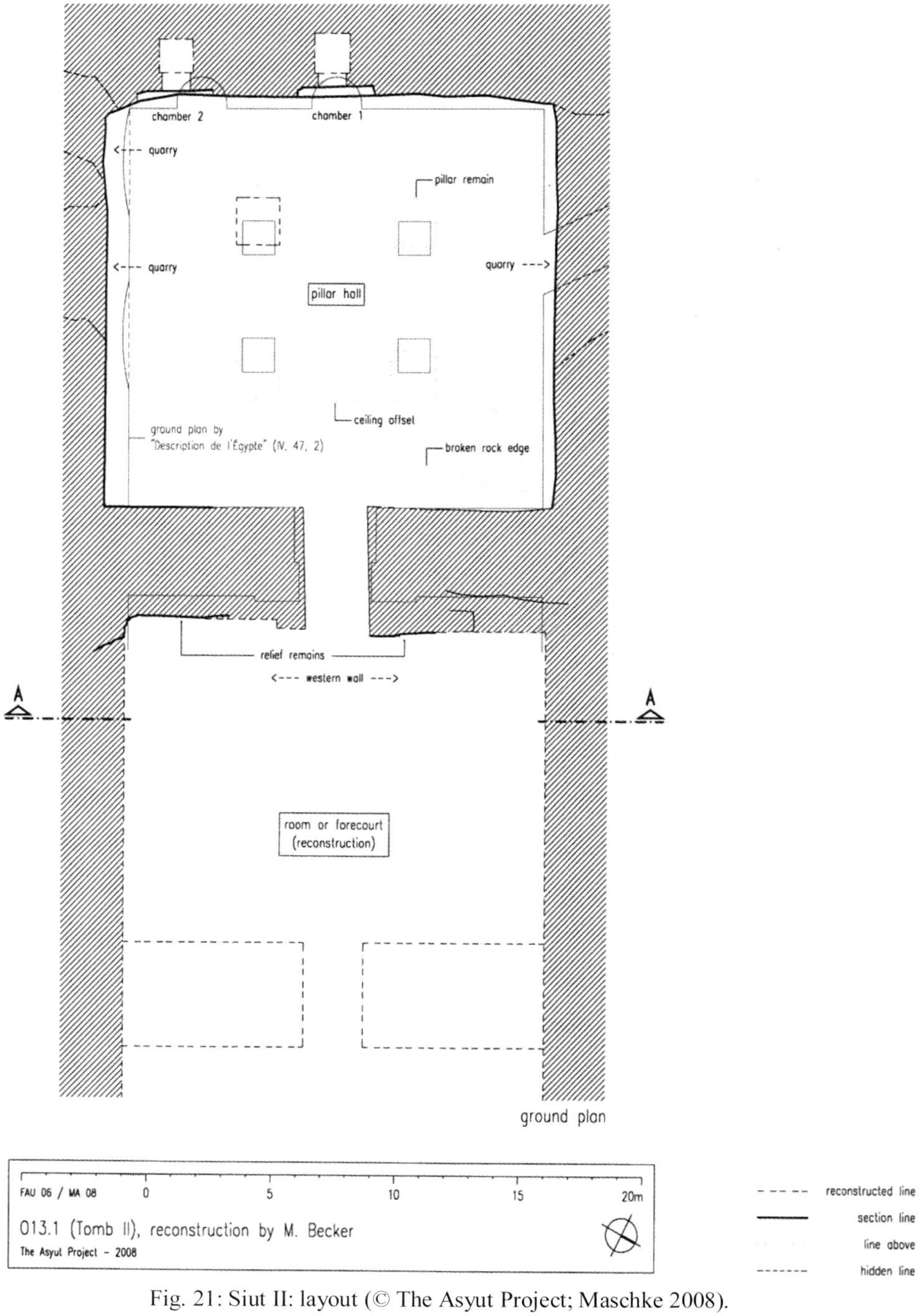

Fig. 21: Siut II: layout (© The Asyut Project; Maschke 2008).

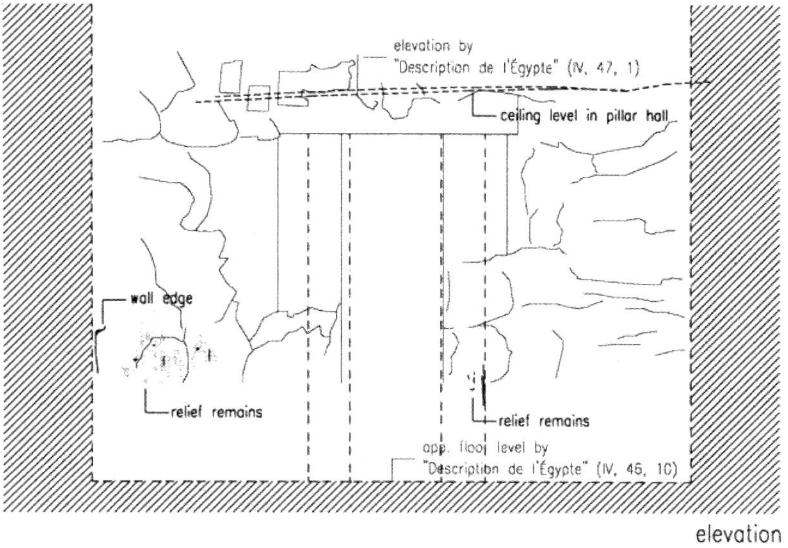

Fig. 22: Siut II: elevation, reconstruction (© The Asyut Project; Maschke 2008).

References:

BRUGSCH 1891: H. Brugsch, *Thesaurus Inscriptionum Aegyptiacarum. Altaegyptische Inschriften. Sechste Abtheilung* (Leipzig 1891; reprint Graz 1968).

DOXEY 1998: D. M. Doxey, *Egyptian Non-Royal Epithets in the Middle Kingdom. A Social and Historical Analysis* (Probleme der Ägyptologie 12, Leiden 1998).

FAULKNER 1973: R. O. Faulkner, *The Ancient Egyptian Coffin Texts. I: Spells 1-354* (Warminster 1973).

GRIFFITH 1889a: F. Ll. Griffith, *The Inscriptions of Siût and Dêr Rîfeh* (London 1889).

GRIFFITH 1889b: F. Ll. Griffith, The Inscriptions of Siût and Dêr Rîfeh, in: *The Babylonian and Oriental Record* 3 (1888-89), 121-129; 164-168; 174-184; 244-252.

JONES 2000: D. Jones, *An Index of Ancient Egyptian Titles, Epithets and Phrases of the Old Kingdom* (British Archaeological Reports, International Series 866, Oxford 2000).

KAHL 2007: J. Kahl, *Ancient Asyut. The First Synthesis after 300 Years of Research* (The Asyut Project 1, Wiesbaden 2007).

LEPSIUS 1904: C. R. Lepsius, *Denkmäler aus Aegypten und Aethiopien nach den Zeichnungen der von seiner königlichen Majestät dem Könige von Preussen Friedrich Wilhelm IV nach diesen Ländern gesendeten und in den Jahren 1842-1845 ausgeführten wissenschaftlichen Expedition.* Text. Zweiter Band. Mittelägypten mit dem Faijum, herausgegeben von Eduard Naville unter Mitwirkung von Ludwig Borchardt, bearbeitet von Kurt Sethe (Leipzig 1904).

MARIETTE 1889: A. Mariette-Pacha, *Monuments divers recueillis en Égypte et en Nubie* (Paris 1889).

VAN DER MOLEN 2000: R. van der Molen, *A Hieroglyphic Dictionary of Egyptian Coffin Texts* (Probleme der Ägyptologie 15, Leiden 2000).

MONTET 1930-35: P. Montet, Les tombeaux de Siout et de Deir Rifeh (suite), in: *Kêmi. Revue de philologie et d'archéologie égyptiennes et coptes* 3, 1930-35, 45-111.

PANCKOUCKE 1822: C. L. F. Panckoucke, *Description de l'Égypte ou recueil des observations et des recherches qui ont été faites en Égypte pendant l'Expedition de l'armée française,* Ant. IV, Seconde édition (Paris 1822).

DE ROUGÉ 1877: E. Vicomte de Rougé, *Inscriptions hiéroglyphiques copiés en Égypte pendant la mission scientifique* (Études Égyptologiques 9, Paris 1877).

SPELEERS n.d.: L. Speleers, *Traduction, index et vocabulaire des textes des pyramides égyptiennes* (Brussels n.d.).

WARD 1982: W. A. Ward, *Index of Egyptian Administrative and Religious Titles of the Middle Kingdom* (Beirut 1982).

Wooden Models from Asyut's First Intermediate Period Tombs*

Monika Zöller-Engelhardt

Introduction

Wooden models form one of the largest and most important groups of grave goods during the time from the middle of the Old Kingdom until the end of the Middle Kingdom. As provision and equipment for the afterlife of the deceased, their forms of representation range from simple miniature model food, model weapons and tools to richly equipped and populated scenes of food producing and manufacturing of goods for daily life. Religious objects could be found as models as well (TOOLEY 1995: 10). Particularly numerous are model boats, which often appear in pairs or entire armadas (TOOLEY 1995: 51). Complex workshops with surrounding architecture emerge during the transition from the First Intermediate Period to the Middle Kingdom (cf. DO. ARNOLD 2005).

Asyut was one of the major centers of production for high quality wooden models in Ancient Egypt and they form the characteristic element of grave goods in the First Intermediate Period and the Middle Kingdom:

> Mais l'élément charactéristique du matérial funéraire d'Assiout est l'abondance et la grande variété de modèles en bois qui reproduisent les différentes activités de la vie quotidienne destinées à garantir la vie éternelle au défunt.
> (LEOSPO 1998: 672-674).

Various museums display high quality wooden model objects coming from the Asyut necropolis, collected by early researchers mainly at the beginning of the twentieth century. Unfortunately these early excavations were often inadequately conducted and documented and hence causing severe problems for the following missions (KAHL 2007: 21-33, cf. also J. Kahl in this volume). In addition, most of the tombs have already been robbed or rearranged in Pharaonic and Coptic history and suffered greatly from stone quarrying and environmental influences in modern times (KAHL 2007: 3-4). It is thus one of the major tasks of the Asyut Project not only to document and describe the discovered artifacts but, in a second step, to anchor them in time and place.

Comparison material to wooden models from Asyut is easily found in nearly every Egyptian collection around the world. For instance, the grave goods from the undisturbed tomb of Nakhti,[1] now divided between several collections in Egypt (Egyptian Museum, Cairo), Europe (Louvre Museum, Paris) and the United States (Museum of Fine Arts,

* I would like to thank Tobias Dany for his advice regarding my English.

1 Excavated by Chassinat and Palanque in 1903 (CHASSINAT/PALANQUE 1911: iii, 29-135), the tomb is refilled today. Its position can only be located by means of a photography given in the excavation publication (ibd.: Pl.1; KAHL 2007: 93).

Boston), are a remarkable example for the composition of late Eleventh or early Twelfth Dynasty[2] burial equipment. Consisting of the material found in the side chambers of four shafts – belonging to the tomb owner and family members or at least special members of Nakhtis entourage (CHASSINAT/PALANQUE 1911: 142-143) – and the aboveground hall, the objects include among other several offering bearers (e.g. Cairo JE 36291; Cairo JE 36290; Louvre E 12029), one granary (Louvre E 11938), one slaughtering scene (Boston MFA Acc.no. 04.1781), several model boats (e.g. Louvre E 12027) as well as numerous tool and weapon models (e.g. a model quiver [Louvre E 12016]; model lances [Louvre E 12017]; model adzes [Louvre E 12005]; models shields [Louvre E 11988]).[3]

Further examples of Asyut's model artwork can be found in the British Museum in London (e.g. an Old Kingdom model peasant with hoe [London BM EA 45195]; a food producing scene [London BM EA 45197]), in the Museo Egizio in Turin (e.g. model boat Turin S.8657) and also in the Louvre Museum in Paris (e.g. model boat Louvre E 11993).

Yet the most famous artworks from Asyut are clearly the often cited two battalions of model soldiers (CG 257/JE 30969 and CG 258/JE 30986) from the tomb of Mesehti (RYAN 1988: 13; cf. KAHL 2007: 28, 82-83). The exquisite embodiment of the figures, each with individual facial features, height and varying weapon and clothing design, gives them a very lifelike and unique appearance. More than any other artwork these figures represent the elaborated design of wooden models from Asyut.

The short overview over the comparison material is essential to the examination of the recently discovered wooden model material, since, for the most part, the objects are fragmentary and often in bad condition.[4] Each of the following reconstruction attempts is based on the extensive study of comparison material ideally from Asyut itself, but also from other finding spots.[5] Especially the model material found in the tomb of the local nomarch Iti-ibi (Tomb Siut III/N12.1) (Pl. 18) allows the reconstruction of an enormous burial equipment of excellent workmanship only comparable to the most elaborated previous model finds.[6]

Tomb Siut III (N12.1)

The architecture of Tomb III (N12.1) consists of an aboveground great hall with four burial shafts, each one of them displaying a side chamber branching off to the south (Pl. 24). The

2 The exact date of Nakhti's Tomb is still a matter of debate. While stylistic datings suggest late Eleventh Dynasty (TOOLEY 1989: 35, with further reference), orthography (SCHENKEL 1962: 118) and pottery (SEIDLMAYER 1990: 350-351) seem more consistent with a Twelfth Dynasty dating (KAHL 2007: 95).

3 For a more detailed listing cf. TOOLEY 1989: 35.

4 For a short summary of the discovered objects cf. ZÖLLER 2007b: 87-88.

5 A detailed examination of Egyptian wooden model material is provided by TOOLEY 1989, TOOLEY 1995 and TOOLEY 2001. For comparison material cf. also the works of GARSTANG 1907; REISNER 1913; PETRIE 1917; WINLOCK 1955; GÖTTLICHER/WERNER 1971; GLANVILLE/FAULKNER 1972; DI. ARNOLD 1981; LANDSTRÖM 1974; JONES 1995.

6 The material has been studied in detail in ZÖLLER 2007a. The publication of the finds and results from Tomb III (N12.1) is in preparation.

rear part of the tomb is enlarged by three niches of differing size, which were installed during later reuse of the tomb (KAHL 2007: 76).

The finding situation is problematic, since the tomb has not only been plundered in antiquity, but has also been object to the excavation work of early researchers, who left numerous traces of their presence (KAHL/EL-KHADRAGY/VERHOEVEN 2005: 160; KAHL 2007: 28-29, 31-33).

Nevertheless, every shaft (apart from Shaft 1, see below) or side chamber, respectively, contained remains of grave goods, partially consisting of wooden models. Although the context is disturbed, there is some evidence that the objects could have belonged to the original burial equipment (see below in: Conclusion).

Tomb Siut III (N12.1): Shaft 1

In 2004 the Asyut Project Team started cleaning the front part of the inner hall's surface and Shaft 1 (Pl. 24). Surprisingly, Shaft 1 held a huge amount of fragmentary material in a depth between 30 and 90 centimeters (KAHL/EL-KHADRAGY/VERHOEVEN 2005: 160): not only fragments of wooden models, but also numerous faience and clay shabtis, fragments of offering trays (cf. the contribution of Andrea Kilian elsewhere in this publication), coffin fragments, pottery and other miscellaneous objects.

It became evident that the material had been collected by the early researchers from all over the necropolis (KAHL/EL-KHADRAGY/VERHOEVEN 2005: 160). Due to its fragmentary condition it was considered to be worthless and left behind by them. The side chamber of Shaft 1 did not contain any model material.

The retrieved model fragments included, among others, various figure fragments (Figs. 1, 2), mostly arms, some remains of model boat equipment (like oars) and several further fragments, which could – due to the mixed context – not be related to scenic or architectural complexes or boats, respectively. It cannot be decided whether any of the material from Shaft 1 belonged to the original burial context.

Tomb Siut III (N12.1): Shaft 2

In 2005 the cleaning of Tomb III was continued with the remaining three shafts and surface area (KAHL/EL-KHADRAGY/VERHOEVEN 2006: 243-244). Contrary to the finding situation of Shaft 1, the remaining shafts yielded more consistent wooden model material. Especially

Fig. 1: Part of female model figure (© The Asyut Project; Zöller).

Fig. 2: Part of model figure (© The Asyut Project; Zöller).

the side chamber of Shaft 2 held model fragments which clearly belong to one set of grave goods. This is recognizable because of their homogeneous character and distinct intensive colouring (Pl. 6b-c). The model arms and legs as well as the parts of bodies of model figures are of a simple, less-detailed design. The models are not of poor quality as the diligent painting and accurate modeling prove.

Of the retrieved fragments from the side chamber of Shaft 2 at least the following wooden model structures could be reconstructed:

- one female offering bearer (comparable in size and design with the previously mentioned examples from the tomb of Nakhti; CHASSINAT/PALANQUE 1911: 30-31 with Fig. 2, 32-34, 49, Pl. 4, 9, 10), documented by a pair of model bird's wings (Pl. 6a);
- at least one food producing scene (several model arms clearly belonging to female grinding figurines [cf. BREASTED 1948: Pl. 34a, 37a; JØRGENSEN 1996: 21, Fig. 8] and a wooden model beer jar demonstrate that one food producing scene must have existed, which included a grinding process and beer production);
- at least one model boat, evidenced by several model oars and model oar fragments (Fig. 3);
- and one singular figure of larger size[7] without scenic context.

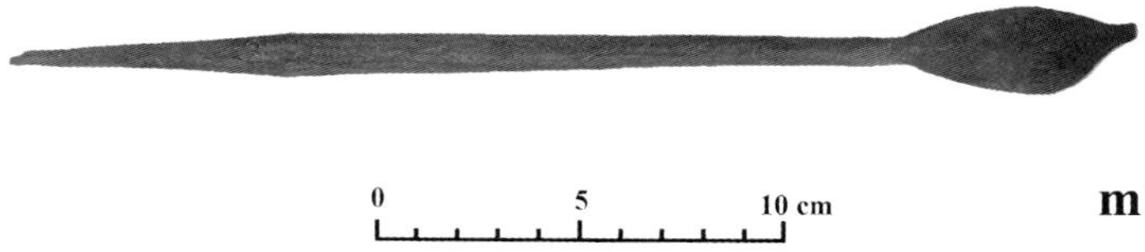

m123

Fig. 3: Wooden model oar (© The Asyut Project; Zöller).

Tomb Siut III (N12.1): Shaft 4

Shaft 4 provided a special finding situation: The shaft had obviously not been disturbed since antiquity or at least since the Coptic period and yielded several secondary burials in the main shaft (KAHL 2007: 76; KAHL/EL-KHADRAGY/VERHOEVEN 2006: 243).

At the bottom of the shaft, and also in the side chamber, various wooden model objects could be retrieved. The similarity in design, size and colouring of the objects from the main shaft to the objects from the side chamber is so evident that could be stated that they belonged to the same model equipment. Shaft 4 contained the best preserved model items and components, including several completely preserved model figures, model equipment and utensils.

Considering the model finds of Shaft 4 and its side chamber, one can reconstruct the following wooden model structures:

7 Individual model figures without scenic context are rare. An example from Asyut is the "man with a hoe" (BM EA 45197), dating to the Old Kingdom.

- at least one offering bearer (size and design according to the previously mentioned objects, cf. Shaft 2 above) (Fig. 4-5);
- a granary structure suggested by granary model utensils;
- a food producing scene with corn grinding, storage, beer production and baking as well as (probably meat) cooking (cf. the equipment of kitchen tender R and the butcher shop E from the tomb of Meket-Re, WINLOCK 1955: Pls. 44, 61) as the objects of model equipment show (Fig. 6-7);
- and probably two model boats, their original presence being documented by remains of oars and mast rests.

Fig. 4: Bird's wings belonging to offering bearer (© The Asyut Project; Zöller).

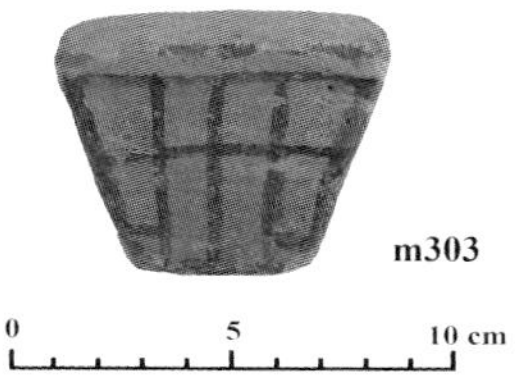

Fig. 5: Basket of offering bearer (© The Asyut Project; Zöller).

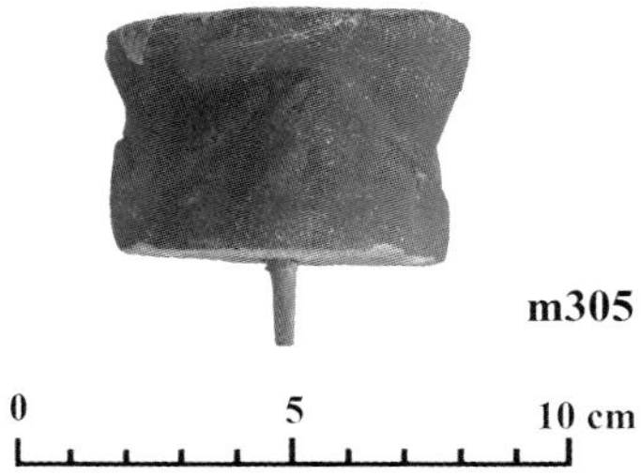

Fig. 6: Brazier with bowl for cooking (© The Asyut Project; Zöller).

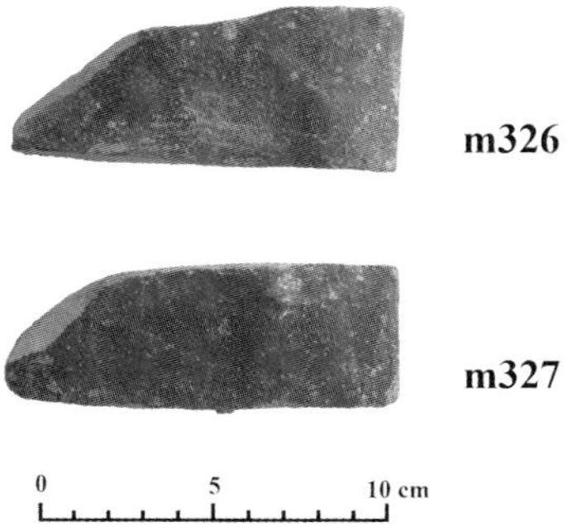

Fig. 7: Grinding tables (© The Asyut Project; Zöller).

The original context of the model figures cannot be determined with certainty, although, due to the body posture, it can be assumed that the squatting figures represent oarsmen (cf. Fig. 8; for comparison examples cf. BREASTED 1948: Pls. 69b, 72b, 96a-b; REISNER 1913: Pl. 2, CG 4801), while the standing figures may be the crew of a sailing boat,[8] but they could also belong to a scenic context.

8 This suggested reconstruction would be based on the assumption that wooden model burial equipments including two or more model boats often displayed one model boat equipped for sailing and one for rowing (cf. TOOLEY 1995: 51). This cannot be determined with certainty for the present context.

Tomb Siut III (N12.1): Shaft 3

The largest amount of wooden model material was discovered in the side chamber of Shaft 3. The items also featured the best quality in workmanship, visible in careful carving and painting and the highest diversity of activities. Additionally, the side chamber held a great number of wooden model tool and weapon handles.

More than 60 model arm fragments could be identified alongside with several model figure heads and bodies, hands, legs and feet.

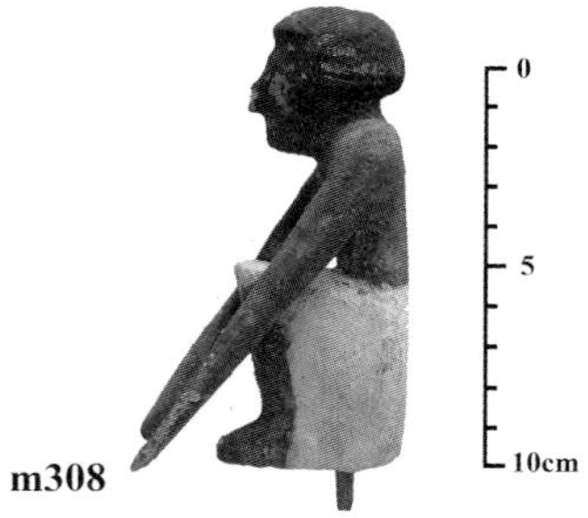

Fig. 8: Model figure, probably oarsman (© The Asyut Project; Zöller).

Numerous utensils, such as vessels (Fig. 9), vats or a model fan (Fig. 10), were discovered among the finds.

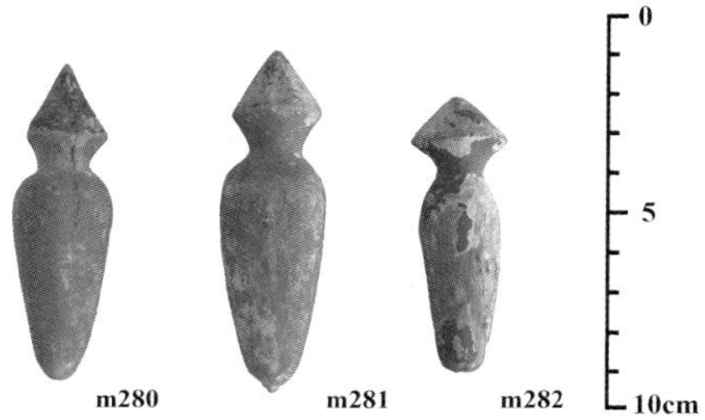

Fig. 9: Model vessels (© The Asyut Project; Zöller).

Wooden model architectural elements, such as walls of model buildings (Pl. 6d) and a base, could be identified among the objects.

In addition, various model boat components complete the impression of a richly equipped model arrangement. If all retrieved model elements, which form just a fraction of the original structures, actually belonged to one grave good equipment (and although the individual stylistic features – especially of the arm fragments – do not correlate in all cases, particularly the wooden model tool and weapon corpus is very homogeneous [see below]), it must have been enormous.

The discovered items from the burial chamber of Shaft 3 allow the assumption of the following elements:

- one offering bearer,
- one granary,
- one bakery/brewery scene,
- one slaughtering scene,
- two or three model boats.

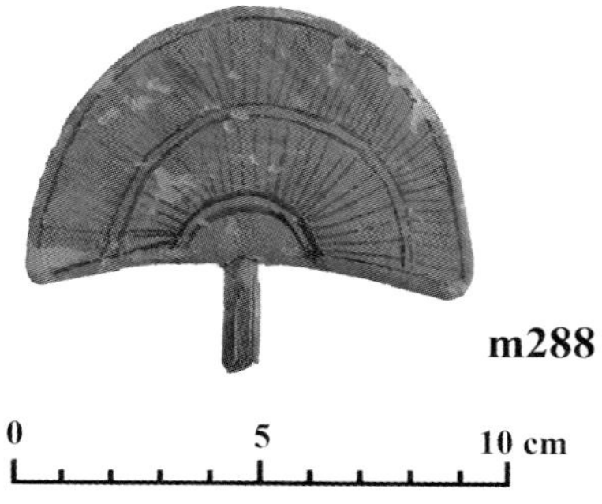

Fig. 10: Model fan (© The Asyut Project; Zöller).

In addition to this already large amount of model equipment, the side chamber of Shaft 3 contained the handles of numerous (model)[9] axes, adzes and chisels, alongside with model shields, probably model quivers as well as sticks and staves. Surprisingly, not one fragment

9 Since the axes, adzes and chisels originally seem to have had metal blades, the model character of these items is unclear. Nevertheless, size and the accompanying model material indicate that they were not actual tools or weapons, especially since they do not show any signs of use.

of the metal blades was detected in the side chamber, although corroded traces at the contact areas of the handles show that there originally must have been blades. The objects are of a very homogeneous character regarding workmanship, design and decoration.

Combining the handle fragments of the different kinds of tools and weapons, the burial chamber held at least the following items:

- 28 axes (all of near-identical design; Fig. 11),
- 45 adzes (displaying two different types; Fig 12-13),
- 41 shield models[10] (showing traces of different colour designs),
- 4 chisels (firmer chisels, cf. KILLEN 1994: 21),
- probably model quivers,[11]
- and about 26 sticks or staves.

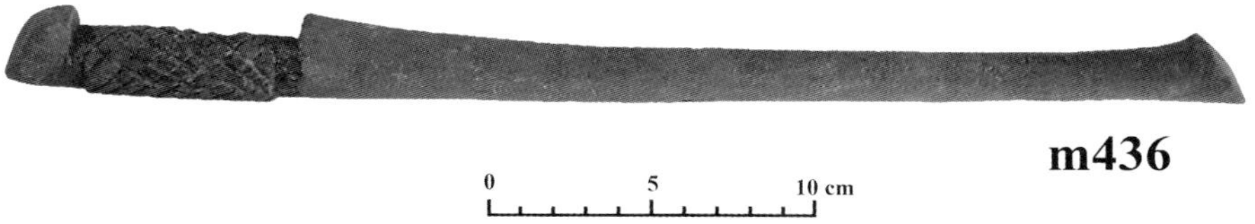

Fig. 11: Handle of axe (© The Asyut Project; Zöller).

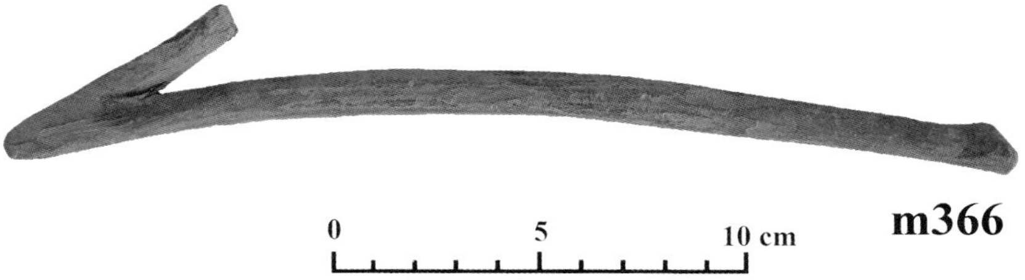

Fig. 12: Handle of adze, type A (© The Asyut Project; Zöller).

10 None of the shield models was completely preserved; the total number is counted by the preserved shield handles (Fig. 14).

11 Among the miscellaneous finds were about 40 sharpened heads of sticks, too, which could have formed heads of model arrows. Yet, the fragments do not show distinct marks of their probable original function.

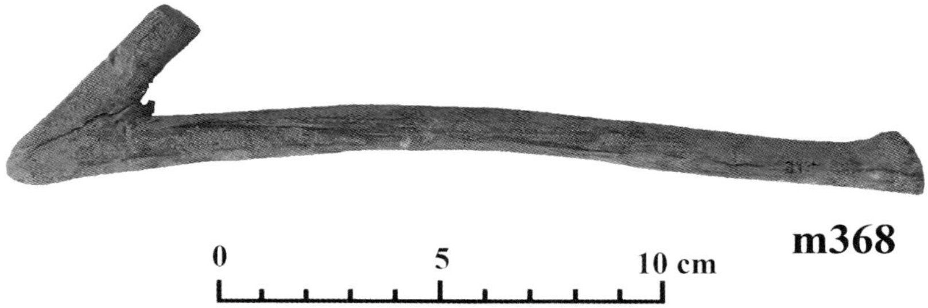

Fig. 13: Handle of adze, type B (© The Asyut Project; Zöller).

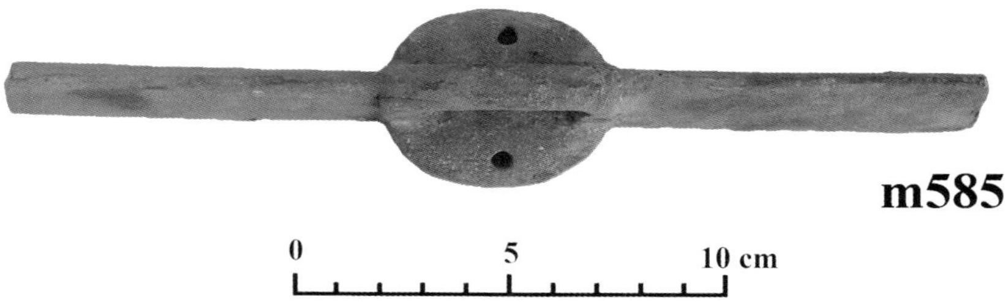

Fig. 14: Handle of model shield (© The Asyut Project; Zöller).

Tomb Siut III (N12.1): Surface

The surface finds inside the hall of Tomb III (N12.1) and the Coptic niches in the tomb's rear part were less extraordinary. Only a few model fragments could be detected, which could due to their context not definitely be assigned to one of the shaft's equipments. The surface finds yielded among other some model figure fragments such as arms or feet. Furthermore, a model grain measure and a grain sack were discovered (size and design according to the objects discovered in Shaft 4 and its side chamber) as well as two fragments of oars.

Tomb Siut IV (N12.2)

Tomb IV (N12.2), the tomb of Iti-ibi's successor, Khety II, is directly adjacent to Tomb III (N12.1). Its architecture consists of a rectangular aboveground hall, originally supported by four pillars (Pl. 26-27). Two large rectangular shafts are cut into the limestone ground, which were covered by a layer of mixed debris, that was in turn partly covered by a probable Coptic mud and lime plaster floor when it was recovered by the Asyut Project team in 2004 and 2005 (EL-KHADRAGY 2006: 83; KAHL/EL-KHADRAGY/VERHOEVEN 2005:

163-164; KAHL/EL-KHADRAGY/VERHOEVEN 2006: 244). Shaft 1, located in the front part of the tomb before the first row of pillars, shows two side chambers branching off to the north and to the south at the bottom of the shaft. Shaft 2 displays a somewhat more complex structure, with two side chambers branching off to the north and three chambers extending to the south, probably resulting from later reuse of the shaft (EL-KHADRAGY 2006: 83). Both shafts contained some wooden model objects (see below).

The tomb had obviously been plundered in antiquity as well and the excavations of the early researchers again left their marks: One of the rectangular niches, cut into the northern wall, held a deposit of rejected material left behind by early excavators, either Palanque or Hogarth (EL-KHADRAGY 2006: 90), who used Tomb IV (N12.2) as a magazine (CHASSINAT/PALANQUE 1911: 1-2) or a camp (RYAN 1988: 59). The separated items included fragmentary wooden model material (see below).

Tomb Siut IV (N12.2): Shaft 1

The shaft filling contained several objects belonging to wooden model boats, including two fragments of one large rudder (Pl. 7c) and an oval half-rounded item with flat contact area displaying two wooden dowels. The object probably formed part of the hull of a wooden model boat. The upper part of a mast rest and two fragments of the arm of a model figure were the remaining model items in the shaft filling.

The southern side chamber held one model vessel of oval shape with a small lid and two round model vats with red painting (Pl. 7d). Furthermore, the right arm of a large model figure or statuette and a large red object with unknown function were discovered.

The fragments are too sparse for a reconstruction attempt of the original scenic or boat context.

Tomb Siut IV (N12.2): Shaft 2

The cleaning of Shaft 2 brought several wooden model fragments. In the shaft filling one model arm with traces of yellow paint was discovered. In greater depth the shaft held the heavily damaged bodies of two standing, male wooden model figures, both with red skin and white apron. The fragment of another figure (Fig. 15) was found near the bottom of the shaft. Only the upper rear part of the figurine was

Fig. 15: Part of model figure, rear side (© The Asyut Project; Zöller).

preserved, displaying a black short wig, probably yellow skin, divided by a green line crossing the back diagonally. Due to their poor condition the original function or context of the three figures cannot be reconstructed.

The filling contained some more fragments which, based on their material, design or painting could be associated to wooden model structures, but their original position and function is unclear.

The upper northern side chamber held two wooden model figures (Pl. 7a-b) and a separate model arm fragment. The first figurine represents a male carrier figure balancing a rectangular basket on his head. The left arm is directed upwards to support the weight. The male figure's skin is painted yellow, the apron white. The second figurine depicts a female with shoulder-length black hair wearing a long white dress. The skin is painted in a light brown colour. The figure's left arm is bent at the elbow and lies in front of the body. The opposite arm and the lower part of the figure are lost.

The separate arm is in poor condition but does not belong to either of the aforementioned models.

Tomb Siut IV (N12.2): Niche and Surface

The cleaning of the surface and especially of the first niche in the northern wall (KAHL/EL-KHADRAGY/VERHOEVEN 2005: 163-164) uncovered a couple of wooden model fragments, including several model figure arms, some small fragments of model architecture and the body of a squatting model figure. The latter is poorly preserved without any remains of colouring. The extremities and the head are lost as well.

Interesting are two small legs of model furniture, both in lion-paw design, but obviously from two different pieces of furniture. The items could have belonged to biers like the ones found on wooden model funerary barks (compare e.g. GLANVILLE/FAULKNER 1972: Pl. 3, Figs. a-b).

The few scattered surface finds are too fragmentary for any reconstruction attempt and seem not to belong to the same grave good equipment.

Conclusion

The cleaning of the Tombs III (N12.1) and Tomb IV (N12.2) of the local nomarchs Iti-ibi and Khety II produced surprising results: Although both tombs had been plundered in antiquity and excavated by early researchers at the beginning of the twentieth century, a large amount of material could still be discovered during the recent works of The Asyut Project.

Especially the wooden model material discovered in Shafts 2, 3 and 4 and their side chambers, respectively, in Tomb III (N12.1) was particularly interesting.

Due to several factors it could be concluded that the items form a part of the original grave goods equipment of the tomb:

a. Their finding position in the side chamber suggests that the objects had been placed there intentionally since they could not have gotten there by refilling the shafts.[12]
b. In addition, the few model objects discovered in the shaft's fillings do not correlate stylistically with the homogeneous model groups from the side chambers.[13] The model fragments, especially from the side chambers of Shaft 2 and 4, show a great stylistic conformity and each one of them belonged to a particular set of model grave goods. The models from the side chamber of Shaft 3 show a greater diversity in workmanship – apart from the weapon and tool handles, which show a clear accordance – which does not mean that they did not belong to one model equipment.[14]
c. The composition of the different models for each side chamber shows a representative cross-section of a model grave goods equipment for Asyut at the end of the First Intermediate Period, each including at least one offering bearer, a granary structure, (a) model boat(s) and a food producing or processing scene.

Thus, it can be assumed that the wooden model objects belonged to the original grave goods equipment of Tomb III.

The same argumentation cannot fully be applied to the finds of Tomb IV since the fragments are too sparse to allow reconstructions of complete scenes or boats. The presence of a few fragments in the side chambers of Shaft 1 and 2 indicates the original character of these shafts and that the tomb owner and his wife were actually buried here (cf. EL-KHADRAGY 2006: 83-84, 89).

Interesting is a strong stylistic similarity between the workmanship of the wooden model figures from the northern side chamber of Shaft 2 in Tomb IV (N12.2) and the features of the model figures from the side chamber of Shaft 4 in Tomb III (N12.1) (Fig. 16). It seems that the figures can be dated to the same time frame and were possibly even manufactured in the same workshop.

In conclusion, it can be stated that the recently discovered fragments of wooden model scenes, boats and statuettes comprise remains of a richly equipped grave goods composition of a high quality standard. The fragments from the side chambers of the different shafts of Tomb III display a variety of activities, scenes and boats, perfectly suiting a typical Asyut First Intermediate Period burial, including offering bearers, granaries and boats as well as wooden model shields, tools and weapons. In Tomb IV (N12.2) the same amount of material could not be retrieved so that statements about the original grave goods compilation in this context remain difficult.

12 This applies particularly for the finding situation of Shaft 3, which offered only sparse model fragments at a low depth in the shaft filling, none at the bottom of the shaft but all the more in the side chamber itself.

13 The few wooden model fragments detected in the filling near the bottom of Shaft 2 are clearly distinct from the very homogeneous group from the side chamber. In contrast, the fragments discovered at the bottom of Shaft 4 clearly do belong to the fragments found in the side chamber but the finding context was different for this shaft (see above).

14 It is possible, that (especially large compilations of) wooden model grave goods show a diversity in workmanship within one model equipment due to differences in the natural material wood itself and different manufacturers working in one workshop (cf. DI. ARNOLD 1981: 35; TOOLEY 1989: 381).

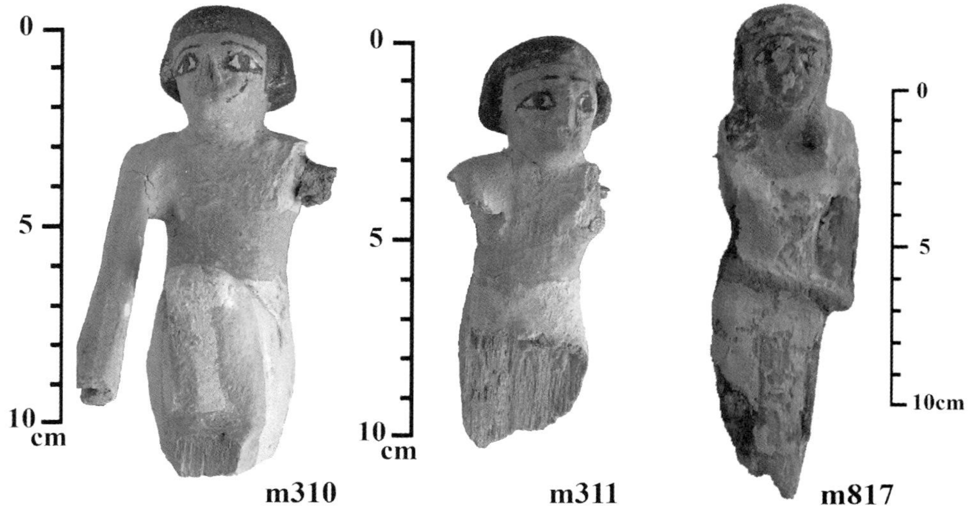

Fig. 16: Stylistic comparison between model figures from Tomb III – Shaft 4, side chamber (m310, m311) and Tomb IV – Shaft 2, side chamber (m817) (© The Asyut Project; Zöller).

Unless the remaining material of the burial shafts has been examined, at least the wooden model material indicates the original character of the shafts in Tomb III (N12.1) and Tomb IV (N12.2). If the material is actually contemporary (see discussion above) we see the remains of an enormous grave goods equipment reflecting the social rank and wealth of the tomb owners.

References:

DI. ARNOLD 1981: Di. Arnold, *Der Tempel des Königs Mentuhotep von Deir el-Bahari III. Die königlichen Beigaben* (Archäologische Veröffentlichungen 23, Mainz 1981).

DO. ARNOLD 2005: Do. Arnold, The Architecture of Meketre's Slaughterhouse and Other Early Twelfth Dynasty Wooden Models, in: P. Janósi (ed.), *Structure and Significance. Thoughts on Ancient Egyptian Architecture* (Untersuchungen der Zweigstelle Kairo des Österreichischen Archäologischen Instituts 25, Denkschriften der Gesamtakademie 33, Vienna 2005) 1-65.

BREASTED 1948: J. H. Breasted, *Egyptian Servant Statues* (The Bollingen Series 13, Washington 1948).

CHASSINAT/PALANQUE 1911: É. Chassinat/Ch. Palanque, *Une campagne des fouilles dans la nécropole d'Assiout* (Mémoires publiés par les membres de l'Institut Français d'Archéologie Orientale du Caire 24, Cairo 1911).

EL-KHADRAGY 2006: M. El-Khadragy, New Discoveries in the Tomb of Khety II at Asyut, in: *The Bulletin of the Australian Centre for Egyptology* 17, 2006, 79-95.

GARSTANG 1907: J. Garstang, *The Burial Customs of Ancient Egypt. As Illustrated by Tombs of the Middle Kingdom* (London 1907).

GLANVILLE/FAULKNER 1972: St. R. K. Glanville/R. O. Faulkner, *Wooden Model Boats* (Catalogue of Egyptian Antiquities in the British Museum II, London 1972).

GÖTTLICHER/WERNER 1971: A. Göttlicher/W. Werner, *Schiffsmodelle im Alten Ägypten* (Wiesbaden 1971).

JONES 1995: D. Jones, *Boats* (London 1995).

JØRGENSEN 1996: M. Jørgensen, *Catalogue Egypt I (3000-1550 B.C.) Ny Carlsberg Glyptotek* (Copenhagen 1996).

KAHL 2007: J. Kahl, *Ancient Asyut. The First Synthesis after 300 Years of Research* (The Asyut Project 1, Wiesbaden 2007).

KAHL/EL-KHADRAGY/VERHOEVEN 2005: J. Kahl/M. El-Khadragy/U. Verhoeven, The Asyut Project: Fieldwork Season 2004, in: *Studien zur Altägyptischen Kultur* 33, 2005, 159-167.

KAHL/EL-KHADRAGY/VERHOEVEN 2006: J. Kahl/M. El-Khadragy/U. Verhoeven, The Asyut Project. Third season of fieldwork, in: *Studien zur Altägyptischen Kultur* 34, 2006, 241-249.

KILLEN 1994: G. Killen, *Egyptian Woodworking and Furniture* (Shire Egyptology 21, Princes Risborough 1994).

LANDSTRÖM 1974: B. Landström, *Die Schiffe der Pharaonen. Altägyptische Schiffsbaukunst von 4000 bis 600 v. Chr.* (Munich 1974).

LEOSPO 1998: E. Leospo, Assiout entre la Première Période Intermédiaire et le Moyen Empire (Fouilles Schiaparelli), in: Ch. Eyre (ed.), *Seventh International Congress of Egyptologists* (Orientalia Lovaniensia Analecta 82, Leuven 1998), 667-676.

PETRIE 1917: W. M. F. Petrie, *Tools and Weapons* (British School of Archaeology in Egypt 30, London 1917).

REISNER 1913: G. A. Reisner, *Models of Ships and Boats* (Catalogue Général des Antiquités Égyptiennes du Musée du Caire Nos. 4798-4976 et 5034-5200, Cairo 1913).

RYAN 1988: D. P. Ryan, *The Archaeological Excavations of David George Hogarth at Asyut, Egypt* (Cincinnati 1988).

SCHENKEL 1962: W. Schenkel, *Frühmittelägyptische Studien* (Bonner Orientalistische Studien, Neue Serie 13, Bonn 1962).

SEIDLMAYER 1990: St. J. Seidlmayer, *Gräberfelder aus dem Übergang vom Alten zum Mittleren Reich. Studien zur Archäologie der Ersten Zwischenzeit* (Studien zur Archäologie und Geschichte Altägyptens 1, Heidelberg 1990).

TOOLEY 1989: A. M. J. Tooley, *Middle Kingdom Burial Customs. A Study of Wooden Models and Related Material* (unpubl. Ph.D., Liverpool 1989).

TOOLEY 1995: A. M. J. Tooley, *Egyptian Models and Scenes* (Shire Egyptology 22, Princes Risborough 1995).

TOOLEY 2001: A. M. J. Tooley, in: *The Oxford Encyclopedia of Ancient Egypt* II (Oxford 2001), 424-425, s.v. Models.

WINLOCK 1955: H. E. Winlock, *Models of Daily Life from the Tomb of Meket-Rē*ᶜ *at Thebes* (Publications of the Metropolitan Museum of Art, Egyptian Expedition 18, Cambridge 1955).

ZÖLLER 2007a: M. Zöller, *Holzmodelle aus dem Grab des Gaufürsten Jtj-jbj (Siut III) in Assiut/Mittelägypten* (2 vols., unpubl. M.A. thesis, Mainz 2007).

ZÖLLER 2007b: M. Zöller, Wooden Models from Asyut, in: J. Kahl/M. El-Khadragy/U. Verhoeven, The Asyut Project: Fourth Season of Fieldwork (2006), in: *Studien zur Altägyptischen Kultur* 36, 2007, 87-88.

Internet References (28/01/2010):
http://www.britishmuseum.org/research/search_the_collection_database.aspx
http://cartelen.louvre.fr/cartelen/visite?srv=crt_frm_rs&langue=en&initCritere=true
http://www.museoegizio.it/pages/museum.jsp
http://www.mfa.org/collections/search_art.asp
http://www.globalegyptianmuseum.org/

Pottery Offering Trays: General Observations and New Material from Asyut

Andrea Kilian

Introduction

During the field campaigns conducted by The Asyut Project from 2004 until 2008 a considerable amount of fragmented pottery offering trays was unearthed. There is still no specific term which could be used when referring to these objects. In German they are spoken of as e.g. "Opferplatten", "Opferteller" or "Opfertafel"; in English they are known e.g. as "(pottery) offering trays" or "offering plates".

Some of these terms are not just referring to the objects that are topic of this article. In the following, the term "offering trays" therefore will be used to refer to trays in various shapes made by hand, formed out of clay. They have to be distinguished from the kind of offering tables which are similar in composition, but always made out of stone. Besides, the latter can bear inscriptions, while offering trays never show any kind of inscription. Pottery offering trays usually feature a rim and may contain different applications representing canals, basins, and various offerings such as oxen, bread, vegetables and more. Because they are often very crudely made, not much interest had been paid to them so far.

This paper presents a study on pottery offering trays in general and material from Asyut in particular. For that reason, the history of research and the current thesis about trays will be sketched before focusing on layout, distribution, chronology and use of the trays. Finally, the new finds from Asyut and their relevance will be discussed.

History of research

The list of publications dealing with these objects is not very extensive. The first to write about pottery offering trays was Petrie, mentioning them in his publication about his excavations in Kahun, Gurob and Hawara (PETRIE 1890: 24-25). In the report about his work in Rifeh, he states that offering trays developed into soul houses and represent their most simple form (PETRIE 1907: 15).

Petrie's opinion remains valid until today; offering trays are mentioned only marginally or listed without providing the context of their discovery, or even without any further description. The excavators largely referred to Petrie's work when dating their own material.

Only an article written by Kuentz in 1961, which dealt with offering tables, contains a short chapter on offering trays. Unfortunately, Kuentz has not been able to bring his article to an end, and so it was printed incomplete years later (KUENTZ 1981: 248-255).

In the 1970s Slater worked with the finds made by Fisher in Dendereh and analysed the formal development of offering trays (SLATER 1974: 301-315). Tooley studied types, development and regional aspects of the trays (TOOLEY 1989: 249-304).

The first and hitherto only detailed article on this subject was published in 1975 by Niwinski (NIWINSKI 1975). He was the first to consider origin, development, dating criteria and distribution area of the trays as well as reasons for their appearance and use. Several short papers followed; the latest article by Leclère having been printed in 2001 (LECLÈRE 2001). It contains a list of almost all sites on which pottery offering trays and soul houses have been found up to the present.

Theses about offering trays

Offering trays have been found throughout Egypt, from Lisht in the north to the fortresses of Buhen and Mirgissa in Nubia, but until today there are no trays known coming from the Delta. The origin of offering trays is not yet clear. It is largely assumed that they developed from stone offering tables and are their cheaper substitute (cf. PETRIE 1907: 15), which made them affordable for the poorer populace. They seem to appear during the First Intermediate Period and cease to exist after the Thirteenth Dynasty, while stone offering tables are used throughout the Egyptian History until the Late Period. Another thesis states that offering trays were used exclusively during the Twelfth Dynasty and neither before nor after it (NIWINSKI 1975: 95; NIWINSKI 1984: 810).

As mentioned above, it is generally believed that pottery offering trays were used as cheap substitutes for stone offering tables. The first examples, assumed to be true copies of the tables, were rectangular shaped. During the course of time, they became round, changing their appearance gradually while spreading from Lower to Upper Egypt, presuming that the origin of the trays lies somewhere in Lower Egypt, possibly around Lisht (NIWINSKI 1975: 93; NIWINSKI 1984: 806-807).

Design of pottery offering trays

Pottery offering trays are formed by hand out of a very rough Nile clay (the fabric of the fragments found in Asyut is Nile clay C, according to the Vienna system, cf. NORDSTRÖM/BOURRIAU 1993: 173sqq.).[1] Almost all of them possess a rim or wall and some kind of water outlet, such as spouts or a hole in the surrounding wall. Very few trays are washed with white colour, some are coloured red. Others do not have any kind of additional colouring at all. Sometimes they are carefully burnished. None of the trays bears any signs of inscription.

The shapes of the trays vary from rectangular to rounded, oval or horseshoe-shaped. Several applications can be added to the trays, mostly models of food offerings (like oxen, bread, vegetables) or architectural elements concerning water distribution, such as basins or canals. Slater describes 44 trays coming from the excavation of Fisher in Dendereh that bear no applications at all, but unfortunately she does not state why she addresses them as offering trays instead of assuming them to be simple dinner plates or bread moulds (SLATER 1974: 302).

Generally, offering trays can be equipped with the following elements:

- Architectural: dividing walls, channels, basins, and spouts. If the tray is square, the spout is protruding, while with round or oval specimens simple holes are piercing the

1 I would like to express my thanks to Jochem Kahl who analysed the fabrics involved.

surrounding wall. The wall of horseshoe-shaped forms normally reduces its height towards an open front into which the canals are leading.

- Offering models:
  - animals: bound oxen, head and leg of oxen, fowl.
  - bread: round, square, oblong and conical forms.
  - other: on some trays oblong objects can be found. The meaning of these is not yet clear; they can be interpreted as cucumber, bread or ribs of an ox.
- Other: *ḥs*-vases, small bowls and seats can be added to the trays.
- Singular depictions: a round container with elongated neck (MINAULT-GOUT 1995: 307, Fig. 12), an apparently scratched vessel stand for a pair of scratched Hes-vases (PETRIE 1925: Pl. 28, 710), a feather (?) (WAINWRIGHT 1926: 170; see also British Museum EA 46613, unpublished, which shows the same item and also originates from Asyut).

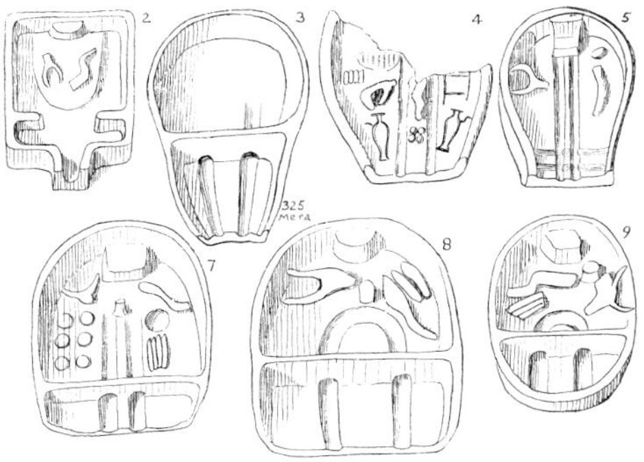

Fig. 1: Trays from Dendereh (detail after PETRIE 1900: Pl. 19).

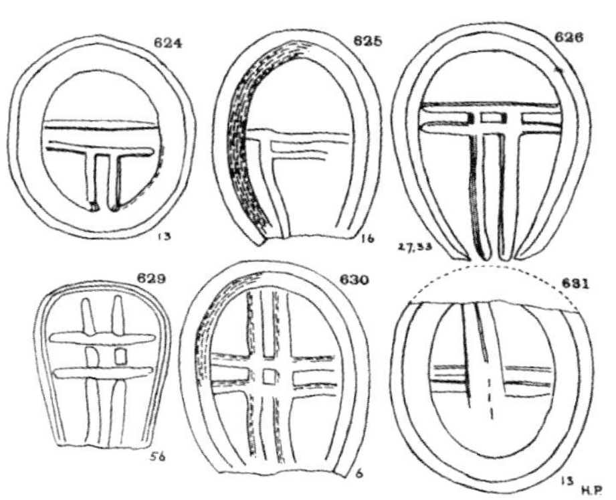

Fig. 2: Trays from Qurna (detail after PETRIE 1909: Pl. 21).

All of these elements can be combined with each other without following any rules; even a bound ox with its head still attached to its body can be combined with a separated head. Mostly, the offering models are only very crudely made. Some of them are so stylised that comparisons with stone offering tables or stelae are necessary to discover the meaning of an application.

The designs of the trays vary with respect to their regional provenance.[2]

The trays of Dendereh very often show a seat placed against the back wall opposite the water outlet (Fig. 1). They are mostly oval or horseshoe-shaped and show two parallel canals or a single U-shaped canal with the bend in the rear part. Sometimes they have dividing walls, often pierced by the canals. One of the trays from Dendereh is special in that it shows double walls (SLATER 1974: 306).

The by far greatest part of the trays from Qurna consists only of canals, mostly arranged parallel to each other, leading from the back to the front and crossed at right angles by one or two additional canals (Fig. 2). Others consist of only two canals ema-

2 The following results have been gained through the study of offering trays listed in Table 1. Further research was done in KILIAN 2009: 81-100.

nating from two basins, and only very few bear heads and legs of oxen or bread as food offerings. Apparently there are only very few rectangular trays known from Qurna, the remaining ones being oval or sometimes round.

In Armant the trays are mostly round (Fig. 3). All of the 13 published trays display bound oxen, often with head, a leg and the characteristic Armantian conical loaf of bread. The canals are mostly T-shaped, the offerings being arranged behind the canals.

Trays from Esna are of a simple design, often only displaying canals and basins. Quite unusually, they sometimes do not feature an outflow. As a rare exception, some of the trays from Esna do not possess a rim, but are flat with canals and basins deepened into the surface (DOWNES 1974: 94, Fig. 65).

In El Kab the trays are mainly horseshoe-shaped or oval, characteristically containing numerous parallel canals leading from the middle of the tray to an open front (Fig. 4). These kinds of canals are also very characteristic for the trays from Esna. They can also be found on trays from Edfu, where troughs, bowls or small dishes frequently are added to the trays (Fig. 5).

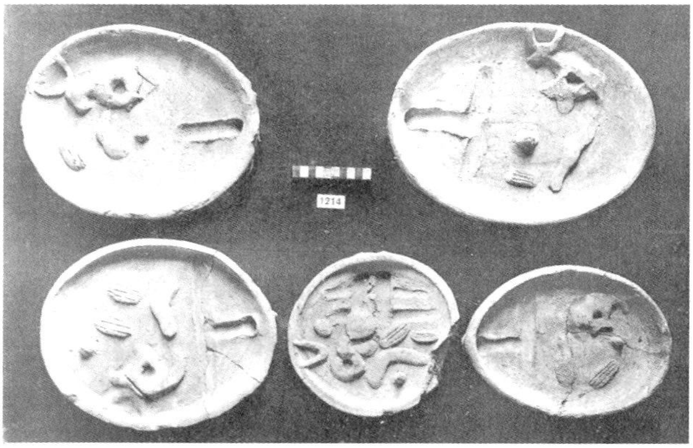

Fig. 3: Trays from Armant
(after MOND/MYERS 1937: Pl. 22.5).

Concerning the shape of the trays itself, the following distribution is to be noticed:

Rectangular trays can be found almost everywhere, starting from Kahun in the north to Uronarti in the south and even in the oases, namely in Balat. The main focus of their distribution lies in Asyut and Deir Rifeh.

Oval trays range from Dendereh over Qurna and Armant to Qubbet el-Hawa. Some

Fig. 4: Tray from El Kab
(detail after QUIBELL 1897: Pl. 5.4).

Fig. 5: Tray from Edfu
(after MICHAŁOWSKI 1938a: Pl. 42.3).

single items were discovered in Deir Rifeh, Gebelein and Esna. No oval trays have been found north of Deir Rifeh.

Round trays come from Thebes, especially Armant, but also Qurna and El-Tarif. Very few originate from between Dendereh as the northern border and Gebelein as the southern border in their distribution.

Horseshoe shapes spread from Asyut as northernmost part over Dendereh and Qurna to Qubbet el-Hawa as southernmost part of their occurrence.

Regarding the composition of the trays, it can be observed that canals, basins, heads and legs of oxen as well as round bread loaves can be found on trays from all over Egypt.

Bound oxen can be found only in the regions from Asyut to Gebelein, whereas heads of oxen occur within almost the entire distribution area with exception of the oases. Birds are displayed very rarely; until now only three examples from Kahun (PETRIE 1891: Pl. 4.23), Abydos (PETRIE 1925: Pl. 28.710) and Balat (MINAULT-GOUT 1995: 307, Fig. 12) are known, being now complemented by two fragments from Asyut (OT24; OT25). Vases of the *ḥs*-type are depicted quite seldom and often in combination with birds.

Conical loaves of bread are to be found especially in Armant, with some rare examples in Kahun, Asyut and Deir Rifeh. Triangular loaves of bread are known from Asyut and on soul houses from Deir Rifeh.

Unfortunately, it was not possible to obtain a typology of offering trays. Instead, in accordance with Tooley, one can speak of special "trends" (TOOLEY 1989: 297) at different locations: Although different local specifications can be observed, it cannot be concluded that special trays may only be found exclusively in one single place. For example, some of the trays from Qubbet el-Hawa very much resemble those from the Theban area, namely those from Qurna and El-Tarif (cf. EDEL 2008a: 1289, Fig. 8, 9, 10; ARNOLD 1973: Pl. 68, a-b).

Very interesting is the fact that almost no tray completely equals another. Some are very similar, but almost always differing in some detail. Although almost all of the Asyutian trays conducted by the Asyut Project are formed out of Nile Clay C (see above), it has clearly been visible which fragments fit together, on the one hand due to the craftmanship, on the other because of small differences in the fabric. That speaks against a mass production of these objects. However, one has to bear in mind that there are only very few objects under discussion in Asyut with less than 40 trays having been unearthed, compared to other locations such as Dendereh with over 300 trays (SLATER 1974: 301).

Furthermore, the Asyutian fragments have been found in a context that does not allow any conclusions regarding chronology, so there are no further hints if the differences in design and fabric could be due to the course of time.

Placement of the trays

According to Petrie (PETRIE 1907: 14), offering trays were positioned on top of shallow graves. Unfortunately, these objects are not very well recorded in excavation reports. Nevertheless, there are several hints that the mouth of a shaft was not the only location offering trays were placed on.

In Asyut, Armant (MOND/MYERS 1937: 59) and Edfou (MICHAŁOWSKI 1938b: 82, 84) the trays have been discovered inside the burial chambers, on two occasions being arranged close to the head of the entombed (e.g. RYAN 1988: Tomb XVIII, 37-38; MICHAŁOWSKI 1938b: 82). In Dendereh they had not only been placed on top of pits, but also in offering places and in burials (SLATER 1974: 311). On Qubbet el-Hawa one was found in front of the entrance of tomb QH 206 a, most likely in a cultic context (EDEL 2008b: 1944-1945.). E.g. in Mostagedda (BRUNTON 1937: 110), the Saff el-Dawaba (ARNOLD 1972: 24-26) and on Qubbet el-Hawa (EDEL 2008b: 1764sqq.) they were revealed in the debris inside the shafts. In Karnak (LAUFFRAY 1980: 47-48), Buhen (EMERY 1979: 151), Mirgissa (DUNHAM 1967: 160) and Uronarti (DUNHAM 1967: 55) they were not connected to the necropolis at all, but were located in the town or fort, respectively.

It seems as if the positioning of the trays is as variable as their design and differs from place to place.

Chronology, origin and development

None of the trays was found in a precisely dated context, but concluding from the given archaeological evidence, offering trays seem to have been in use from the First Intermediate Period until the Thirteenth Dynasty. In Balat they have been found in a mastaba in an archaeological context being dated to the First Intermediate Period (MINAULT-GOUT 1980: 277; VERCOUTTER 1980: 372). Most of them come from Middle Kingdom sites, such as the Nubian forts or the settlement of the workers of the pyramid of Senwosret II in Kahun (cf. Table 1). In Thebes, they have been found on sites which were used until the Thirteenth Dynasty (MOND/MYERS 1937: 22). This shows that they cannot be dated exclusively to the Twelfth Dynasty.

The Römer- und Pelizaeus-Museum Hildesheim carried out a thermo-luminescence analysis on a tray with the result of 1600 BCE $\pm$ 20 % (MARTIN-PARDEY 1991: 147). This yields a possible time span from 1920-1280 BCE indicating that the earliest date for the tray involved is during the Middle Kingdom; the most probable date is the Second Intermediate Period and the latest possible is the New Kingdom.

Current evidence does not allow any definite conclusions about the origin of the trays. While Leclère assumes the Theban area as origin (LÈCLERE 2001: 99), Tooley says that "The area between Ballas and el-Minsha exhibits all kinds of trays and 'soul-houses', indicating an equal influence from the south and the north on the ateliers in this region." (TOOLEY 1989: 294-295.) But as this region shows the greatest variety in the design of offering trays, the trays may as well have developed in this area, spreading north with preference of the rectangular forms, while round forms were preferred in the south.

While Niwinski believes that the offering trays developed out of stone offering tables (NIWINSKI 1975: 97) and that they suffered from a formal decadence (meaning the simpler the design, the younger the tray), Slater's investigation points in the opposite direction. In her examination of the finds from Dendereh she observes a development from simple or even plain trays to more complex designs. In comparison with accompanying material and relating it to the use of the burial ground, she comes to the conclusion that the simplest trays date to the First Intermediate Period, while the main part dates to the Middle Kingdom

(SLATER 1974: 402), developing more complex designs by adding canals, basins and offerings (SLATER 1974: 307, 312).

Use of offering trays

Due to the poor documentation of offering trays and their finding context, their utilisation can only be guessed.

Slater assumes them to be substitutes for cult places, as in Dendereh only few such structures have been found (SLATER 1974: 311). Aufrère thinks that the trays may symbolize the tomb itself, the base of the tray corresponding to the courtyard, the spout working as door or entrance (AUFRÈRE 1992, 21; see also JÉQUIER 1910: 213). Emery suggests they could be votive offerings, as he found the trays in Buhen in rooms underneath the temple of the New Kingdom. But he also mentions they could have been brought into the town by children, having retrieved them from the necropolis and using them as toys, or having been unused objects stored in town (EMERY 1979: 151).

The function of the trays is closely related with the location they were originally placed at. Located in a cult chamber or close to the shaft mouth, they may have been used in libation ceremonies, the canals serving as outflow for water poured out onto the tray and thus becoming magically loaded with the energy provided by the offerings (VERHOEVEN 1997: 481). In this context, the red colour of some trays probably symbolizes life and regeneration (WILKINSON 1999: 106). The white colour indicates that the tray, after being covered with it, hasn't been used again, because the white colour is not very durable and vanishes when getting into contact with fluids.

Seiler assumes that white colour has been used to purify vessels before they could be used in cultic contexts, and that they have been coloured again after use to cover the traces (SEILER 2005: 117). That may also be true with offering trays and could explain red washed trays that are covered with white colour as well.

When placed inside the sarcophagus chamber, the tray could not have been used for the cult of the dead. In this case, its function must be that of a burial object. The applied offerings are models used as substitutes to nourish the tomb owner in the afterlife, while canals, basins and *ḥs*-vases could probably symbolize the ritual of the libation. The square blocks on some of the trays are interpreted as seats on which the deceased could take place during the ceremony.

Some of the trays do not show any applications at all but only canals and basins. Niwinski assumes that the libation gained such great importance that only canals and basins would suffice to guarantee the function of the tray (NIWINSKI 1984: 811-812, n. 4).

Unfortunately, the ancient Egyptian name of the trays is not conveyed, so we cannot gather any information from it.

Pottery offering trays in relation to stone offering tables

As mentioned above, it has often been assumed that pottery trays had been used as cheap substitutes for stone offering tables. This topic cannot be discussed here in detail, but there are some differences between the two types to be mentioned.

While tables can bear inscriptions, this is never the case with trays: they are always anepigraphic. Besides, tables are almost always square, while trays show a wide range of forms from square to round bases.

The offerings on stone tables are often depicted more delicately than those on trays and show a wider range, e.g. images of figs and grapes. In contrast, the ox head is mostly shown without its horns, while when depicted on trays, it is always sculptured with horns.

The main elements on stone tables of the Middle Kingdom are a mat with a *ḥtp*-bread on top. Mat and bread are often combined with two *ḥs*-vases. This combination is so typical that Hölzl speaks of it as "kanonische Dekoration" (HÖLZL 2002: 72-73). *Ḥs*-vases are quite rare on trays, while mat and bread are not displayed at all.

So it seems possible that the trays did not emerge from stone tables, but developed independently.

Offering trays from Asyut

Most of the tray fragments discovered by The Asyut Project have been found in Shaft 1 of Tomb III, a shaft with several layers of material left behind by former excavators on the site of Asyut. 30 fragments were retrieved here, and only some of these fragments partly matched. The remaining fragments were found in several spots in Tomb III (Coptic niche), Tomb IV ("Hogarth's Depot"; Shaft 1; Shaft 2), the so-called Tomb of the Dogs; N13.1 (Shaft 1, Shaft 2), step 7 in front of N13.1 (Shaft 1.36), N12.3 (side chamber) and on the surface close to Tomb II. The total of 48 fragments belongs to no more than 32 different trays. Only two of them could be reconstructed to more than 50 % of their original size. None of the offering tray fragments discovered by The Asyut Project has been found *in situ*. Nevertheless, these tray fragments provided important new facts about offering trays in general.

All of the discovered fragments apparently belonged to offering trays, none of them showing explicit traces of connection to soul houses which are so well-attested in the neighbouring area of Deir Rifeh.

In Asyut, a wide variety of forms can be distinguished. Some of the trays had a white wash or were coloured red (Pl. 9a), but mostly the surface was too poorly preserved to allow any statements about the surface treatment. Three fragments display inner dividing walls (cf. Fig. 6), two show basins and three bear *ḥs*-vases (Pl. 9a). Round and square bread loaves occur, as well as heads and legs of oxen and bound oxen with and also without head (Fig. 7).

Fig. 6: Tray from Asyut with dividing wall, OT40 = S05/St.1281 (© The Asyut Project; Kilian).

But Asyut also shows some unique features on the tray fragments. One is a piece of meat imitating the *jwꜥ*-hieroglyph (Gardiner Sign-list F44; Pl. 8e).

Another notable piece is a corner fragment of a tray with its wall still preserved (Pl. 8a). This wall is decorated with white dots on the outside and thus is unique with this kind of decoration.

Another unique feature is the head of an animal whose horns are curving sideways to the front of its face, reminiscent of a ram's head (Pl. 8 b-d). It is clearly distinguishable from the well-attested heads of oxen. In addition the animal is not facing the inside of the tray, but seems to be peering outside, standing on its neck and looking over the edge. It is the first known piece of this peculiar design.

Additional new information is provided by the discovery of a depicted triangular loaf of bread on one of the trays (Pl. 9b), as this has to date not been found in any other location in Egypt but on soul houses from Deir Rifeh (cf. Fitzwilliam Museum, Cambridge, No. E.47.1907).

Fig. 7: Head, leg and bound ox; OT6 = S04/132 (© The Asyut Project; Kilian).

Until recently, only rectangularly shaped trays had been discovered on the site of Asyut. However the recent discovery of two fragmented oval trays in the material from Tomb III has suggested the existence of non-rectangular shaped trays in Asyut (Pl. 9c). This provides new information about the distribution of the trays and suggests that the round/oval forms were spread all over Egypt. The assumed development from north to south and from a rectangular shape to a round form can thus no longer be supported.

More information can be gained from the publication of Ryan, who worked on the documentation of the excavations of Hogarth in Asyut (RYAN 1988). Ryan sums up the results of the excavation conducted by Hogarth in 1906/1907 and describes the findings tomb by tomb. According to the evidence there, fragments of pottery offering trays have been found together with fragments of wooden models (RYAN 1988: Tombs XIII (30-31), Tomb XXXV (59), Tomb LI (80); see also PETRIE 1921: 66; CHASSINAT/PALANQUE 1911: 164). They often seem to have been discovered inside burial chambers (at least as indicated by fragments detected there, because most of the tombs were found disturbed).

One tomb was discovered intact by Chassinat and Palanque; there the offering tray was found together with wooden models, pottery, a wooden statue of the deceased and other grave goods inside the burial chamber (CHASSINAT/PALANQUE 1911: 164; Pl. 34). While the wooden objects are of good quality and craftsmanship, the offering tray is of inferior quality.

Furthermore, in some Asyutian tombs both pottery offering trays as well as stone offering tables were discovered together in the same tomb (RYAN 1988: Tombs XIII, p. 30-31; XXVII, p. 47-49; XXXV, p. 59; XXXVI, p. 60; XLVII, p. 76; LI, p. 80). It seems as if pottery offering trays had been placed inside the burial chamber, whereas the stone offering trays were situated in front of it. As almost all tombs have been found robbed, this cannot be stated with certainty. It nevertheless indicates that the two objects may have served different functions. This would contradict the thesis that offering trays had been used as cheap substitutes for offering tables. So while they seem to occur mainly in "poorer" funerals, they can also be found in "wealthier" ones. In the case of the tomb found intact by Chassinat and Palanque (CHASSINAT/PALANQUE 1911: 164; Pl. 34), the quality of the tray does not appear to have any connection with the wealth of its owner.

Despite the fact that only fragmentary material has been discovered during the archaeological fieldwork done by The Asyut Project, these fragments have added a considerable amount of new information on the subject of offering trays in general.

Table 1: Publications presenting or mentioning offering trays that were studied for this paper (abbreviations of literature not mentioned in the text according to the *Lexikon der Ägyptologie* VII. Nachträge, Korrekturen und Indices, Wiesbaden 1992, IX – XL).

Balat:	Minault-Gout 1980: 277, Pl. 66.
	Minault-Gout, A., *Balat* II, FIFAO 33, 1992, 27, Fig. 9; 49, 124, Pl. 42.
	Minault-Gout 1995: 307, Fig. 12; 308.
	Vercoutter, J., in: *BIFAO* 79, 1979, 458.
Saqqara:	Seipel, W., *Ägypten. Götter, Gräber und die Kunst. 4000 Jahre Jenseitsglaube* 1 (Linz 1989) 97, Fig. 63b.
	Lunsingh Scheurleer, R. A., *Egypte. Geschenk van de Nijl,* (Amsterdam 1992) 90, Cat.-No. 58; p. 205-206.
Kahun	Petrie 1890: 24sqq., Pl. 13.
	Petrie 1891: 9, Pl. 4, Fig. 20, 23.
Sedment	*Sedment* I, 8, Pl. 13, 37, 38, 39.
Ehnasya	Petrie 1921: 66.
Deir el-Bersheh	Kamal, A. Bey, Fouilles à Déïr-el-Barshe (Mars-Avril 1900), in: *ASAE* 2, 1901, 38 f.
Meir	Kamal, A. Bey, Rapport sur les fouilles exécutées dans la zone comprise entre Deïrut au nord et Deîr el-Ganadlah, au sud, in: *ASAE* 11, 1911, 14.
	Niwinski 1975: 86.
	Kuentz 1981: 249, footnote 5.
Asyut	Chassinat/Palanque 1911: 164, Pl. 34.1.
	Wainwright 1926: 160-166 (161-162), Fig. p. 170.
	Kamal, A. Bey, Fouilles à Deir Dronka et à Assiout (1913-1914), in: *ASAE* 16, 1916, 65-114 (70, No. 34).
	Niwinski 1975: 88, footnote 60.
	Ryan 1988: Excavation Report: 30-31; 34; 37; 41; 46; 48; 55; 59-60; 65; 76; 80.
Deir Rifeh	Petrie 1907: 11-20, Pl. 14.
Mostagedda	Brunton, G., *Mostagedda and the Tasian Culture* (London 1937) 110, Pl. 62. 11.
Abydos	Petrie 1925: 11, Pl. 28.
Hu	Petrie, W. M. F., *Diospolis parva. The Cemeteries of Abadiyeh and Hu 1898-1899* (EEF 20, London 1901) 43, Pl. 25.
	Capart, J., Rapport sur une fouille faite du 14 au 20 Février 1927 dans la nécropole de Héou, in: *ASAE* 27, 1927, 48.
Dendereh	Petrie 1900: 26, Pl. 19.
Deir el-Ballas	*Naqada and Ballas,* 8, 42, Pl. 44.
El-Tarif	Arnold 1972: 13-31 (26-30); 27, Fig. 7; Pl. 13 b, c; Pl. 16 a-c.
	Arnold 1973: 135-162 (142, 150); Pl. 68 a-d; 69 a.
	Arnold, Di., *Gräber des Alten und Mittleren Reiches in El-Tarif* (AV 17, 1976) 23, 34.
Qurna	Petrie 1909: 4, Pl. 20-21.
	Galan, J., www.excavacionegipto.com, Campagna 2007 (see now also M. J. López Grande, Field notes from Dra Abu el-Naga on the First Intermediate Period/Early Middle Kingdom Pottery, in: *Under the Potter's Tree. Studies on Ancient Egypt Presented to Janine Bourriau on the Occasion of Her 70th Birthday* (OLA 204, Leuven 2011) 598, Fig. 2e).

	RUMMEL, U. (ed.), *Begegnung mit der Vergangenheit. 100 Jahre in Ägypten,* (Katalog zur Sonderausstellung im Ägyptischen Museum in Kairo, Cairo 2007) 34, No. 18.
Deir el-Bahari	CARNAVON, CARTER, H., *Five Years' Explorations at Thebes. A Record of Work Done 1907-1911* (Oxford 1912) 28, Pl. 18; 54, Pl. 47.
	NIWINSKI, A., Miscellanea de Deir el-Bahari, in: *MDAIK* 41, 1985, 199.
Gournet Murrai	BRESCIANI, E., in: *EVO* 3, 1980, 4-7, Fig. 3, Pl. 6.
Karnak	LAUFFRAY, J., Les travaux du Centre Franco-Égyptien d'étude des temples de Karnak de 1973 à 1977, in: *Cahiers de Karnak* 6, 1980, 1-65 (47-48).
	AZIM, M., La fouille de la cour du VIIIe pylône, in: *Cahiers de Karnak* 6, 1980, 91-127 (161).
	DEBONO, F., Rapport préliminaire sur les résultats de l'étude des objets de la fouille des installations du moyen Empire et « Hyksos » à l'est du lac sacré de Karnak, in: *Cahiers de Karnak* 7, 1982, 377-383 (380, 381).
Armant	BIENKOWSKI, P., SOUTHWORTH, E., *Egyptian Antiquities in the Liverpool Museum* I (Warminster 1986) 31.
	Bucheum I, 77.
	MOND/MYERS 1937: 59-60, 63, Pl. 22, Fig. 5-6.
Tôd	NIWINSKI 1975: 102, footnote 79.
Gebelein	DONADONI ROVERI, A. M., Gebelein, in: Robins, G., *Beyond the Pyramids. Egyptian Regional Art from the Museo Egizio, Turin* (Atlanta 1990) 84.
Esna	BIENKOWSKI, P., SOUTHWORTH, E., *Egyptian Antiquities in the Liverpool Museum* I (Warminster 1986) 48.
	BIENKOWSKI, P., TOOLEY, A. M. J., *Gifts of the Nile. Ancient Egyptian Arts and Crafts in the Liverpool Museum* (London 1995) 80.
	DOWNES 1974: 93-94, Fig. 63, 65, 118, 121.
El Kab	*El Kab,*18; Pl. 5, Fig. 4.
	Sayce, A. H., III. - Excavations 1904, in: A. H. Sayce/S. Clarke, Report on Certain Excavations Made at El-Kab During the Years 1901, 1902, 1903, 1904, in: *ASAE* 6, 1905, 251.
Edfu	MICHAŁOWSKI 1938a: 121, 179-180, 183-184, 189, 192-193. Pl. 42, Fig. 2-4.
	MICHAŁOWSKI 1938b: 67, 82, 84, Fig. 47, 305-306, Pl. 40, 42.
Qubbet el-Hawa	EDEL 2008a: 1192, Fig. 4, 5; 1196, Fig. 9; 1288sq., Fig. 7-10; 1293; 1294, Fig. 15; 1310, Fig. 10-13.
	EDEL 2008b: 1768, 1777; 1781, Fig. 64, 65; 1956 f.; 1961, Fig. 260; 1962, Fig. 268; 1995, Fig. 43.
	NIWINSKI 1975: 112, additional note.
	NIWINSKI 1984: 806, n. 2 s.v. Seelenhaus (und Opferplatte).
Qubban	*Arch. Survey of Nubia* 1910-1911, 49, 56, 59, 66, 68-69.
Aniba	STEINDORFF, G., *Aniba* I (Glückstadt 1935) 41, ID., *Aniba* III (Glückstadt 1935) Pl. 16, b 1.2.
Buhen	EMERY 1979: 151-152, Pl. 55, 1457.1459.1551.1584; Pl. 104, 1551.
Mirgissa	DUNHAM 1967: 160, Pl. 90.C.
Uronarti	DUNHAM 1967: 43, Pl. 44.A, 49-50, 55, 112, Fig. 4.

References:

ARNOLD 1972: Di. Arnold, Bericht über die vom Deutschen Archäologischen Institut Kairo im *Mnṯw-ḥtp*-Tempel in El-Târif unternommenen Arbeiten, in: *Mitteilungen des Deutschen Archäologischen Instituts Abteilung Kairo* 28, 1972, 13-31.

ARNOLD 1973: Di. Arnold, Bericht über die vom Deutschen Archäologischen Institut Kairo im Winter 1971/72 in El-Târif durchgeführten Arbeiten, in: *Mitteilungen des Deutschen Archäologischen Instituts Abteilung Kairo* 29, 1973, 135-162.

AUFRÈRE 1992: S. Aufrère, *Portes pour l'au-delà. L'Égypte, le Nil et le «Champ des Offrandes»* (Lattes 1992).

BRUNTON 1937: G. Brunton, *Mostagedda and the Tasian Culture* (British Museum Expedition to Middle Egypt. First and Second Years 1928, 1929, London 1937).

CHASSINAT/PALANQUE 1911: É. Chassinat, Ch. Palanque, *Une campagne de fouilles dans la nécropole d'Assiout* (Mémoires publiés par les membres de l'Institut Français d'Archéologie Orientale du Caire 24, Cairo 1911).

DOWNES 1974: D. Downes, *The Excavations at Esna 1905-1906* (Warminster 1974).

DUNHAM 1967: D. Dunham, *Uronarti, Shalfak, Mirgissa* (Second Cataract Forts 2, Boston 1967).

EDEL 2008a: E. Edel (eds. K.-J. Seyfried, G. Vieler), *Die Felsgräbernekropole der Qubbet el-Hawa bei Assuan* 1, 2 (Paderborn et al. 2008).

EDEL 2008b: E. Edel (eds. K.-J. Seyfried, G. Vieler), *Die Felsgräbernekropole der Qubbet el-Hawa bei Assuan* 1, 3 (Paderborn et al. 2008).

EMERY 1979: W. B. Emery, *The Fortress of Buhen. The Archaeological Report* (Egypt Exploration Society 49, London 1979).

HÖLZL 2002: R. Hölzl, *Ägyptische Opfertafeln und Kultbecken. Eine Form- und Funktionsanalyse für das Alte, Mittlere und Neue Reich* (Hildesheimer Ägyptologische Beiträge 45, Hildesheim 2002).

JÉQUIER 1910: G. Jéquier, Les tables d'offrandes égyptiennes, in: *Sphinx* 13, Uppsala 1910, 205-226.

KILIAN 2009: A. Kilian, *Tönerne Opferteller der 1. Zwischenzeit und des Mittleren Reiches aus Mittelägypten,* 2 vols. (unpubl. M.A. thesis, Mainz 2009).

KUENTZ 1981: Ch. Kuentz, Bassins et tables d'offrandes, in: *Bulletin de l'Institut Français d'Archéologie Orientale* 81 Suppl., 1981, 243-282.

LAUFFRAY 1980: J. Lauffray, Les travaux du Centre Franco-Égyptien d'étude des temples de Karnak de 1972 à 1977, in: *Cahiers de Karnak* 6, 1980, 1-65.

LECLÈRE 2001: F. Leclère, Les «Maisons d'âme» égyptiennes: une tentative de mise au point, in: B. Muller (ed.), *«Maquettes architecturales» de l'antiquité.* (Regards croisés, travaux du Centre de Recherche sur le Proche-Orient et la Grèce Antiques 17, Paris 2001) 99-121.

MARTIN-PARDEY 1991: E. Martin-Pardey, *Grabbeigaben, Nachträge und Ergänzungen* (Corpus Antiquitatum Aegyptiacarum. Pelizaeus Museum Hildesheim Lieferung 6, Mainz 1991).

MICHALOWSKI 1938a: K. Michałowski et al., *Tell Edfou 1938, Fouilles Franco-Polonaises, Rapports II* (Cairo 1938).

MICHALOWSKI 1938b: K. Michałowski et al., *Tell Edfou 1938, Fouilles Franco-Polonaises, Rapports III* (Cairo 1938).

MINAULT-GOUT 1980: A. Minault-Gout, Rapport préliminaire sur les première et seconde campagnes de fouilles du mastaba II à Balat (Oasis de Dakleh) 1979-1980, in: *Bulletin de l'Institut Français d'Archéologie Orientale* 80, 1980, 271-286.

MINAULT-GOUT 1995: A. Minault-Gout, Les mastabas miniatures de Balat ou les cimetières secondaires du mastaba II, in: *Bulletin de l'Institut Français d'Archéologie Orientale* 95, 1995, 297-328.

MOND/MYERS 1937: R. Mond, O. H. Myers, *Cemeteries of Armant* I (The Egypt Exploration Society 42.1, London 1937).

NIWINSKI 1975: A. Niwinski, Plateaux d'offrandes et maisons d'âmes. Genèse, évolution et fonction dans le culte de morts au temps de la XIIe dynastie, in: *Etudes et Travaux* 8, 1975, 73-112.

NIWINSKI 1984: A. Niwinski, in: *Lexikon der Ägyptologie* V (Wiesbaden 1984), s.v. Seelenhaus (und Opferplatte), 806-813.

NORDSTRÖM/BOURRIAU 1993: Ceramic Technology: Clays and Fabrics, in: Do. Arnold/J. Bourriau (eds.), *An Introduction to Ancient Egyptian Pottery* (Sonderschriften des Deutschen Archäologischen Instituts 17, Mainz 1993).

PETRIE 1890: W. M. F. Petrie, *Kahun, Gurob, and Hawara* (London 1890).

PETRIE 1891: W. M. F. Petrie, *Illahun, Kahun and Gurob* (Warminster 1891).

PETRIE 1900: W. M. F. Petrie, *Dendereh 1898* (The Egypt Exploration Fund 17, London 1900).

PETRIE 1907: W. M. F. Petrie, *Gizeh and Rifeh* (British School of Archaeology in Egypt 13, London 1907).

PETRIE 1909: W. M. F. Petrie, *Qurneh* (British School of Archaeology in Egypt 16, London 1909).

PETRIE 1921: W. M. F. Petrie, Discoveries in Herakleopolis, in: *Ancient Egypt* 1921, 65-69.

PETRIE 1925: W. M. F. Petrie, *Tombs of the Courtiers and Oxyrhynkhos* (British School of Archaeology in Egypt 37, London 1925).

QUIBELL 1897: J. E. Quibell, *El Kab* (Egyptian Research Account 3, London 1989).

RYAN 1988: D. P. Ryan, *The Archaeological Excavations of David George Hogarth at Asyut, Egypt 1906/1907* (Cincinnati 1988).

SEILER 2005: A. Seiler, *Tradition und Wandel. Die Keramik als Spiegel der Kulturentwicklung Thebens in der Zweiten Zwischenzeit* (Sonderschriften des Deutschen Archäologischen Instituts Kairo 32, Mainz 2005).

SLATER 1974: R. A. Slater, *The Archaeology of Dendereh in the First Intermediate Period* (Pennsylvania 1974).

TOOLEY 1989: A. M. J. Tooley, *Middle Kingdom Burial Customs. A Study of Wooden Models and Related Material*, unpubl. Ph.D. (Liverpool 1989).

VERCOUTTER 1980: J. Vercoutter, Les Travaux de l'Institut Français d'Archéologie Orientale en 1979-1980, in: *Bulletin de l'Institut Français d'Archéologie Orientale* 80, 1980, 369-392.

VERHOEVEN 1997: U. Verhoeven, Der Totenkult, in: R. Schulz/M. Seidel (eds.), *Ägypten. Die Welt der Pharaonen* (Cologne 1997) 480-489.

WAINWRIGHT 1926: G. Wainwright, A subsidiary burial in Hap-Zefi's tomb at Assiut, in: *Annales du Service des Antiquités de l'Égypte* 26, 1926, 160-166.

WILKINSON 1999: R. H. Wilkinson, *Symbol & Magic in Egyptian Art* (London 1999).

An Overview of Islamic Pottery

Abd El-Naser Yasin

During seven seasons of fieldwork, a large number of Islamic pottery objects has been discovered and classified as follows:

1. Unglazed Earthenware
   The excavation provided us with various fragments of unglazed vessels, mostly water jugs and *koullal*. Examples of this kind of pottery are:

a. A remarkable number of matching fragments that constitute a large part of a jar. This jar is decorated with interlacing incised figures, in the midst of which are circles. The circles are divided into three zones. In the intermediate zone there is a figure similar to a crescent or a horseshoe (Fig. 1; Pl. 10a), which may refer to a certain state official heraldry in the Mamluk rule, namely the horseshoe rank (MAYER 1933: 25). This heraldry was a symbol of a person who was very important both in peace and war times, Prince Amir Akhor, who was the supervisor of the Sultanic stables.

b. A number of fragments of jar or *koulla* necks and filters. Dating these fragments is difficult because most of them have no decoration, while the others have simple decoration only (Fig. 2).

2. Glazed Earthenware
   The most common forms of pottery found during the fieldwork are those made of glazed earthenware. The objects, which belong to this kind of pottery, are decorated by using the incised, carved and painted techniques in the slip under a polychrome transparent glaze. Most of the decorations are stylized plant motifs and inscriptions with the Mamluk *Thuluth* calligraphy. Examples of this kind of glazed earthenware are:

a. A fragment of a bowl corpus, decorated on the inside and the outside with inscriptions in the Mamluk *Thuluth* calligraphy (Fig. 3), it is quite similar to a certain object from Mamluk pottery (GRUBE 1976: Pl. 95).

b. A relatively large fragment of a bowl corpus and its base, decorated on the outside with painting of abstract plant motifs and on the inside with incised geometric motifs (Figs. 4-6).

c. A fragment of a bowl base attached to a small part of its corpus, decorated with an interlaced triangular motif (Fig. 7), a typical style of many bowl decorations, which belong to the Mamluk Period (BAHGAT/MASSOUL 1930: 84, Pl. 50).

d. A fragment of an upper part of a bowl. The upper edge of the interior of the bowl is decorated with a border of abstract plant motifs (Fig. 8). It is noticeable that the motifs used in the excavated bowl are very similar to the planting patterns, which decorate a Mamluk bowl of the eighth *Hijri* century/the fourteenth century CE (ATIL 1981: Pl. 73).

e. A fragment of a bowl base attached to a small part of its corpus. The base is decorated with a multi-petal rosette (Fig. 9), painted in light green against a dark-green background. The colours and rosette motif of the excavated fragment are a typical style of a Mamluk glazed pottery (ATIL 1981: Pl. 93).
f. A bowl, the interior and exterior of its surfaces are glazed. Although its exterior is characterized by the absence of decorations, its interior has carved motifs under the glaze (Pl. 10b).

3. Monochrome-glazed pottery

Among the pottery objects found during fieldwork are a number of undecorated bowl fragments with green or yellowish-brown glazes. Some fragments have both glaze colours: green glaze on the inside and yellowish-brown glaze on the outside. Examples of this kind of pottery are:

a. A fragment of a bowl base and a part of the corpus, the base is circular and relatively high. The interior surface is coated with green transparent glaze, while the exterior surface is coated with yellowish-brown glaze (Fig. 10).
b. A number of bowl fragments, which may belong to one or more bowls, with green transparent glaze (Pl. 11a). One of the fragments has simple motifs incised under the glaze. The motifs bring to mind the Mamluk watermark or stamp symbols popular especially in pottery, which are believed to be used as an indicator of a certain job, a position or a social class.

4. Underglazed-painted pottery

Among the pottery finds of the excavation were two fragments characterized by a more fragile and whiter clay (Pl. 11b). One of these two fragments is an upper part of a bowl corpus; the other is a part of the same bowl. The interior and exterior of the two fragments are decorated with simple light-blue and greenish-black motifs. This decoration style, a typical style of a Mamluk underglazed bowl, belongs to the 8th *Hijri* century/the fourteenth century CE (ATIL 1981: Pls. 73, 77, 83).

5. Imitation of Tang pottery

The Tang Dynasty of China had produced a unique type of pottery. It is characterized by the simple dots or stripes decorations (ZHIYAN/WEN 1989: Pls. 20, 25). The Tang pottery had been imported by Muslim countries, including Egypt. The imitation of the Tang pottery had spread throughout Egypt since the Tulunid until the end of the Mamluk reign. Some of the excavations' pottery finds are imitations of the Tang Chinese pottery. Examples of this kind of pottery are:

a. A fragment of a bowl base attached to a small part of the bowl corpus. The interior of the bowl base is decorated with yellow dots within which are smaller green dots (Fig. 11). It is painted under transparent glaze. The design on this fragment resembles a design on a Mamluk underglazed bowl (FRANÇOIS 1999: Pl. 5, no. 99).
b. A fragment of a bowl, decorated on the inside with vertical stripes of different colours: green, yellow, and reddish-yellow.

6. Chinese Porcelain:
Porcelain is famous Chinese pottery made of white coherent and solid material. The decoration is painted in blue against a white background and underglazed. This type of pottery was exported to the Near East since the third century of *Hijra*/ninth century CE (LANE 1971: 21). It is well known that Egypt had imported large quantities of Chinese porcelain produced during the reign of the Chinese royal family of "Minge" (1368-1644 CE). Mamluk pottery makers were interested in imitating porcelain, however, they did not quite succeed.

The fieldwork in Asyut has discovered fragments of porcelain. When reassembled, they created a bowl corpus and only part of its base. The interior of one fragment is decorated in blue against a white background, but is plain in its exterior. The bowl corpus is decorated as an open flower (Fig. 12).

Obviously this bowl is not locally or homemade, but a product of China. This is evident from the purity of its material and colours as well as the open flower, which was a very common decorative element in Chinese pottery, although some Egyptian artefacts, particularly during the Mamluk period, had similar decorative elements, but its representation was different from the Chinese style.

To sum up, we can safely assume that most of the pottery discovered in the western mountain of Asyut belongs to the Mamluk Period. However, this does not mean that we did not find pottery belonging to other periods, such as the Ottoman Period, of which many fragments of pipes were found (Fig. 13).

Now we come to the question: Who used this pottery?

We know that the area, in which the pottery was discovered, was originally an ancient Egyptian cemetery that was used as a residential area as well as for worship by Christian friars. It is not possible that such Ottoman pipes were used by those friars, but rather by some Mamluks, who found refuge in this area during the French Campaign in Egypt.

It is difficult to assume that the pottery was used by Christian friars for a number of reasons:

1. This highly decorated pottery does not correspond with the simple life of friars. This pottery, whether local or of foreign origin, is not only varied in shape and type, but is also similar to that commonly used in the Mamluk ruling centers in Cairo.
2. The horseshoe heraldry or rank, which was the symbol of a Mamluk prince, was inscribed on one of the discovered objects. Another object was decorated with a "stamp", which signifies a job of some Mamluk ruling class.

These two points lead us to another question about the possibility and the reason behind the existence of Mamluks in that area.

Historical sources tell us that Mamluks launched a number of punitive campaigns against the Arab rebels living in Upper Egypt. Asyut was known to be one of the strongholds of rebellion against the Mamluk reign. Historical references also tell us that the Mamluks reached the western mountain of Asyut, where the objects were found, to suppress one of those rebellions (MAQRIZI 1997: 346; IBN TAGHRIBARDI 1992: 120-122).

One of the strongest rebellions actually took place in 701 *Hijri*/1301 CE, during the reign of Sultan Elnasser Mohamed Ibn Qalawoon. The Mamluk army reached the western mountain of Asyut and surrounded the Arab rebels, who escaped into the mountains and the ancient Egyptian cemetery. Finally the Mamluks were able to take over and resolutely defeat the rebels.

The military campaign was so huge that it was led by 20 princes, the most renowned being the vice-sultan "Salar", Prince "Baybars Elgashinkir" and Prince "Sonkor Elaaser".

Based on this information we can safely say that the finds of Mamluk pottery discovered in the Western Mountain of Asyut belong to the Mamluk military campaign. It is well known that different pots and jars were usually carried for the use of military officers and soldiers during such campaigns. Since this particular campaign included 20 princes, it would be quite natural for them to carry the best types of ware with them; like the ware which was discovered in the excavation.

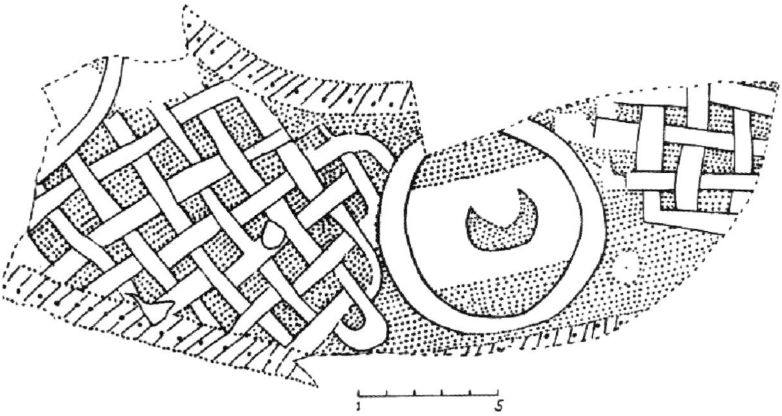

Fig. 1: S06/st574, unglazed earthenware (© The Asyut Project; drawing: A. El-Naser Yasin).

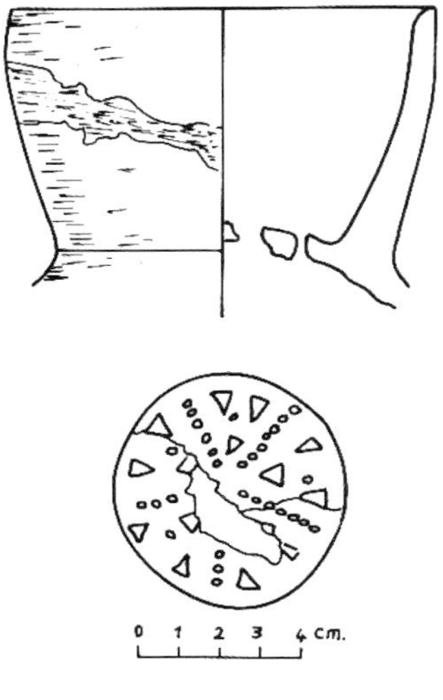

Fig. 2: S07/st210 (© The Asyut Project; drawing: A. El-Naser Yasin/S. Shafik).

Fig. 3: S04/st351 (© The Asyut Project; drawing: A. El-Naser Yasin).

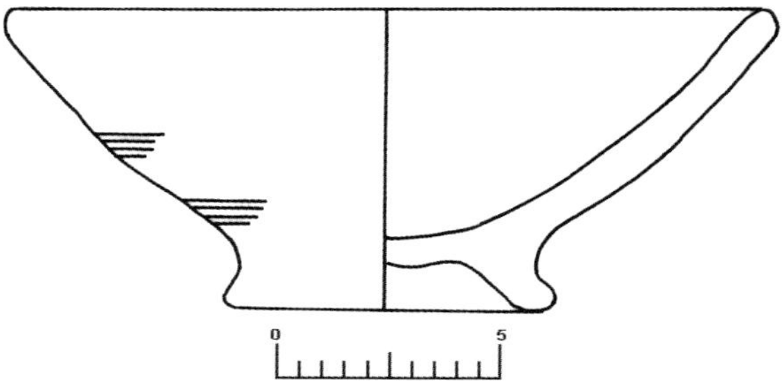

Fig. 4: S06/st359 (© The Asyut Project; drawing: A. El-Naser Yasin).

Fig. 5: S06/st359, outside (© The Asyut Project; drawing: A. El-Naser Yasin).

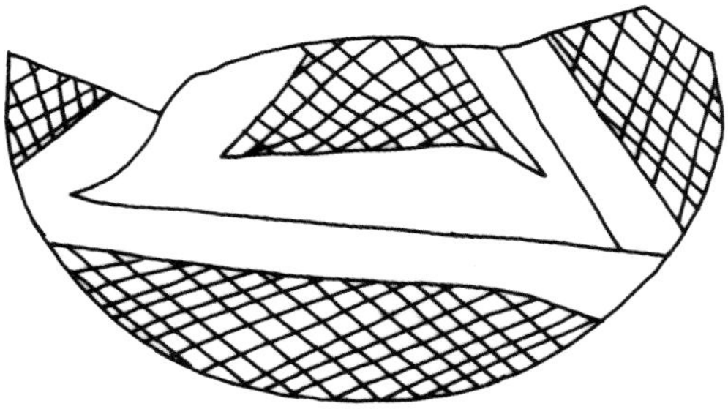

Fig. 6: S06/st359, inside (© The Asyut Project; drawing: A. El-Naser Yasin).

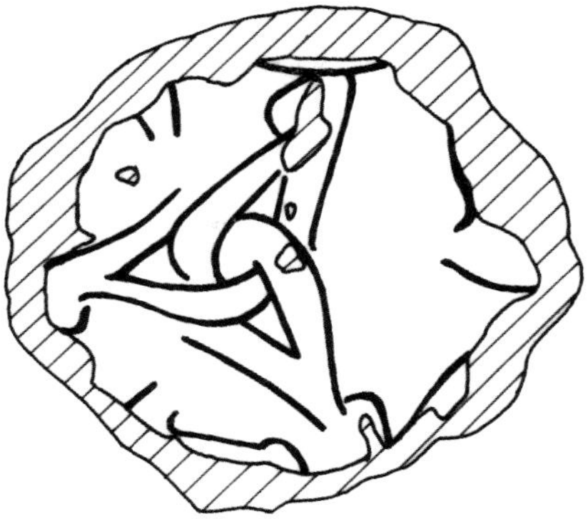

Fig. 7: S06/st217 (© The Asyut Project; drawing: A. El-Naser Yasin).

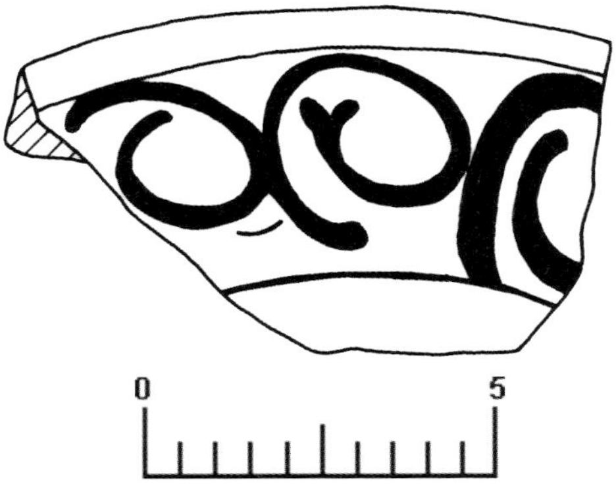

Fig. 8: S04/st292 C (© The Asyut Project; drawing: A. El-Naser Yasin).

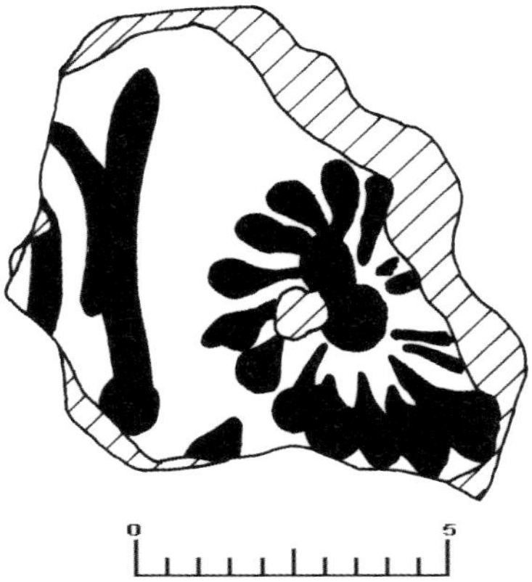

Fig. 9: S05/st1261 B (© The Asyut Project; drawing: A. El-Naser Yasin).

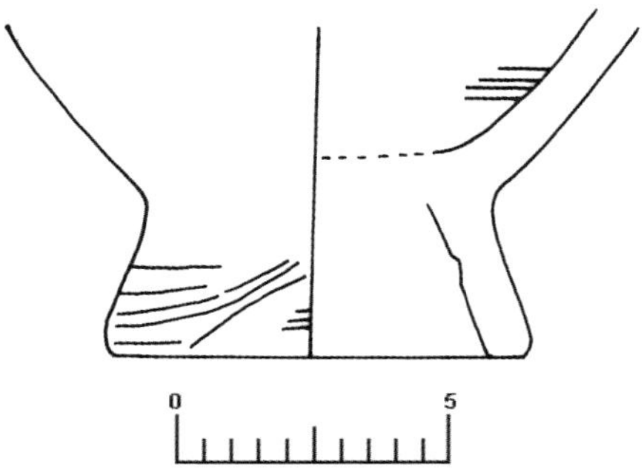

Fig. 10: S05/st256 B (© The Asyut Project; drawing: A. El-Naser Yasin).

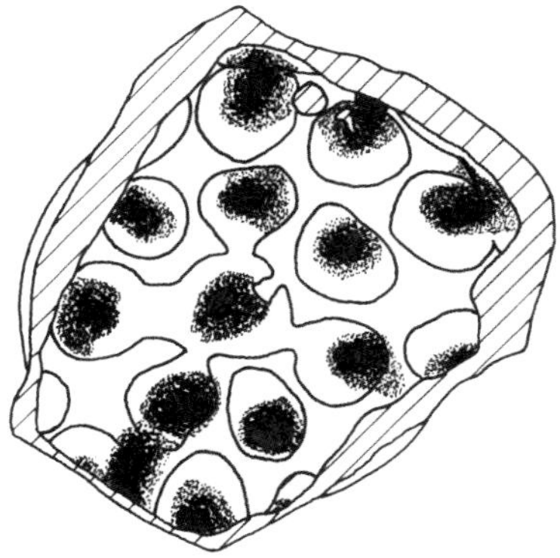

Fig. 11: S06/st81 A (© The Asyut Project; drawing: A. El-Naser Yasin).

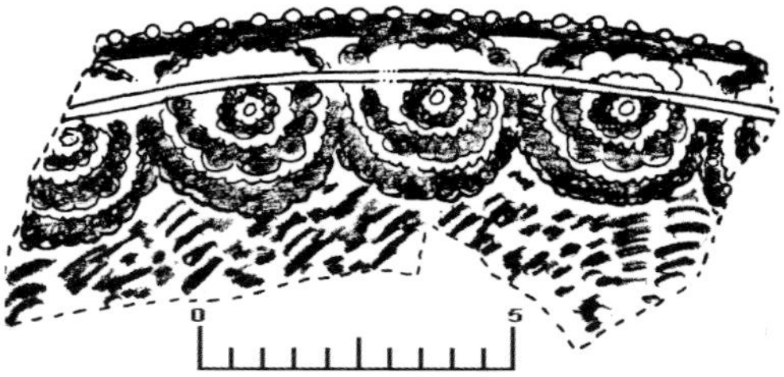

Fig. 12: S04/st15 + S05/st64 (© The Asyut Project; drawing: A. El-Naser Yasin).

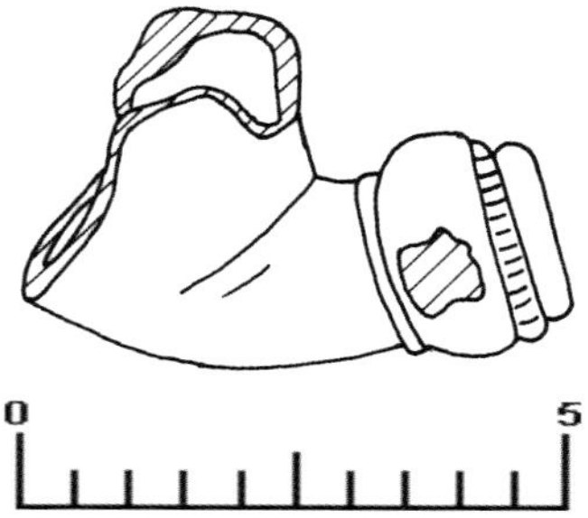

Fig. 13: S04/st366 (© The Asyut Project; drawing: A. El-Naser Yasin/S. Shafik).

References:

ATIL 1981: E. Atil, *Renaissance of Islam: Art of the Mamluks* (Washington 1981).
BAHGAT/MASSOUL 1930: A. Bahgat/F. Massoul, *La Céramique Musulman de l'Égypte* (Cairo 1930).
FRANÇOIS 1999: V. François, *Céramiques Médiévales à Alexandrie: contribution à l'histoire économique de la ville* (Études Alexandrines 2, Cairo 1999).
IBN TAGHRIBARDI 1992: Ibn Taghribardi, *El-Nogom el-Zahera* (Beirut 1992).
GRUBE 1976: E. J. Grube, *Islamic Pottery of the Eighth to the Fifteenth Century in the Keir Collection* (London 1976).
LANE 1971: A. Lane, *Later Islamic Pottery: Persia, Syria, Egypt, Turkey* (London 1971).
MAQRIZI 1997: Al-Maqrizi, *Kitab al-Suluk* 1, Beirut 1997.
MAYER 1933: L. A. Mayer, *Saracenic Heraldry* (Oxford 1933).
ZHIYAN/WEN 1989: L. Zhiyan/C. Wen, *Chinese Pottery and Porcelain* (Beijing 1989).

Human Bones from Tombs of the Old Kingdom

Magdalena Patolla

Introduction

This study deals with human skeletal remains from the Middle-Egyptian necropolis Gebel Asyut al-gharbi, step 7 (Pl. 20). Biological traces on skeletal material serve as a basis for individual findings, which offer a unique access in reconstructing daily life, environmental and living conditions in prehistoric populations and allow an insight into the population structure. Hence, human material is a primary source of information for population-related statements (RÖSING et al. 2005).

Due to the settlement and research history the bone material on Gebel Asyut al-gharbi is often in poor condition. On the one hand the human residues are fragmented, on the other hand their spatial and temporal origin is unknown in most cases. Indeed, almost complete skeletons were partly found on step 7, which demonstrate closed find complexes and allow an osteoanthropological examination by means of morphognostic and palaeodemographic patterns.

The determination of the age and sex distribution provides indications for the demographic structure of the sample which can be examined in connection with social, cultural and economic parameters (ACSÁDI/NEMESKÉRI 1970). Based on the funeral type and circumstances, the Asyut skeletons most probably represent a special social group or partial population such as a high-ranking and privileged upper class, family members of the tomb owner, officials, civil servants or followers.

The health state of the sample, i.e. occurance and degree of severity of certain disease patterns, permits a conclusion of possible life circumstances and environmental circumstances such as hygiene, residential situation or labour conditions. Repetitively performed movements and special working practices can lead to above-average wear and tear of joints and spine. Dental pathologies can provide information about nutrition, food preparation, oral hygiene and possibly medical interventions (ORSCHIEDT 1996).

Goodman/Armelagos arranged a model of stress interpretation in archaeological populations (Fig. 1; GOODMAN/ARMELAGOS 1989). Stress is meant as detectable physical change of the osseous structure. Skeletal indicators of stress reflect living conditions, diet workload and disease susceptibility in a population. On the basis of this data reconstruction of environmental conditions, cultural systems and host resistance factors is possible.

In connection with the archaeological report a reliable image of the Asyut living population in the Old Kingdom can be reconstructed. Because the fieldwork on step 7 and the anthropological data collection of the skeletal material are not finished yet, the present study shows preliminary results. The presentation of the skeletal series refers to descriptive and explorative statistical calculations. Detailed information on a population and inter-population level can be given only after completed collection and evaluation of the osteological data. More reliable and detailed archaeological information as well as a completion of the anthropological data collection is necessary to calculate a life table, capturing inter-population differences and interpretation of the anthropological results in comparison to other sites of the Old Kingdom.

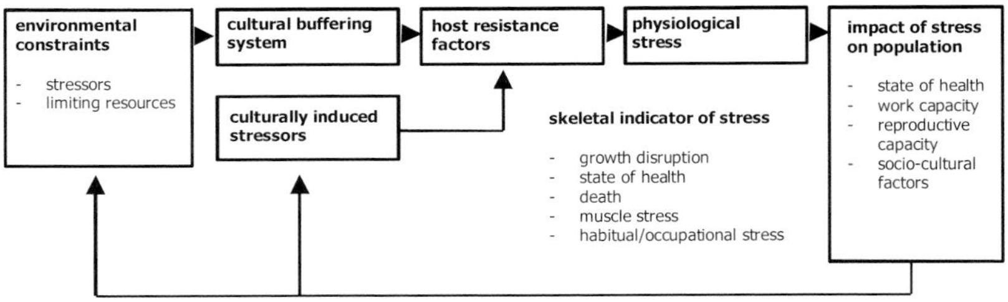

Fig. 1: Model of stress in archaeological populations (GOODMAN/ARMELAGOS 1989).

Material

The site is located on the seventh geological layer of the Gebel Asyut al-gharbi, accordingly named step 7, and is located in the south of Tomb N13.1 (Pl. 20-21). Step 7 consists of a total of 61 shafts in four terraces, which probably formed a plain in earlier times. In the north it is not possible to detect the border, because the area is damaged due to quarrying. The shafts or grave pits are 1-1.5 m deep. Some of them contain a sidechamber or a niche, but are very similar in building structure, except in terms of size and state of preservation. In the course of the pottery analysis some of these shafts can be dated into the Old Kingdom. The chronological order of the shafts is not fully determined yet. Thus they remain a central point of investigation for future fieldwork.

The skeletons were consistently buried in the crouched position, no characteristic artificial or natural mummification traces are visible. The burials are north-south orientated, with view to the east. Children were also buried on their back. As grave goods pottery, head rests, woven baskets and sometimes a necklace and plants have been excavated (cf. the contribution of Jochem Kahl in this volume, p. 10-11). Often the shafts and side-chambers were robbed in ancient time.

Methods

Measuring distances and indices are collected from cranium and post cranium (BRÄUER 1988). The body height is calculated according to regression formulas by PEARSON 1899.

Morphognostic methods on skull and particular pelvis (ACSÁDI/NEMESKÉRI 1970, PHENICE 1969) permit a rather reliable sex determination. The vertical diameter of head of humerus and femur (DITTRICK 1979; DITTRICK/SUCHEY 2005; STEWART 1979) complete sexing. Discriminant analysis with data collected from patella (INTRONA et al. 1998) as well as talus and calcaneus (STEELE 1975) are rather not suitable for the Asyut population.

Primary tooth wear (LOVEJOY 1985) and degenerative changes on the pelvis (BROOKS/SUCHEY 1990; LOVEJOY et al. 1985; MEINDL et al. 1985) are suitable for age estimation. Age determination by means of ectocranial closure (MEINDL/LOVEJOY 1985) or sternal rib metamorphosis (IŞCAN et al. 1984, 1985) are rather unreliable methods and merely describe tendencies.

The morphology of the pelvis, lower jaw and their longitudinal values used for discriminant analyses could be an approach to identify the sex of subadults (SCHUTKOWSKI 1990). Biological age can be determined on the basis of continuous growth phases and developmental stages. Different methods can be used for this purpose, e.g. mixed dentition (UBELAKER 1999), ossification of the joints (BROTHWELL 1981), length of the long bones (STLOUKAL/HANÁKOVÁ 1978) and determination of the growth stages of single skeletal elements (BASS 2005; SCHEUER/BLACK 2000).

Tooth state, fragmenting degree, caries, inflammations of the jaw, parodontopathy, tartar and transversal enamel hypoplasias are recorded systematically in the dental findings. Joint damages and defects on the spine, i.e. *spondylarthrosis deformans*, *spondylosis deformans* and Schmorl's nodes are collected according to the recommendations by SCHULTZ 1988. Furthermore cranial and postcranial pathological processes are entirely described. However, not every pathological defect exhibits a specific disease pattern. The individual findings contain all visible pathological damages, whereas the graphics correspond to specific disease patterns at the individual level. In the evaluation descriptive parameters and frequencies are calculated separately for age and sex.

Results

For the calculation of a life table anthropological information of the whole site is required. Detailed archaeological information about social status and profession is necessary for an interpretation of these palaeodemographic analyses. The membership to an economy and higher social class in the Old Kingdom is assumed. In this case a natural age distribution is unlikely (DRENHAUS 1992). On the basis of age and sex distribution it is possible to describe intra-population demographic parameters in the sample.

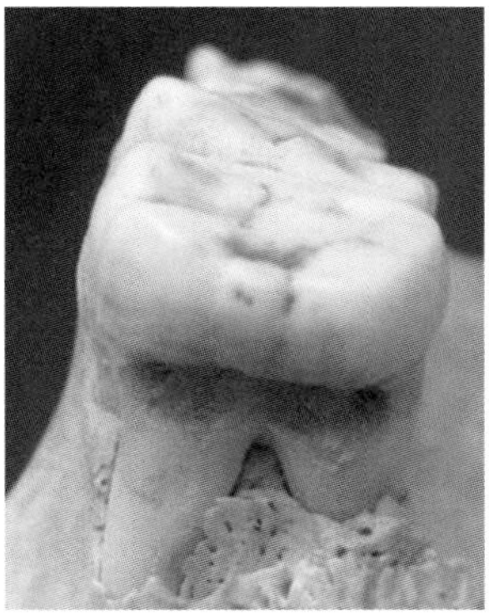

Fig. 2: SK F16: Caries, upper molar (M2) left side (© The Asyut Project; Patolla).

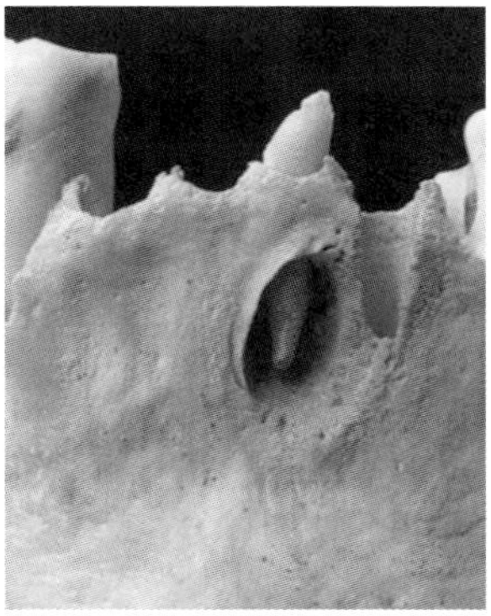

Fig. 3: SK F37: Inflammation of the lower jaw bone, incisor (I1) left side (© The Asyut Project; Patolla).

The total sample contains nineteen individuals with a balanced sex ratio (Pl. 12a). Seven of them have been identified as male, six of them as female and six are indifferent, but with a tendency to a sex. With regard to these tendencies

53 % of the Asyut skeletons are defined as male and 48 % as female. Only few subadults are represented in the sample. A deficiency of children is possible (KÖLBL 2004). Subadult mortality rate is 15 %. Almost 85 % of the people survived the susceptible childhood and an exceptional number of individuals reached the mature age. There are no significant differences in distribution between adult (20-40 years) and mature (40-60 years) age. No age- or sex-specific mortality peak exists in the sample (Pl. 12b). It seems that consequences of stress situations and health risk during pregnancy and maternity are not seen in the present study. This supports the assumption of a privileged part of the population.

The average body height of men is 162.5 cm and that of women is 159.0 cm. The results suggest no indications of poor and unbalanced diet, excessive physical activity patterns and workload, poor living and environmental conditions (WURM/LEIHMEISTER 1986).

For the analysis 17 jaws with 255 teeth were available. More than a half are missing, corresponding to 289 teeth. Altogether 30 teeth exhibit carious lesions (Fig. 2). The very high caries intensity of 11.8 % and caries frequency of 53 % could point to a rather carbohydrate rich nutrition and soft diet. The male sample is more often affected by carious defects. Caries is mostly recognizable in the molars, especially in the lower jaw. According to expectations, caries develops preferably in the molars, as food leftovers effectively accumulate in teeth fissures, and bacteria find a favourable milieu to grow (LARSEN 2002, 2006; ALT 2001). Caries can be diagnosed as early as in the juvenile age. In mature and senile stages there are less carious damages than in the adult age, but with a higher intensity. There is a negative correlation of teeth fissure attrition and occlusal caries defects, because small defects can be grind.

32 teeth in the Asyut sample are affected by inflammatory processes (Fig. 3). Periodontal inflammations are often caused

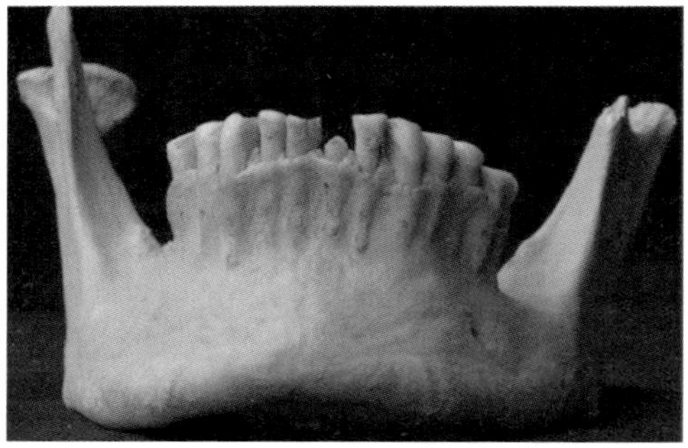

Fig. 4: SK F35: Periodontal damages, lower jaw anterior (© The Asyut Project; Patolla).

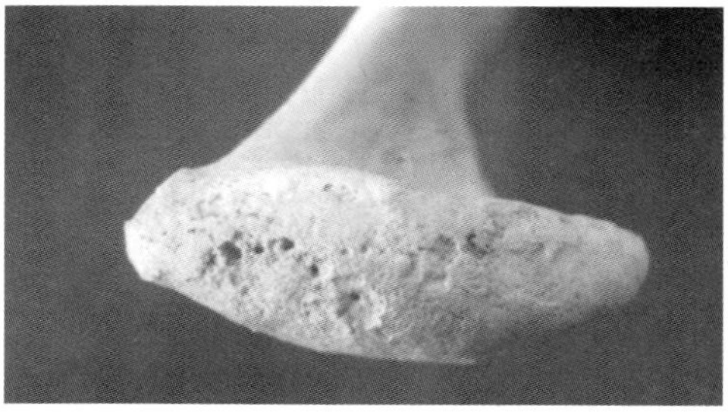

Fig. 5: SK F15: Osteoarthritic changes of the temporomandibular joint, *Caput mandibulae superior*, left side (© The Asyut Project; Patolla).

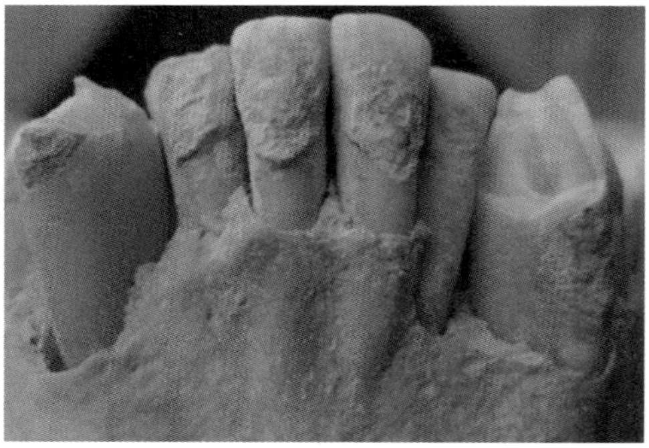

Fig. 6: SK 26: Tartar, lower jaw anterior (© The Asyut Project; Patolla).

by severe caries, attrition, or *gingivitis*, because bacteria can enter more effectively into the jaw bone and lead to inflammatory reactions (ORSCHIEDT 1996). In the maxilla the frequency and intensity is higher than in the mandible. Only three teeth show moderate inflammatory damages in the lower jaw. In the upper jaw especially the molars and the left side are affected. The pattern is similar to the caries distribution.

Periodontal damages are identified in seven individuals (Fig. 4). Overall periodontal diseases are observed with a lower intensity, but with a high frequency in the Asyut population. In the lower jaw almost every tooth shows periodontal damages. Periodontal diseases result from dystrophic (*periodontosis*), inflammatory and traumatic factors (*periodontitis*). Increased biomechanical stress of mastication can also cause a reduction of the osseous structure of the jaw (ORSCHIEDT 1996; Y`EDYNAK/FLEISCH 1983). In this context osteoarthritic changes of the temporomandibular joint can also be developed by accumulating masticatory pressures, which are identified a bit more often in females (Fig. 5).

Slight tartar caused no problems, but passage of time can cause the development of chalk walls, which are only removable by surgery (SCHULTZ 1988). Tartar is found on every tooth in the lower jaw in the sample, particular on the canines (Fig. 6). The highest average values were calculated for the upper molars on the left side. Individual F6 exhibits the most serious tartar.

The degree of the transversal enamel hypoplasia is weak and mainly manifested as multiple and thin enamel furrow preferably on the molars in the Asyut population. While the incidence of the transversal enamel hypoplasia is very low or even missing in childhood and the juvenile stage, the permanent teeth are rather affected. This should not only be regarded as a hint for long-lasting periods of physiological stress, but can also present short term seasonal emergency periods or a constant slight deprivation. The continuing mineral disturbance could have been caused by malnutrition, infections, traumata and intoxications e.g. fluorosis as well as systemic diseases or growth disorders (CARLI-THIELE 1996).

In summary, caries and inflammation are the most existing dental pathologies in the sample without sex-specific differences. Inflammation and transversal enamel hypoplasia are more often diagnosed in the male sample than periodontal damages and tartar. In the female sample periodontal changes are more frequent, followed by transversal enamel hypoplasia and inflammation. Tartar is rare, only one woman is affected. Caries appears in every adult stage, but the intensity increases with age. Inflammatory processes are quite frequent in mature age. Transversal enamel hypoplasia manifests primarily in

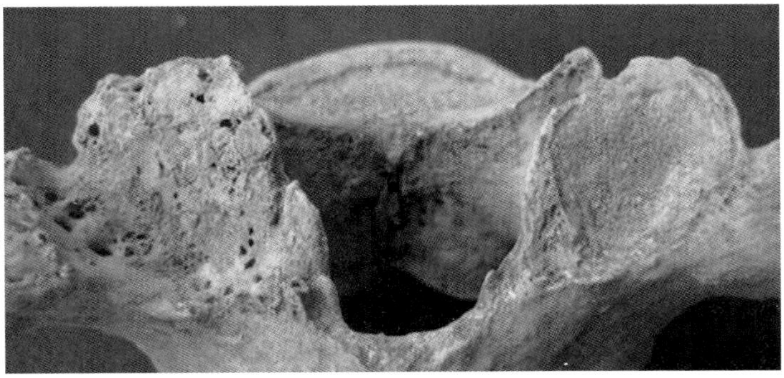

Fig. 7: SK F8: *Thoracic vertebra posterior* showing destruction of the joint surface, *spondylarthrosis deformans* (© The Asyut Project; Patolla).

adult ages. Therefore the severity is most serious in the senile stage. Tartar and periodontal disease have no detectable age-specific peak. To sum up, tartar and caries seem to appear earlier than periodontal lesions and inflammations of the jaw bone (Pl. 13).

Altogether 13 spinal columns have been examined. 25 % of these individuals exhibit spondylopathy, but nearly all skeletons show slight changes with no medical relevance in most cases. The fifth *thoracic vertebra* is mostly missed (n=8.43 %), while the second and sixth *cervical vertebra* and third *thoracic vertebra* are best represented (n=12.86 %).

Degenerative skeletal features like *spondylopathy* or deforming *spondylosis*, *spondylarthritis* as well as degenerative *spondylarthrosis* and Schmorl's nodes are a natural consequence of biological aging. High mobility and regular activities can strain the spinal column additionally. On the contrary, a higher average temperature up to 3° C can effectuate the inhibition of primary and secondarily induced inflammations (JURMAIN 1999; MENNINGER/WAIBEL 1996).

Spondylarthritis can be observed in four individuals in the Asyut sample (Fig. 7). The first and the second thoracic vertebra are least affected by *spondyloarthrosis/ose deformans*. Starting from the middle thoracic vertebra segment, the low mean values increase with highest degree of severity in the lumbar region. In the male population the pathological processes of the cervical intervertebral joints are most frequent and evident, which is most striking at the fifth cervical vertebra. Senile individuals show most serious defects on the cervical segment. An age-related increase is best recognisable on the thoracic spine with no obviously differences between the sexes. An exception are the last three thoracic vertebrae, which exhibit lower values in the male than in the female sample. In the lumbar column there is the same relation, the first and second lumbar vertebra is affected most seriously.

Spondylosis deformans was diagnosed in five individuals with an age-related increase of the mean values, particular in the thoracic und lumbar spine (Fig. 8). In general the males display a higher degree of severity in the cervical and thoracic column. In the male sample the second and third *thoracic vertebra*, in the female sample the fourth and fifth *thoracic vertebra* are most affected. A high mean value is calculated between the eleventh and twelfth *thoracic vertebra* for both sexes. In the female population spondylopathy is more frequent and serious on the lumbar spine, especially between the

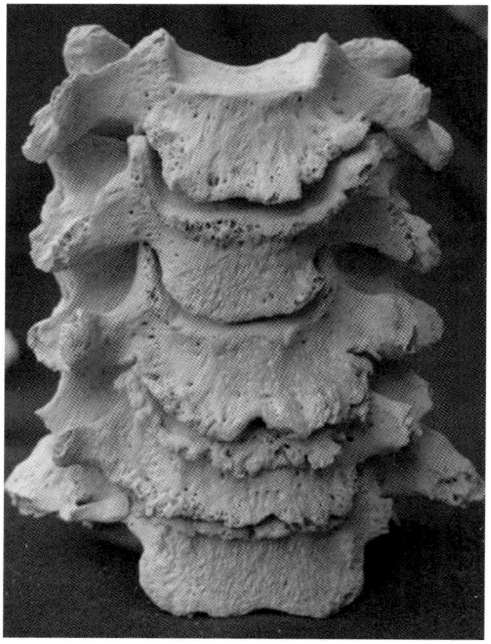

Fig. 8: SK F35: *Thoracic vertebrae* showing deposits of osteophytes, *spondylosis deformans* (© The Asyut Project; Patolla).

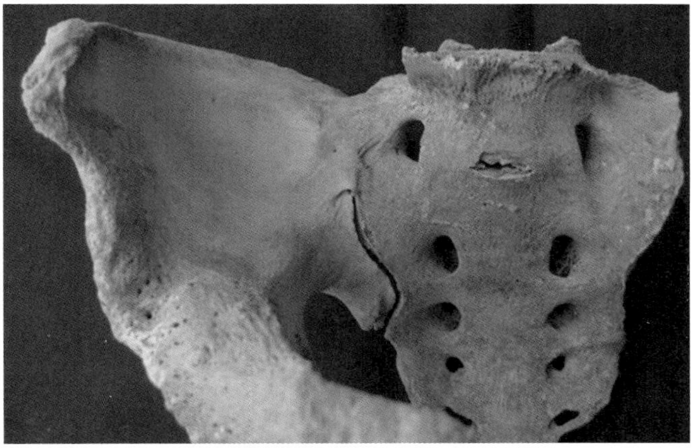

Fig. 9: SK F8: Ossification of ligaments and tendons of pelvis girdle (© The Asyut Project; Patolla).

first and second *lumbar vertebra*. The results can possibly be associated with the physical stress during pregnancy or with the frequent carrying of infants on the arm.

Skeleton F8 displays an entire ossification of ligaments and tendons which can lead to the formation of a steady connection of the pelvic girdle (Fig. 9). This male and skeleton F9 tend to the formation of osseous braces on *corpus vertebrae* and *processus spinosi*. This can be the result of distinctive *spondylosis deformans* where the huge osseous borders grow together to a more or less stiff connection (AUFDERHEIDE/RODRÍGUEZ-MARTIN 1998; CZARNETZKI et al. 1982). Altogether skeleton F8 has most strikingly lesions on the spinal column, which is also true for Schmorl's nodes (JURMAIN 1999; MENNIGER/WAIBEL 1996). Otherwise in the sample, deeper Schmorl's nodes appear only on one column (Fig. 10). Most common damages are visible on the intervertebral discs in the cervical and lumbar region. Schmorl's nodes and other changes of the intervertebral discs in the cervical and thoracic segment appear predominantly in the senile age group, except the lumbar region. In adult and mature defects in the cervical and thoracic region are rare. Numerous, but weakly developed Schmorl's nodes can be observed on the *lumbar vertebrae* in mature individuals. With a few exceptions, Schmorl's nodes exist more often in the male than in the female sample. The degree of severity is less in the female population.

Fig. 10: SK F6: *Thoracic vertebra inferior* showing Schmorl's node where the cartilaginous intervertebral disk has herniated into the bone (© The Asyut Project; Patolla).

Sporadically spondylous pathologies and Schmorl's nodes can be observed in early adult age, but consistently in older individuals. Commonly, pathological defects on the spine increase from cranial to caudal. An influence of above-average physical activity can probably be excluded, because serious damages start at a mature age. Sex-specific differences in intensity and frequency could be due to different functional, occupational and daily activities. Nevertheless a larger sample is necessary to reach reliable conclusions.

More information about joint arthrosis can be taken from the left body side. The hip joint is least preserved. The right upper and lower long bones are more affected by joint arthrosis, especially the shoulder and radioulnar joint. Pathological processes are barely visible on the ankle joint and have higher values on the left body side. The mean values decrease from cranial to caudal, except the hip joint, which has the highest degree of severity, particular in the female population. From this finding it can be deduced that physical load of the upper extremity is higher in males, except the right wrist. In the Asyut sample most diseases are age-dependent in frequency and intensity, particular joint arthrosis and dental pathologies.

Cribra orbitalia and porotic diseases are more numerous in male individuals. Various factors such as diet, infections or acquired iron-deficiency anaemia are possible explanations for porotic pathologies. For a long time *cribra orbitalia* was the most important indicator for iron-deficiency anaemia (Fig. 11). Histological investigations in Nubian populations (n=333) from Missiminia (North Sudan) showed that the hypertrophy suggest other reasons in approximately 60 % of the cases, e.g. osteitis, hypervascularity, blood loss caused by injuries, menstruation, birth or parasitic infestation as well as post-mortem damage. *Cribra orbitalia* is a marker for a high illness susceptibility and physiological stress situations especially during childhood and youth (CARLI-THIELE 1996; WAPLER et al. 2004). As expected *Cribra orbitalia* (n=2) and porotic diseases (n=1) appear already at subadult age, but most frequently in the adult stage and are even visible in one mature individual.

Pacchioni grooves and osteoma are rare in the sample (n=3) and are rather characteristic for the male population (AUFDERHEIDE/RODRÍGUEZ-MARTIN 1998; UHLIG 1982). Traumata are only observed in the male population (n=4). Two males F8 and F28 have one or more fractured ribs, which is typical for crashes and bruises (AUFDERHEIDE/RODRÍGUEZ-MARTIN 1998). Skeleton F28 shows a well healed rib fracture. A broken foot toe is grown together displaced (F34). A sharp slash injury is observed in the forehead of individual F1 and until now the only hint for a possible violent dispute (Fig. 12).

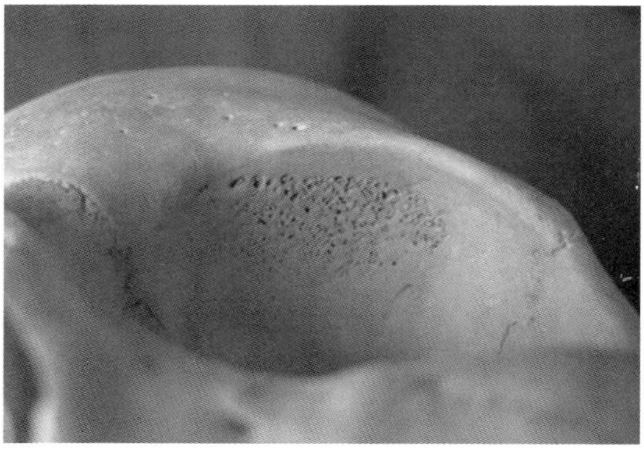

Fig. 11: SK F18: Cribra orbitalia, left *orbita* (© The Asyut Project; Patolla).

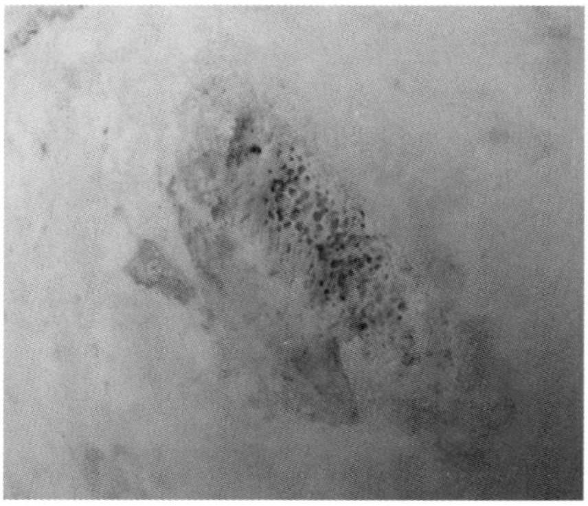

Fig. 12: SK F1: Trauma, *Os frontale* (© The Asyut Project; Patolla).

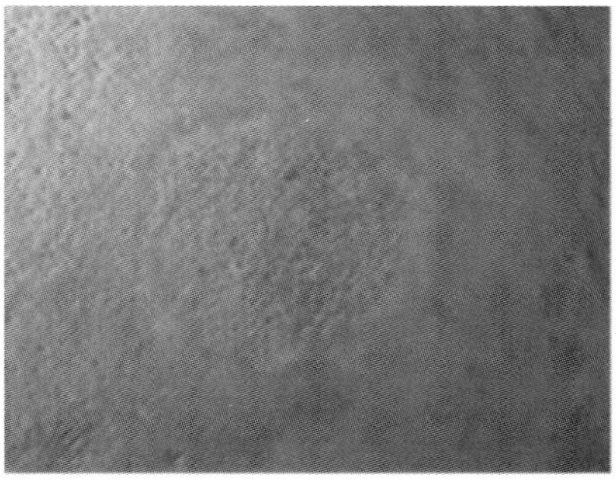

Fig. 13: SK F16: Nonspecific periosteal lesion on the skull (© The Asyut Project; Patolla).

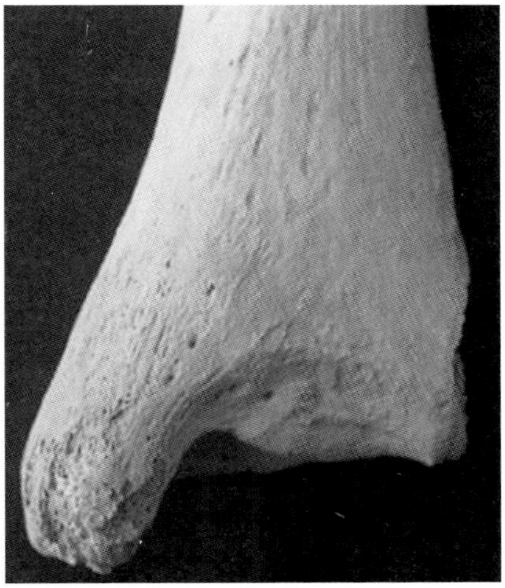

Fig. 14: SK F28: Squatting facet, distal Tibia right side (© The Asyut Project; Patolla).

Nonspecific periosteal inflammations and lesions are signs of poor living and nutrition conditions, because they are mainly caused by multiple stress factors such as parasitic infestation, reduction of mobility, excessive work load and insanitation (SCHULTZ 1988; LARSON et al. 2001). Individual F9 shows osseous appositions on long bones, but several individuals exhibit non-specific small and flat lesions on the skull (Fig. 13). Other clinical pictures and specific features e.g. modifications of the long bones and special symptoms like lytic or infectious lesions are rare in the examined sample.

The males exhibit an insignificantly higher amount of pathologies, which corresponds to the well-known fact that males have a poorer health status than females. This may be due to the fact that children and young men are more susceptible to stress factors and are more exposed to physiological stress. Furthermore, the risk of injury seems to be higher for males.

A further pattern of interest is the squatting position, a balanced posture which requires no strength of musculature. The sole of the foot stands flat on the ground and the flexion of the foot joints thereby exerts pressure on the anterior-distal end of the tibia. This can induce the development of a squatting facet on the talus as well as on the distal tibia (Fig. 14; CAPASSO et al. 1999). Squatting facets are rather present in the female population, except for infants. This leads to the assumption that the individuals presumably spent regularly time in the squatting position and may prefer this to avoid sitting on the dirty and dusty ground.

Summary

Skeletal remains from step 7 on the Gebel Asyut al-gharbi are examined with focus on population structure and health status by means of morphognostic and metric methods. This anthropological study is a preliminary work and results might change, because the fieldwork on step 7 continues; statements on the population level are therefore limited. The sample from the Old Kingdom period consists of 19 individuals with a balanced sex relation. Only three subadults are available for the study, and deficiency of children is possible. Many individuals reached an advanced age. An age- or sex-specific mortality peak cannot be derived. The mean body height is 155.9 cm in females and 162.5 cm in males. This fact implies no evidence for malnutrition or a high workload. The caries intensity and frequency is high and points to a rather carbohydrate rich nutrition and soft diet. Most of the individuals show age-related osteoarthritic changes or dental lesions, which are caused by degenerative processes rather than activity. Pathologies are more often and distinctive in the male population. *Cribra orbitalia* is even observable in the adult-mature stage. Commonly nonspecific diseases are not medically relevant. Systemic or severe disorders are less present. The general state of health can be characterized as inconspicuous and stable. This indicates a low degree of mobility stress (pelvis, morphology of lower limb), malnutrition and physiological stress also during childhood.

Squatting facets are rather typical for the female population and lead to the conclusion that the individuals regularly spent time in the squatting position.

References:

ACSÁDI/NEMESKÉRI 1970: Gy. Acsádi/J. Nemeskéri, *History of Human Life Span and Mortality* (Budapest 1970).

ALT 2001: K. W. Alt, Karies in der Vergangenheit und Gegenwart. Zur Epidemiologie einer Volksseuche, in: A. Kemkes-Grottenthaler/W. Henke (eds.), *Pein und Plagen. Aspekte einer Historischen Epidemiologie* (Edition Archaea, Gelsenkirchen-Schwelm 2001) 156-213.

AUFDERHEIDE/RODRÍGUEZ-MARTÍN 1998: A. C. Aufderheide/C. Rodríguez-Martín, *The Cambridge Encyclopedia of Human Paleopathology* (New York 1998).

BASS 2005: W. M. Bass, *Human Osteology* (Columbia [5]2005).

BRÄUER 1988: G. Bräuer, Osteometrie, in: R. Knußmann (ed.), *Anthropologie – Handbuch der vergleichenden Biologie des Menschen* (Stuttgart 1988) 160-231.

BROOKS/SUCHEY 1990: Sh. Brooks/J. Myers Suchey, Skeletal age determination based on the os pubis: A comparison of the Acsádi - Nemeskéri and Suchey - Brooks methods, in: *Journal of Human Evolution* 5, 1990, 227-238.

BROTHWELL 1981: D. R. Brothwell, *Digging up Bones – the Excavation, Treatment and Study of Human Skeletal Remains* (London [3]1981).

CAPASSO et al. 1999: L. Capasso/K. A. R. Kennedy/C. A. Wilczak, *Atlas of Occupational Markers on Human Remains* (Teramo 1999).

CARLI-THIELE 1996: P. Carli-Thiele, Spuren von Mangelerkrankungen an steinzeitlichen Kinderskeletten, in: M. Schultz (ed.), *Fortschritte in der Paläopathologie und Osteoarchäologie* 1 (Göttingen 1996).

CZARNETZKI et al. 1982: A. Czarnetzki/Ch. Uhlig/R. Wolf, *Menschen des Frühen Mittelalters im Spiegel der Anthropologie und Medizin* (Württembergisches Landesmuseum, Stuttgart 1982).

DITTRICK 1979: J. Dittrick, *Sexual dimorphism of the femur and humerus in prehistoric central California skeletal samples* (California State University, Fullerton 1979).

DITTRICK/SUCHEY 2005: J. Dittrick/J. Myers Suchey, Sex determination of prehistoric central California skeletal remains using discriminant analysis of the femur and humerus, in: *American Journal of Physical Anthropology* 70/1, 2003, 3-9.

DRENHAUS 1992: U. Drenhaus, Methoden der Paläodemographie, in: R. Knußmann (ed.), *Wesen und Methoden der Anthropologie* (Handbuch der vergleichenden Biologie des Menschen 2, Stuttgart 1992) 602-616.

GOODMAN/ARMELAGOS 1989: A. H. Goodman/G. J. Armelagos, Infant and childhood morbidity and mortality risks in archaeological populations, in: *World Archaeology* 21, 1989, 225–243.

INTRONA et al. 1998: F. Introna Jr./G. Di Vella/C. Pietro Campobasso, Sex determination by discriminant analysis of patella measurements, in: *Forensic Sciene International* 95, 1998, 39-45.

IŞCAN et al. 1984: M. Yaşar Işcan/S. R. Loth/R. K. Wright, Metamorphosis at the sternal rib end: A new method to estimate age at death in white males, in: *American Journal of Physical Anthropology* 65, 1984, 147-156.

IŞCAN et al. 1985: M. Yaşar Işcan/S. R. Loth/R. K. Wright, Age estimation from the rib by phase analysis: White females, in: *Journal of Forensic Sciences* 30, 1985, 853-863.

JURMAIN 1999: R. Jurmain, *Stories from the Skeleton. Behavioral Reconstruction in Human Osteology* (Amsterdam 1999).

KÖLBL 2004: S. Kölbl, *Das Kinderdefizit im frühen Mittelalter – Realität oder Hypothese. Zur Deutung demographischer Strukturen in Gräberfeldern* (unpublished Ph.D. thesis, Tübingen 2004).

LARSEN 2002: C. Sp. Larsen, Bioarchaeology: The Lives and Lifestyles of Past People, in: *Journal of Archaeological Research* 10, 2002, 119-166.

LARSEN 2006: C. Sp. Larsen, The Changing Face of Bioarchaeology: An Emerging Interdisciplinary Science, in: J. E. Buikstra/L. A. Beck (ed.), *Bioarchaeology: The Contextual Analysis of Human Remains* (Massachusetts 2006) 359-374.

LOVEJOY 1985: C. O. Lovejoy, Dental Wear in the Libben Population: Its Functional Pattern and Role in the Determination of Adult Skeletal Age at Death, in: *American Journal of Physical Anthropology* 68, 1985, 47-56.

LOVEJOY et al. 1985: C. O. Lovejoy et al., Chronological Metamorphosis of the Auricular Surface of the Ilium: A New Method for the Determination of Adult Skeletal Age at Death, in: *American Journal of Physical Anthropology* 68, 1985, 15-28.

MEINDL et al. 1985: R. S. Meindl et al., A Revised Method of Age Determination using the Os Pubis, with a Review and Tests of Accuracy of other Current Methods of Pubic Symphyseal Aging, in: *American Journal of Physical Anthropology* 68, 1995, 29-45.

MEINDL/LOVEJOY 1985: R. S. Meindl/C. O. Lovejoy, Ectocranial Suture Closure, A Revised Method for the Determination of Skeletal Age at Death based on the Lateral-Anterior Sutures, in: *American Journal of Physical Anthropology* 68, 57-66.

MENNINGER/WAIBEL 1996: M. Menninger/O. Waibel, Spondylopathien, in: A. Czarnetzki (ed.), *Stumme Zeugen ihrer Leiden – Paläopathologische Befunde* (Tübingen 1996) 7-40.

ORSCHIEDT 1996: J. Orschiedt, Zahnerkrankungen, in: A. Czarnetzki (ed.), *Stumme Zeugen ihrer Leiden – Paläopathologische Befunde* (Tübingen 1996) 111-132.

PEARSON 1899: K. Pearson, On the reconstruction of stature of prehistoric races. Mathematic contributions to the theory of evolution, in: *Philosophical Transactions of the Royal Society A* 192, 1899, 169-244.

PHENICE 1969: T. W. Phenice, A newly developed visual method of sexing the Os pubis, in: *American Journal of Physical Anthropology* 30, 1969, 297-301.

RÖSING et al. 2005: F. Rösing et al., Empfehlungen für die forensische Geschlechts- und Altersdiagnose am Skelett, in: *Rechtsmedizin* 15, 2005, 32-38.

SCHEUER/BLACK 2000: L. Scheuer/S. Black, *Developmental Juvenile Osteology* (San Diego 2000).

SCHULTZ 1988: M. Schultz, Paläopathologische Diagnostik, in: R. Knußmann (ed.), *Anthropologie, Handbuch der vergleichenden Biologie des Menschen* (Stuttgart 1988) 480-496.

SCHUTKOWSKI 1990: H. Schutkowski, *Zur Geschlechtsdiagnose von Kinderskeletten – Morphognostische, metrische und diskriminanzanalytische Untersuchungen* (unpublished Ph.D. thesis, Göttingen 1990).

STEELE 1975: D. G. Steele, The Estimation of Sex on the Basis of the Talus and Calcaneus, in: *American Journal of Physical Anthropology* 45, 1975, 581-588.

STEWART 1979, Th. D. Stewart, *Essentials of Forensic Anthropology* (Springfield 1979).

STLOUKAL/HANÁKOVÁ 1978: M. Stloukal/H. Hanáková, Die Länge der Längsknochen altslawischer Bevölkerungen unter besonderer Berücksichtigung von Wachstumsfugen, in: *Homo – Zeitschrift für die vergleichende Forschung am Menschen* 29, 1978, 53-69.

UBELAKER 1999: D. H. Ubelaker, *Human Skeletal Remains – Excavation, Analysis, Interpretation* (Washington, D.C. [3]1999).

UHLIG 1982: Ch. Uhlig, *Zur paläopathologischen Differentialdiagnose von Tumoren an Skelettteilen* (Landesdenkmalamt Baden-Württemberg, Stuttgart 1982).

WAPLER et al. 2004: U. Wapler/E. Crubézy/M. Schultz, Is Cribra Orbitalia Synonymous With Anemia? Analysis and Interpretation of Cranial Pathology in Sudan, in: *American Journal of Physical Anthropology* 123, 2004, 333-339.

WURM/LEIHMEISTER 1986: H. Wurm/H. Leihmeister, Ein Beitrag zur spezifischen Auswahl von Vorschlägen zur Körperhöhenrekonstruktion nach Skelettfunden, zur Vergleichbarkeit von Schätzergebnissen und zur allgemeinen Problematik realistischer Lebendhöhenschätzungen, in: *Gegenbaurs morphologisches Jahrbuch* 132/1, 1986, 69-110.

Y`EDYNAK/FLEISCH 1983: G. y`Edynak/S. Fleisch, Microevolution and Biological Adaptability in the Transition from Food-collecting to Food-producing in the Iron Gates of Yugoslavia, in: *Journal of Human Evolution* 12, 1983, 279-296.

Historic Plant Records from Tombs of Gebel Asyut al-gharbi

Ahmed A. El-Khatib

Summary

Twenty-eight taxa of plant species characteristics of local and neighbouring flora were identified during the inspection of 1080 objects retrieved during fieldwork (including acacia, tamarisk, palm, Christ's Thorn, willow, fig, sycamore fig, cedar, onion, barsah, olive, balanos tree, peach, almond, among others). Variations in the proportions of taxa are interpreted to reconstruct possible human activities associated with plant processing as well as their origin. The analysis of the data shows a pattern of continued utilization of taxa throughout the occupation. This includes the use of different vegetative parts (trunk, branches, fruits and flowers), genera and species of different life forms (trees, shrubs, herbaceous plants). It also reflects the status of trade between the native inhabitants and their neighbour countries.

Introduction

Plant remains found in archaeological sites are key evidence providing information on past territory management and plant uses as well as plant cover and environmental reconstructions (BIRKS et al. 1988; HARVEY/FULLER 2005). They also reflect the status of trade between the native inhabitants and the neighbouring countries. Many authors (HARRIS/HILLMAN 1989; NEUMANN et al. 2003; VAN DER VEEN 1999; ZOHARY/HOPF 2000) report plant exploitation as a fundamental aspect of human cultures. The recovery and identification of plant remains and microfossils have provided archaeologists with the means to reconstruct a more comprehensive view of the past human populations.

"Due to the poor history of research and the deprivation of many of its monuments, Asyut had been forgotten for a long time. …the reconstruction of the history of the ancient necropolis, and thereby of the ancient town and its different fortunes as a city of culture, as a border town and as a wounded city, as well as the determination of various phases and functions concerning the use of the western mountain" (KAHL 2007: 1) were the main goals of The Asyut Project. Accordingly, this botanical research was conducted to identify plant macro remains and reconstruct possible human activities associated with plant species exploitation as well as their origin.

The study area

Asyut was the main town in the 13th province of Upper Egypt in ancient times. It occupies a strategic position at a bend in the river and is still a major regional center. The town was especially important during the Middle Kingdom, when huge rock cut tombs of the governors of the town were built (Pl.14). The study area consists of three tombs, Siut III (N12.1, Pl. 24-25), Siut IV (N12.2, Pl. 26-27), and N13.1 (Pl. 28-29) of the First

Intermediate Period/Eleventh Dynasty, cutting the rocks of Gebel Asyut al-gharbi, Asyut, Egypt. These tombs have been reused during the later periods and were also visited by numerous scholars. They were partly destroyed during the last centuries.

Material and methods

During August-September 2008 an archaeobotanical inspection was conducted at Gebel Asyut al-gharbi as an activity of The Asyut Project, an Egyptian-German cooperation of Sohag University (Egypt) and Johannes Gutenberg-University Mainz (Germany) in the sixth season of fieldwork. Visible plant objects were gathered during the excavation of Tombs Siut III (N12.1), IV (N12.2), and N13.1, from around the mummies within the coffins, materials of baskets and mats, models and other material buried in the debris. They have been transferred to the magazine, where they were classified, examined and identified. The examination of seed-, fruit- and plant-remains was conducted with the naked eye and magnifying lenses. Small samples of the wooden artefacts were removed and prepared for examination using dissecting binocular light microscope (Olympus) and scanning electron microscopy (JSM-5300LV; JEOL). Identification and nomenclature of these plant objects occurred according to TÄCKHOLM 1974 and BOULOS 1995.

Results and discussion

The inspection of 1080 objects showed that they represent the two main categories of the plant kingdom, gymnosperms and angiosperms. The identified objects included seeds, fruits, flowers, reeds, rushes, tree remains and worked wood. The majority of seeds were of native plant species such as the date palm *(Phoenix dactylifera)*, doum palm *(Hyphaene thebaica* Mart.*)*, barsah *(Mimusops schimperi)*, cordia *(Cordia myxa)*, and the common olive *(Olea europaea)*. All of these species were previously described by other authors as ancient and considered the main components of the plant communities during the Pharaonic Period (EL-DIN 2005). Today, the majority of these species is rare and belongs to the almost eradicated flora of Egypt. Other recorded seeds belonged to foreign species, characterizing the flora of the neighbour areas such as Lebanon, Turkey, Syria, and Asia, and included peach *(Prunus persica L.)*, plum *(Prunus domestica)*, almond *(Prunus amygdalus)*, walnut *(Juglans regia)*, and Turkish hazel *(Corylus americana)*.

The fruit objects were represented by the native species juniper *(Juniperus phoenicea)*, cordia *(Cordia myxa)*, balanos tree *(Balanites aegyptiaca)* and Christ's Thorn *(Zizyphus spina-christi)*. Foreign species in this study were represented by cypress, hazel and walnut. It is important to mention here that the last two species may be refuse from visitors during other excavations in recent years. Juniper (al-'ar'ar), including *Juniperus phoenicea*, has been found in ancient Egyptian tombs at multiple sites. The inspected objects included only two floral objects of Asteraceae type called marigold *(Calendula aegyptiaca)* and pine cone *(Pinus halepensis*). Reeds and rushes are among the botanical elements recorded during the inspection of the tombs. Reeds are represented by common reed *(Phragmites australis*) and papyrus plants *(Cyperus papyrus*). Desmostachya or kind of "halfa grass" *(Desmostachya bipinnata)* and cogon grass *(Imperata cylindrica)* represented the rushes species in the inspected objects. These plant objects were found to be the bulk material for basketry, construction and mats manufacture. It is important to mention here that all of these types are native species and constitute the main component of the current flora and plant communities of the swamp- and canal bank habitat in Egypt (EL-KHATIB 1996; 1997; MOHAMED/EL-KHATIB 2001).

The woody type objects of plant remains were acacia *(Acacia nilotica)*, tamarisk *(Tamarix articulata)*, date palm *(Phoenix dactylifera)*, Christ's Thorn *(Zizyphus spina-christi)*, willow *(Salix subserrata)*, sycamore fig *(Ficus sycomorus)*, pine *(Pinus halepensis)*, and oak *(Quercus* sp*)*; cereal type of broom-corn *(Sorghum vulgare)*; vegetable type of onion *(Allium cepa)*; crop type of flax *(Linum usitatissimum)* and fruit type of grape vine *(Vitis vinifera)* and fig *(Ficus carica)*. These remains were found as plant branches detached in the debris. These objects used to be elements of the local flora.

The surviving architecture at many tombs shows considerable use of wood in a wide range of quantity and quality. Much of the wood was probably local. However, good wood had to be imported by local inhabitants. As far back as Old Kingdom Egypt, timber was transported from the neighbour areas to Egypt in multiple shiploads (MEYERS 1997).

The inspected wooden artefacts predominately consisted of local acacia, willow, tamarisk and sycamore fig trees. Other woodcraft objects were made of cypress *(Cupressus sempervirens)*, ebony *(Diospyros sp.)* and cedar *(Cedrus libani)* which were either traded or imported from as far as East Africa, Asia Minor, Lebanon, Syria, Turkey, India, Sri Lanka, Somalia and Greece (WESTERN/MCLEOD 1995). This material denotes that the local wood in general was of softwood nature and used for construction purposes and the manufacturing of boats, models and some farm tools. Imported wood types were of hardwood nature and used for manufacturing coffins, weapons and furniture.

In conclusion, the number of plant remains recorded during this inspection shows 28 species, of which 19 were native and the rest foreign. The majority of foreign species was of woody type and was used for the manufacture of coffins, furniture, models and farming tools.

References:

BIRKS et al. 1988: H. H. Birks, H. J. B. Birks, P. E. Kaland, D. Moe (eds.), *The Cultural Landscape. Past, Present and Future* (Cambridge 1988).

BOULOS 1995: L. Boulos, *Flora of Egypt: Checklist* (Cairo 1995).

EL-DIN 2005: A. G. El-Din Fahmy, Missing plant macro remains as indicators of plant exploitation in predynastic Egypt, in: *Vegetation History and Archaeobotany* 14, 2005, 287-294.

EL-KHATIB 1996: A. A. El-Khatib, On the ecology of the swampy vegetation in Sohag area, Upper Egypt, in: *Pure Science and engineering series* 5/2 (Abhath Al-Yarmouk University) 1996, 51-61.

EL-KHATIB 1997: A. A. El-Khatib, Former and present vegetation of Kraman Island, Upper Egypt, in: *Arab Gulf Journal of Scientific Research* 15/3, 1997, 661-682.

HARRIS/HILLMAN 1989: D. R. Harris, G. Hillman (eds.), Foraging and Farming: The Evolution of Plant Exploitation (One World Archaeology Series 13, London 1989).

HARVEY/FULLER 2005: E. L. Harvey, D. Q. Fuller, Investigating crop processing using phytolith analysis: the example of rice and millets, in: *Journal of Archaeological Science* 32, 2005, 739-752.

KAHL 2007: J. Kahl, *Ancient Asyut. The First Synthesis after 300 Years of Research* (The Asyut Project 1, Wiesbaden 2007).

MEYERS 1997: E. M. Meyers, *The Oxford Encyclopedia of Archaeology in the Near East* (New York 1997).

MOHAMED/EL-KHATIB 2001: M. K. Mohamed, A. A. El-Khatib, Species composition and habitat heterogeneity on the islands of the River Nile, Egypt, in: *Bulletin of the Faculty of Science, Assiut University* 31, 2001, 123-135.

NEUMANN et al. 2003: K. Neumann, A. Butler, S. Kahlheber (eds.), *Food, Fuel and Fields. Progress in African Archaeobotany* (Africa Praehistorica 15, Cologne 2003).

TÄCKHOLM 1974: V. Täckholm, *Student Flora of Egypt* (Cairo ^{2}1974).

VAN DER VEEN 1999: M. van der Veen (ed.), *The Exploitation of Plant Resources in Ancient Africa* (New York 1999).

WESTERN/MCLEOD 1995: A. C. Western, W. McLeod, Woods used in Egyptian Bows and Arrows, in: *The Journal of Egyptian Archaeology* 81, 1995, 77-94.

ZOHARY/HOPF 2000: D. Zohary, M. Hopf, *Domestication of Plants in the Old World – The origin and spread of cultivated plants in West Asia, Europe, and the Nile Valley* (Oxford ^{3}2000).

Plates

Pl. 1a: Tomb N13.1, Graffito N7: reign of Amenhotep III (© Barthel).

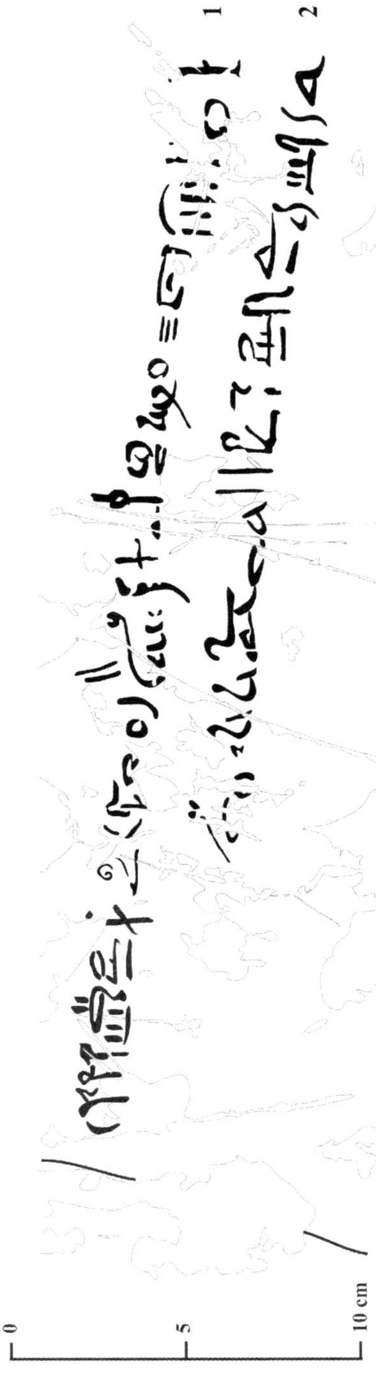

Pl. 1b: Tomb N13.1, Graffito N7: reign of Amenhotep III (© Verhoeven; drawing: S. A. Gülden).

Pl. 2a: Tomb N13.1, Graffito O2: reign of Ramesses XI (© Barthel).

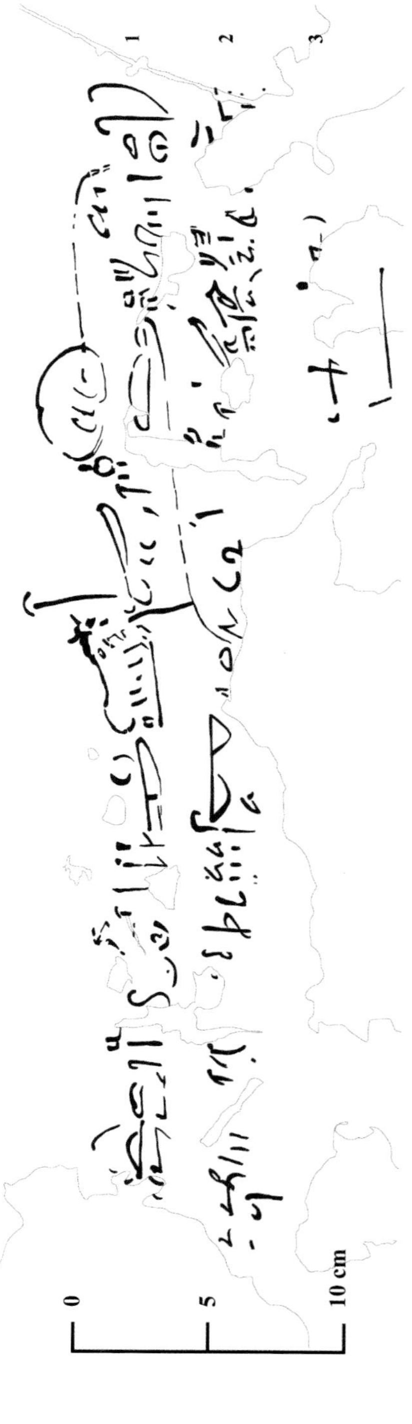

Pl. 2b: Tomb N13.1, Graffito O2: reign of Ramesses XI (© Verhoeven; drawing: S. A. Gülden).

Pl. 3: Tomb N13.1, Graffito N10: scribe Men (© Kahl).

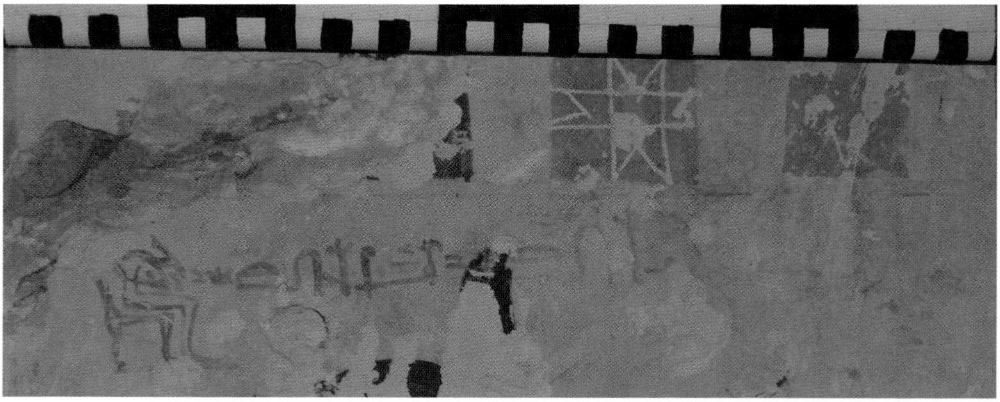

Pl. 4a: Tomb N13.1, Graffito S24: scribe Kha-em-waset (© Kahl).

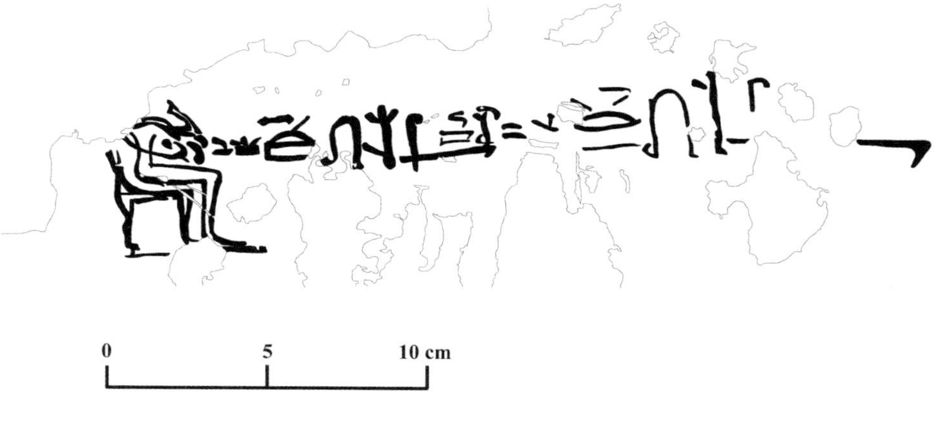

Pl. 4b: Tomb N13.1, Graffito S24: scribe Kha-em-waset
(© Verhoeven; drawing: S. A. Gülden).

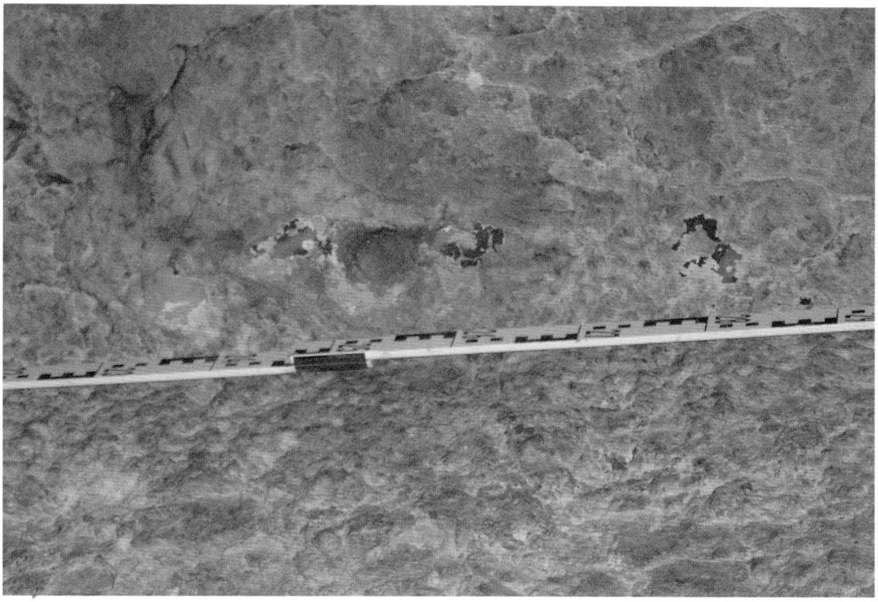

Pl. 5a: Tomb O13.1 (Tomb II): northern niche; remains of colored plaster (© The Asyut Project; Becker 2008).

Pl. 5b: Tomb O13.1 (Tomb II): remains of inscriptions above southern niche (© The Asyut Project; Becker 2008).

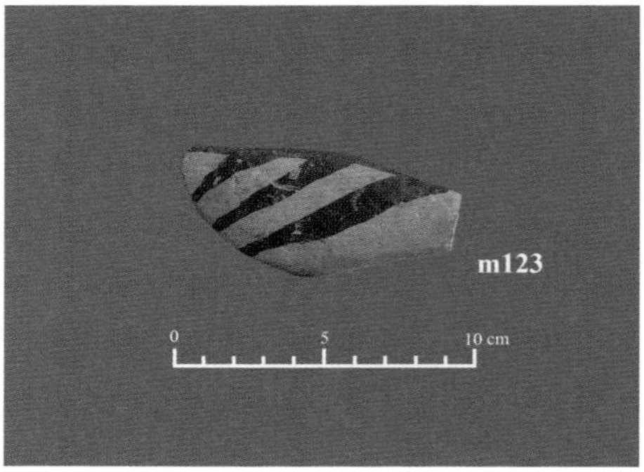

Pl. 6a: Bird's wings belonging to offering bearer (© The Asyut Project; Zöller).

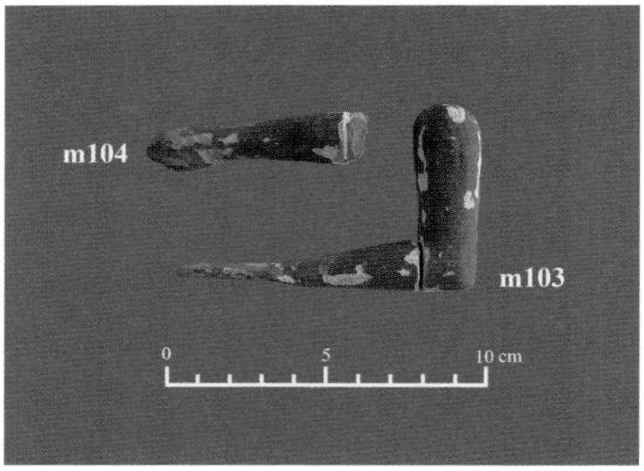

Pl. 6b: Arms of model figures (© The Asyut Project; Zöller).

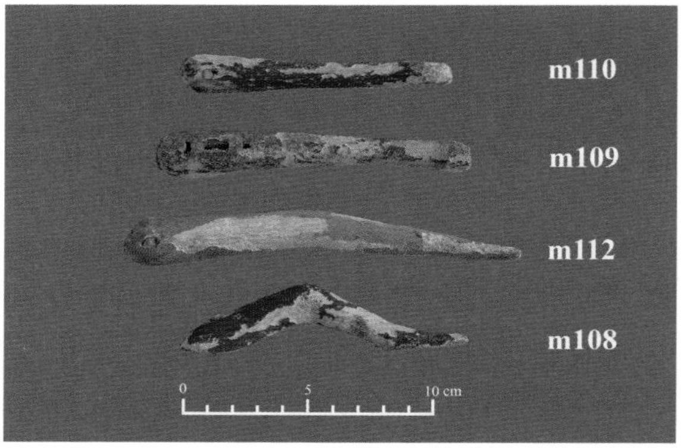

Pl. 6c: Arms of model figures (© The Asyut Project; Zöller).

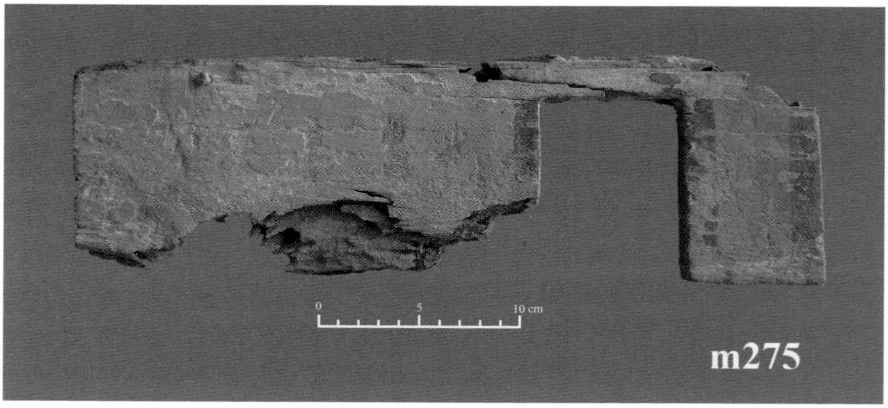

Pl. 6d: Outer wall of model building (© The Asyut Project; Zöller).

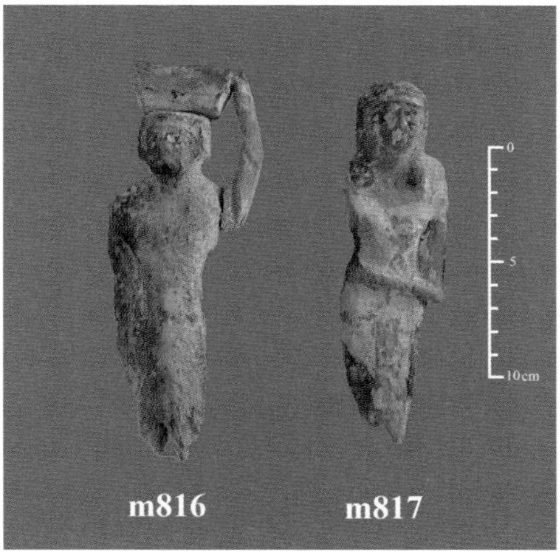

Pl. 7a: Offering bearer and female figure (© The Asyut Project; Zöller).

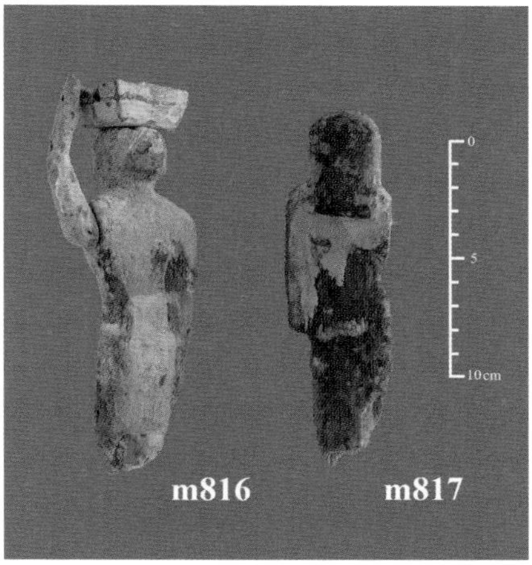

Pl. 7b: Offering bearer and female figure (© The Asyut Project; Zöller).

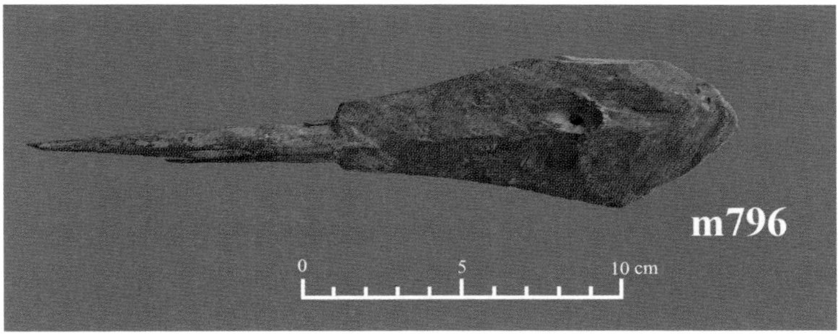

Pl. 7c: Model rudder (© The Asyut Project; Zöller).

Pl. 7d: Model vats (© The Asyut Project; Zöller).

Pl. 8a: Offering tray, decorated with white dots; OT 44 = S06/st426 (© Kahl).

Pl. 8b: OT 28 = S04/st267 B (© Kahl).

Pl. 8c: OT 28 = S04/st267 B, detail (© Kahl).

Pl 8d: OT 28 = S04/st267 B, rear view, detail (© The Asyut Project; Kilian).

Pl. 8e: OT 25 = S04/213, fragment of an oval tray with a kind of fowl and reminiscent of the *jwꜥ*-hieroglyph (© The Asyut Project; Kilian).

Pl. 9a: OT 41 = S05/128, covered with deep red colour and displaying the lower part of a *ḥs*-vase and a square loaf of bread (© The Asyut Project; Kilian).

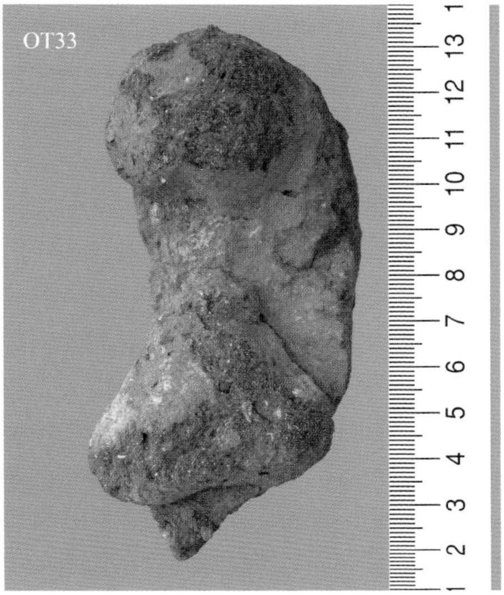

Pl. 9b: Triangular and round loaves of bread; OT 33 = S04/st310.5 (© The Asyut Project; Kilian).

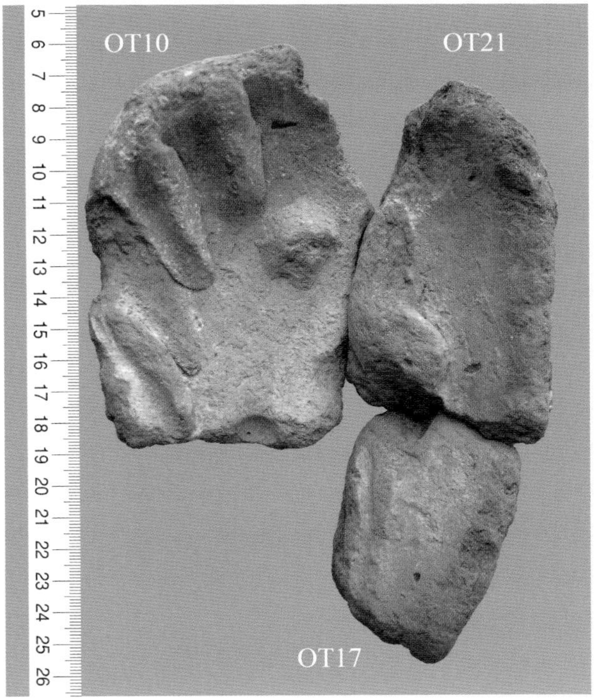

Pl. 9c: Oval tray found in Asyut, OT 10-OT 21-OT 17 = S04/142-S04/173-S04/149 (© Kahl).

Pl. 10a: S06/st574, unglazed earthenware (© The Asyut Project; Yasin/Mahmoud).

Pl. 10b: S07/st253 (© The Asyut Project; Yasin/Abu Bakr).

Pl. 11a: S05/st94 B (© The Asyut Project; Yasin/Mahmoud).

Pl. 11b: S06/st121, fragment of underglazed-painted pottery (© The Asyut Project; Yasin/Mahmoud).

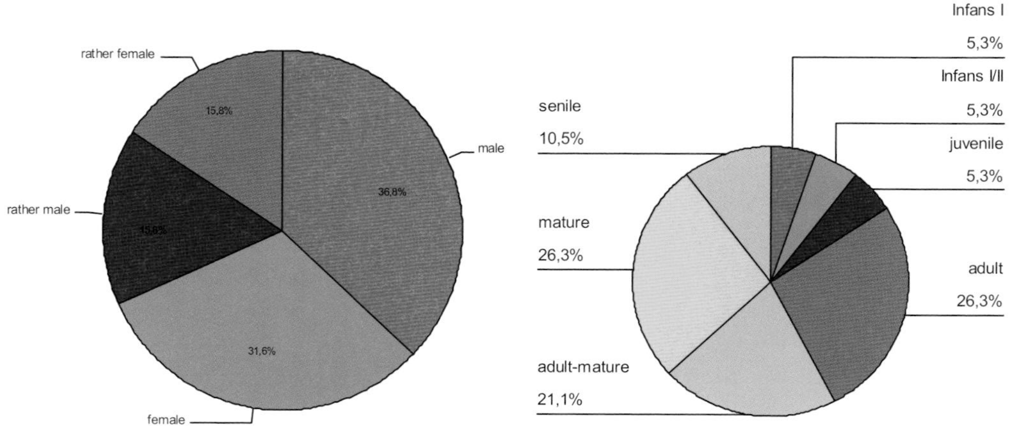

Pl. 12a: Sex and age distribution in the Asyut sample, relative frequency.

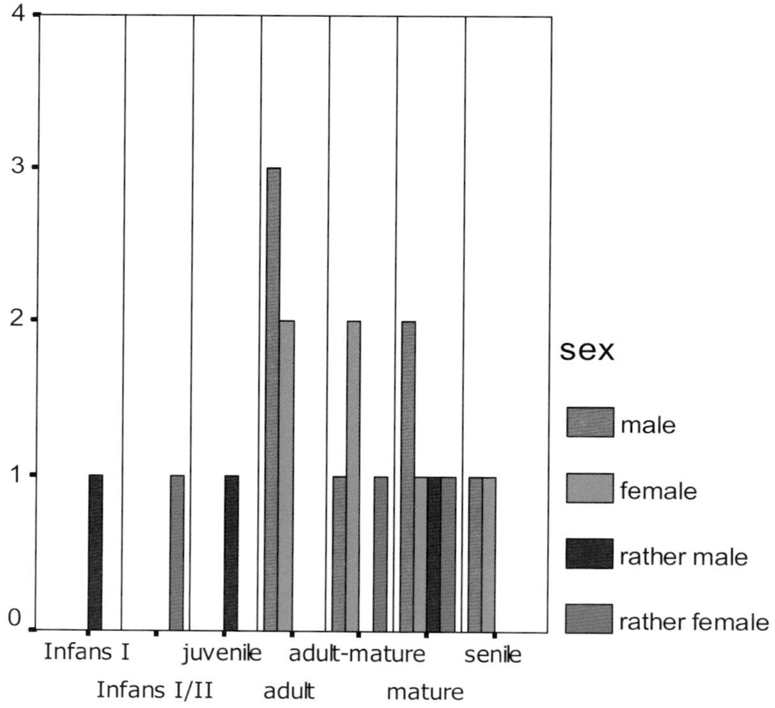

Pl. 12b: Sex and age distribution in the Asyut sample, cross table, absolute frequency.

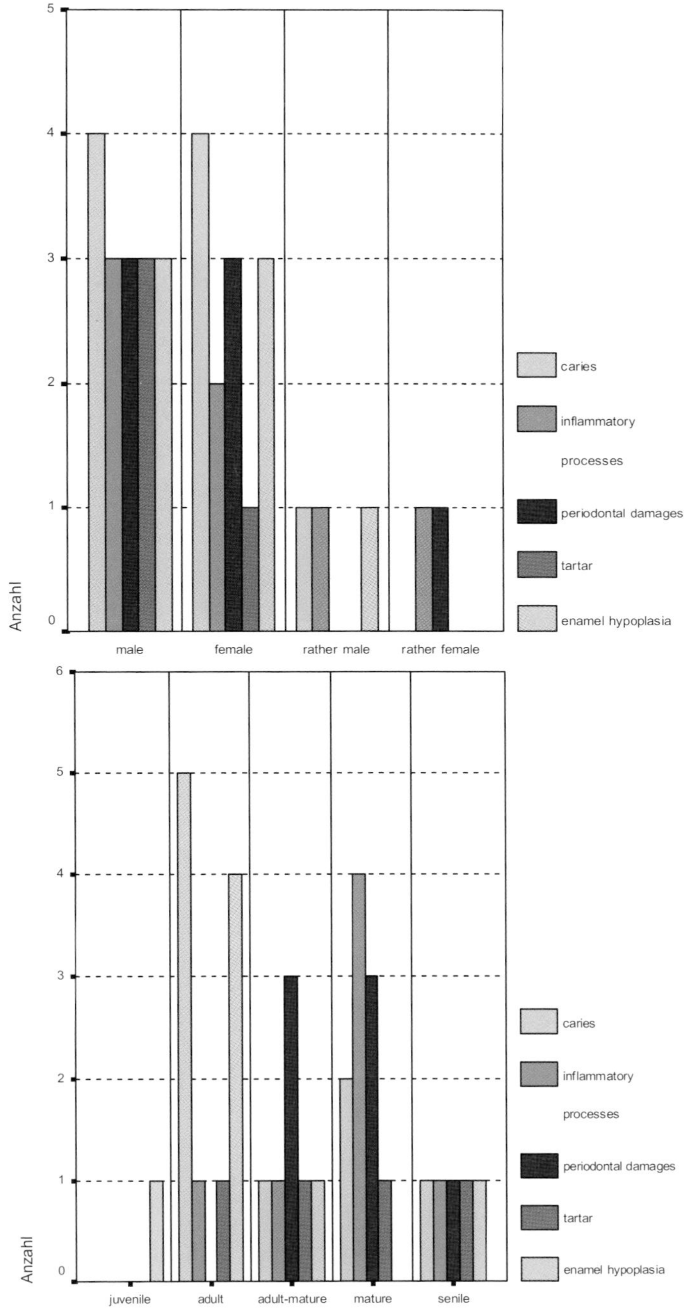

Pl. 13: Sex and age distribution of dental pathologies in the Asyut sample, cross table, absolute frequency.

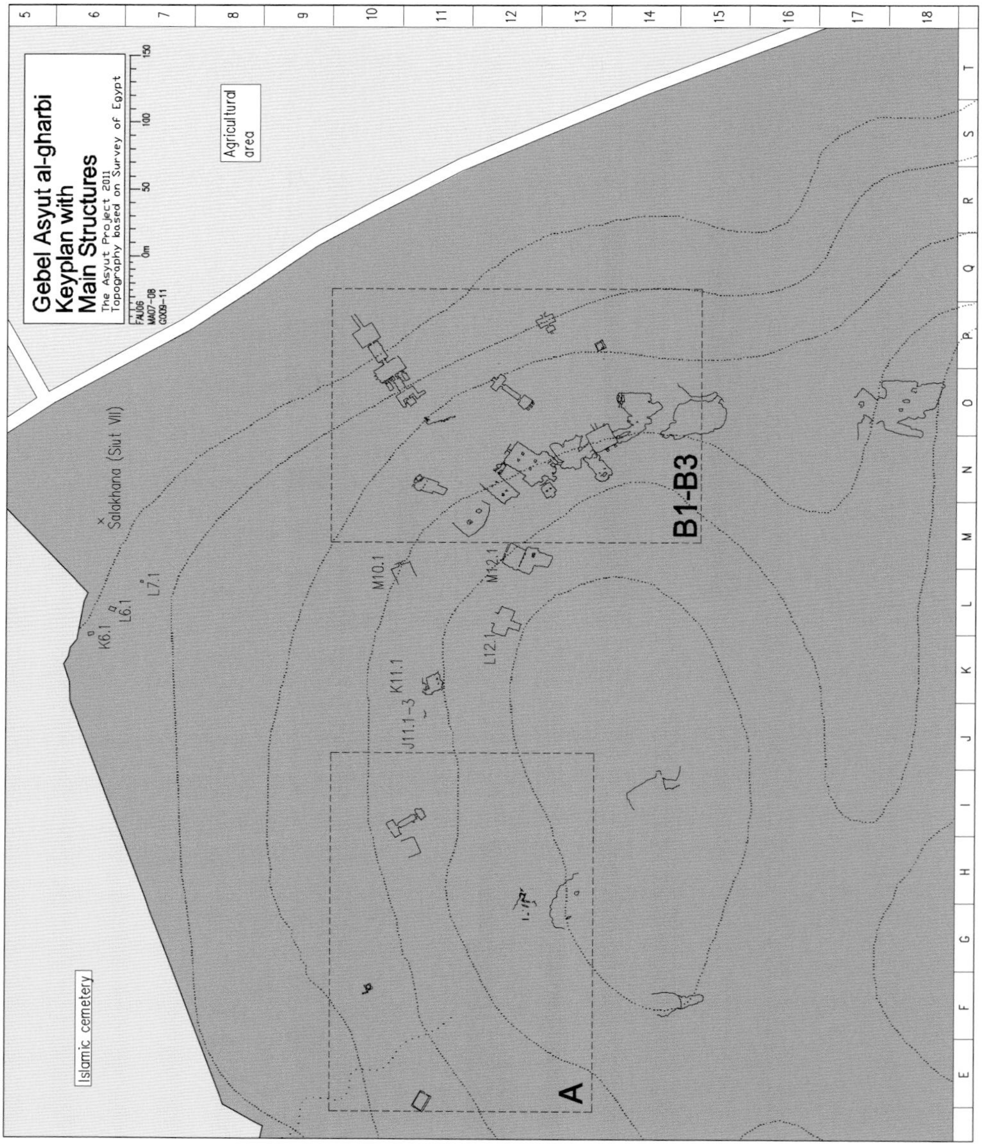

Pl. 14: Gebel Asyut al-gharbi, keyplan with main structures (© The Asyut Project; Fauerbach/Maschke/Goerlich).

Pl. 15: Gebel Asyut al-gharbi, view from north-east (© Barthel 2010).

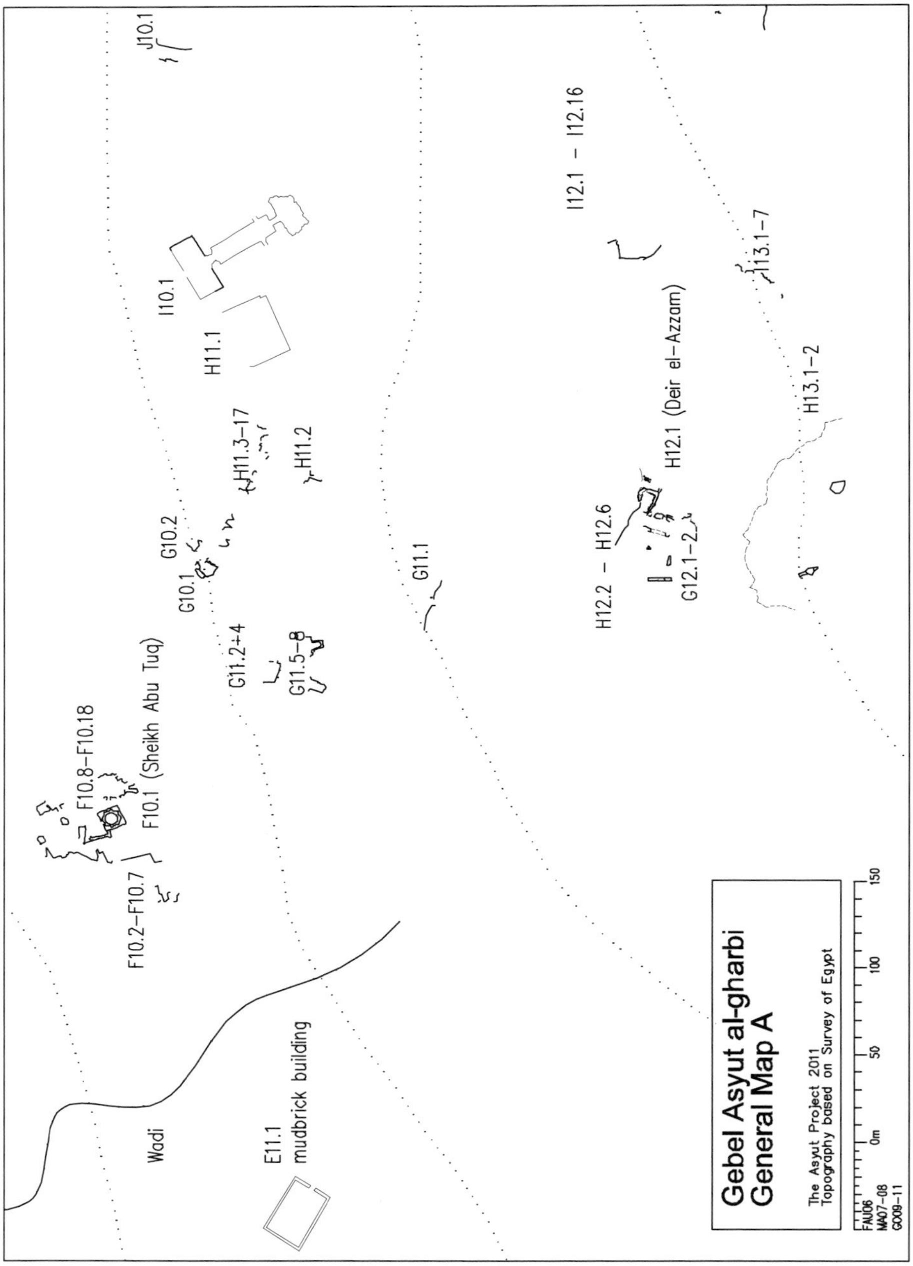

Pl. 16: General Map, section A (cf. Pl. 14), western part of Gebel Asyut al-gharbi.

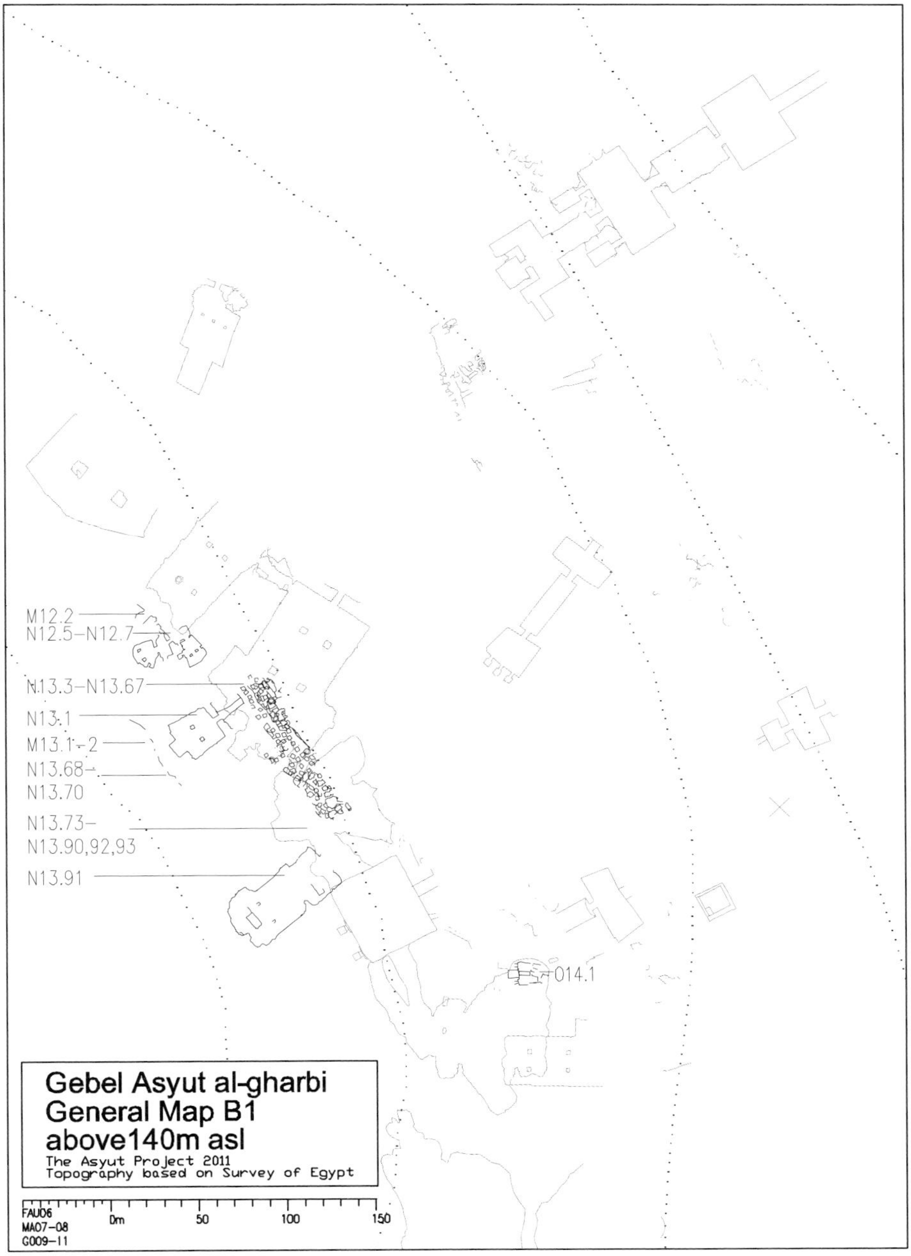

Pl. 17: General Map, section B1 (cf. Pl. 14), step 7.

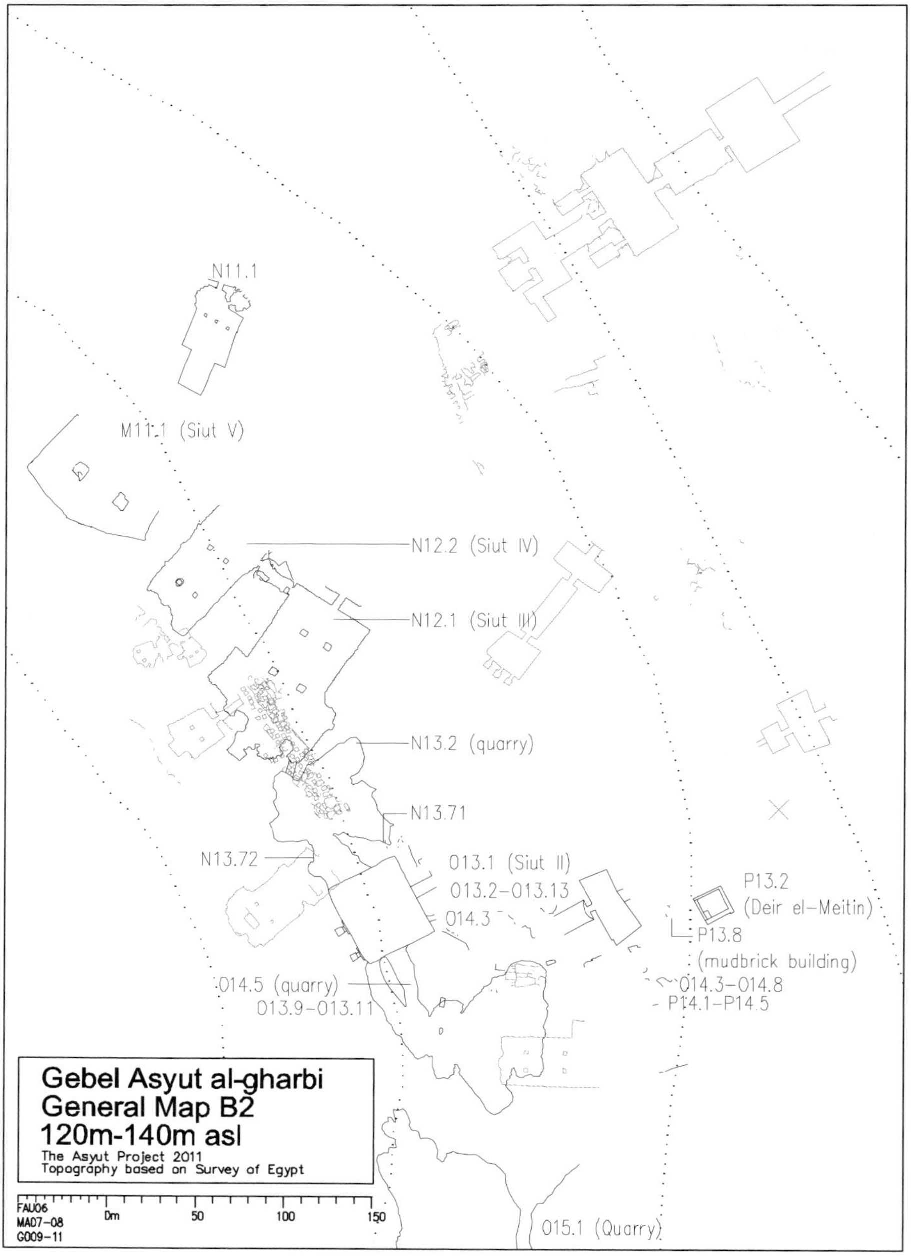

Pl. 18: General Map, section B2, steps 5-6.

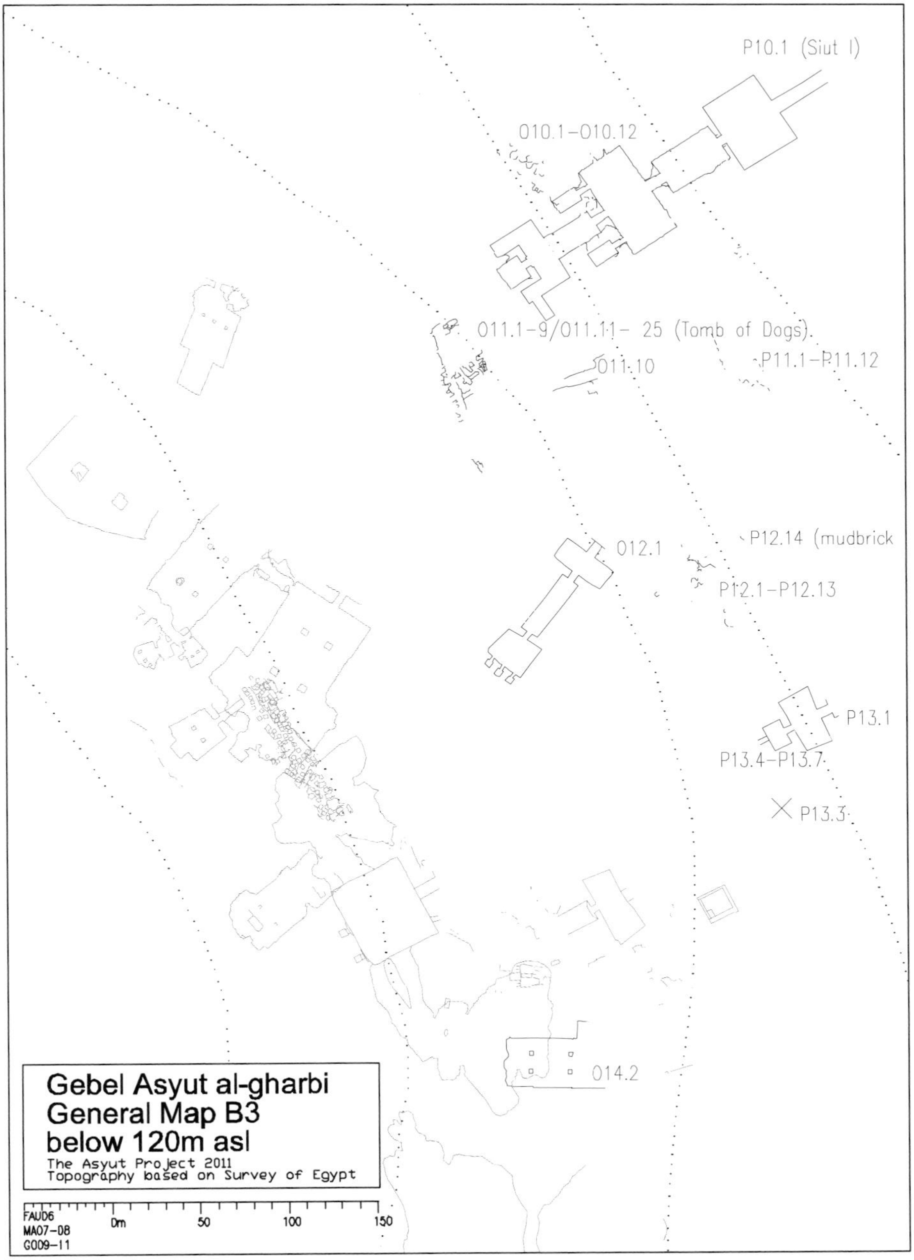

Pl. 19: General Map, section B3, steps 2-4.

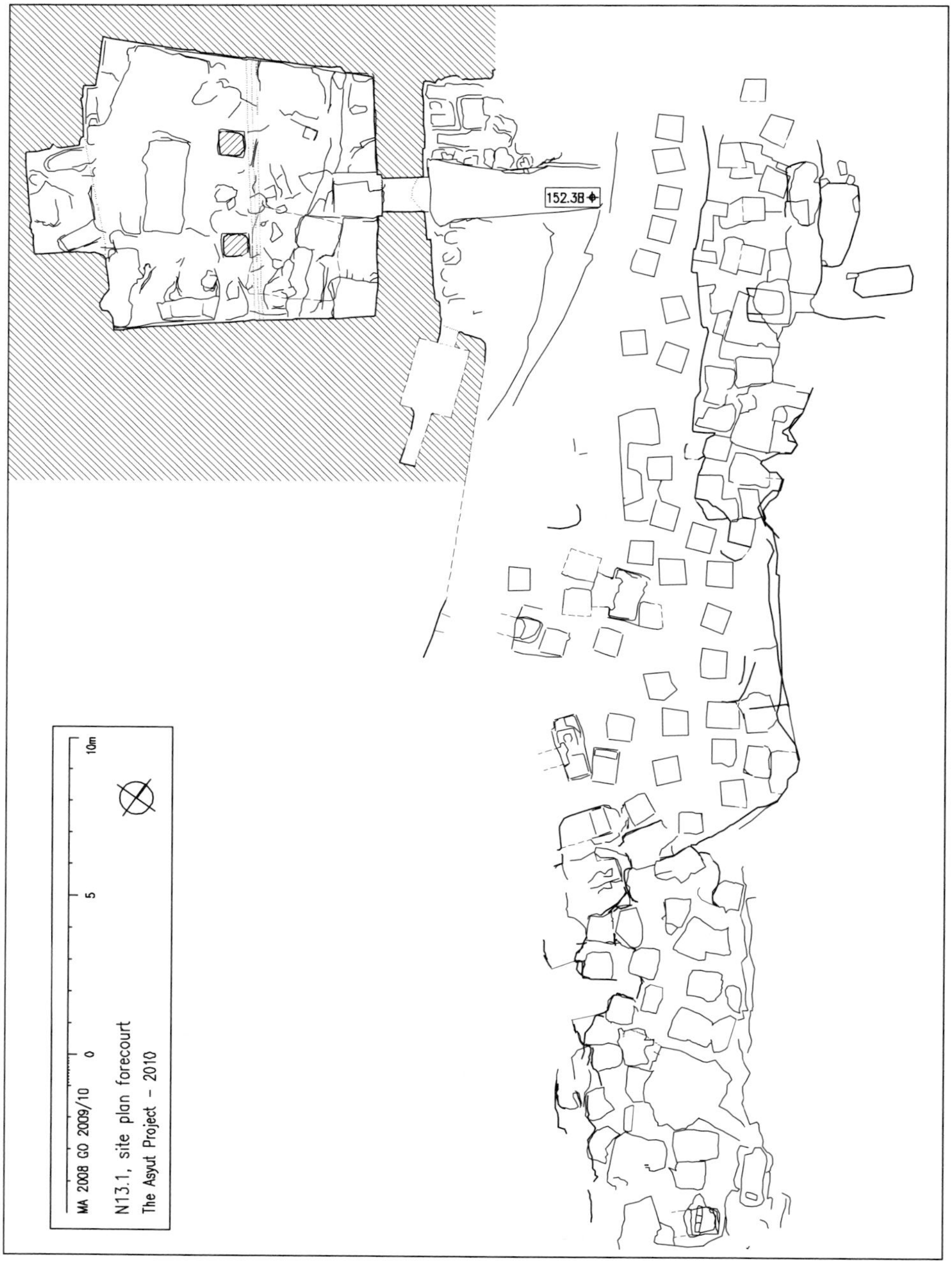

Pl. 20: Shaft tombs on step 7, east of Tomb N13.1.

Pl. 21: Shaft tombs on step 7, view from north (© Barthel 2010).

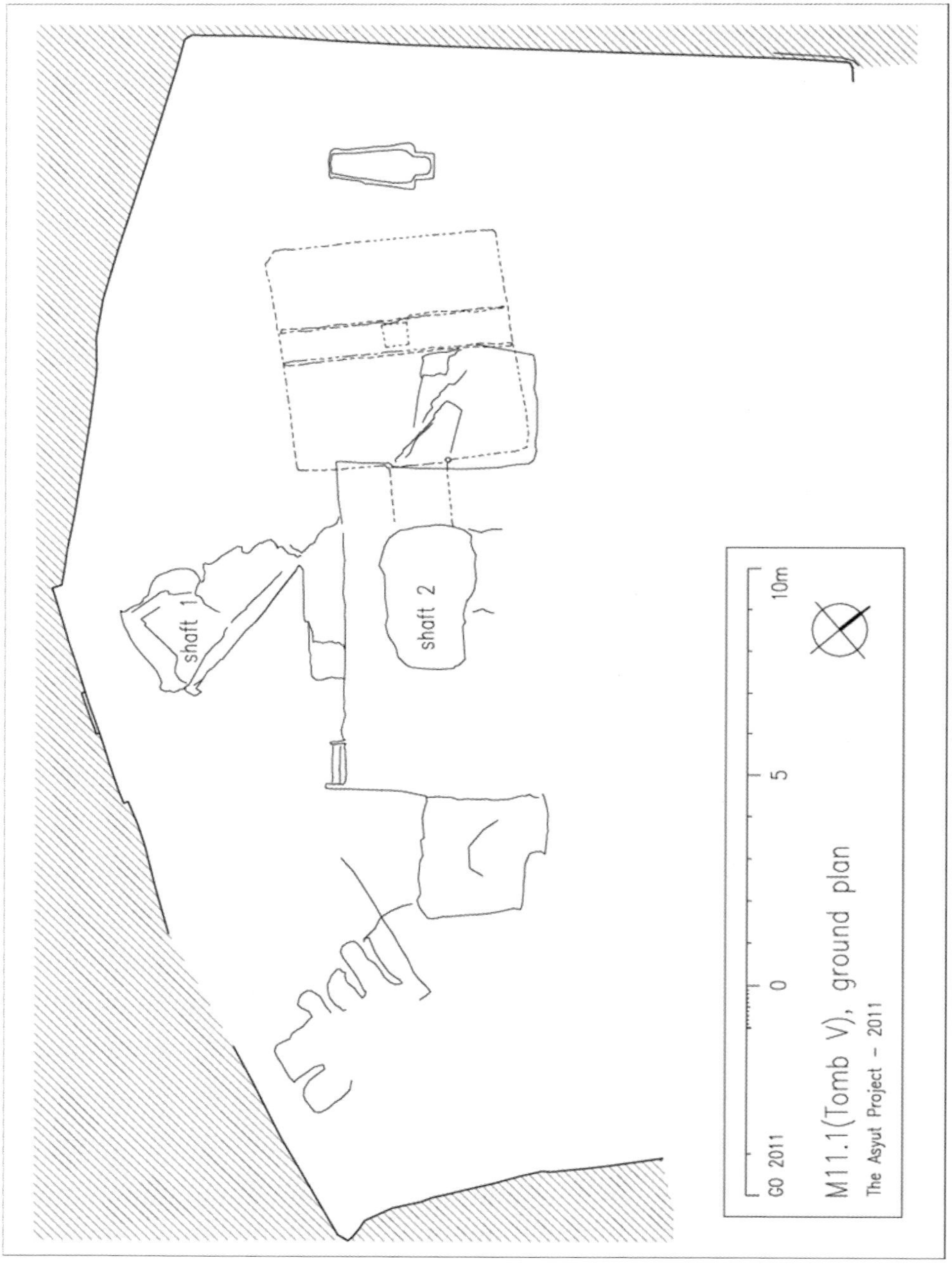

Pl. 22: Tomb M11.1 (Tomb V), ground plan (© The Asyut Project; Goerlich 2011).

Pl. 23: Tomb M11.1 (Tomb V), inner hall with two shafts (© Barthel 2010).

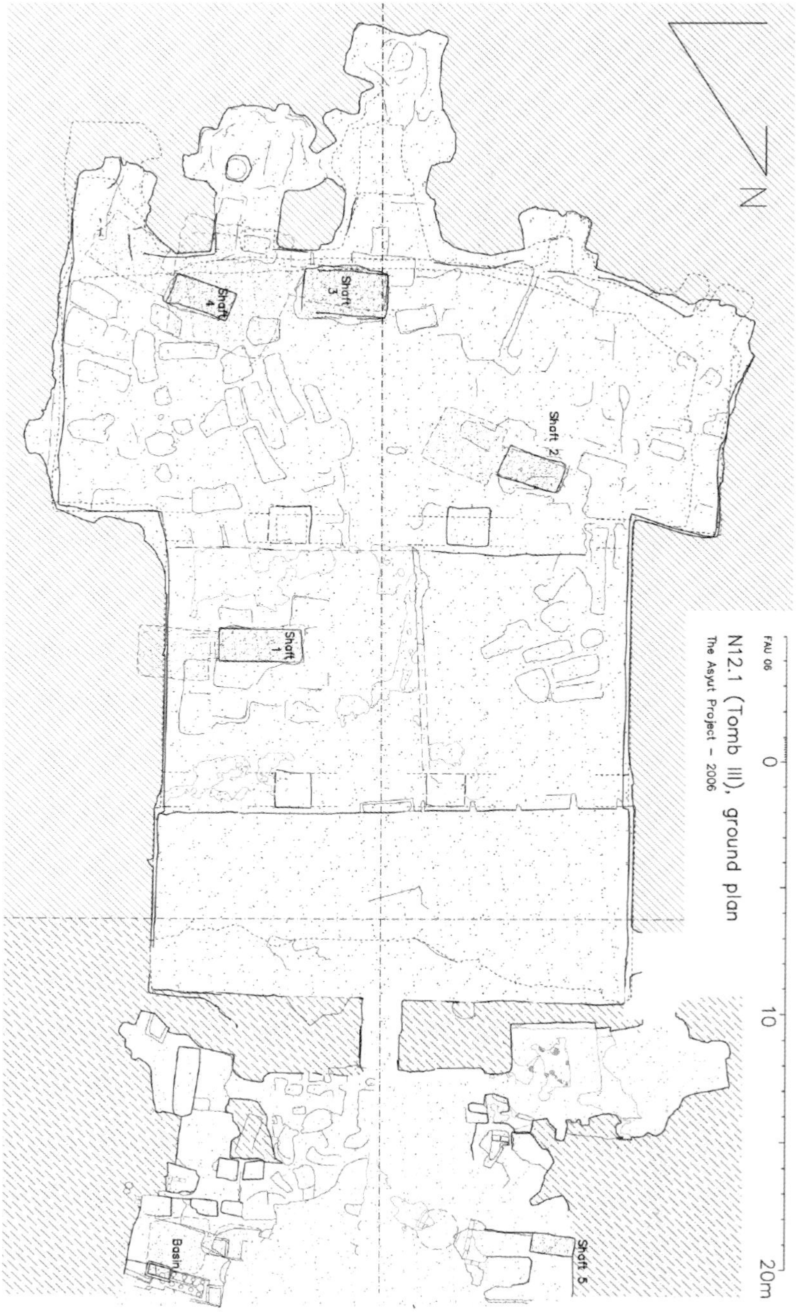

Pl. 24: Tomb N12.1 (Tomb III), ground plan (© The Asyut Project; Fauerbach 2006).

Pl. 25: Tomb N12.1 (Tomb III), view from the entrance area (The Asyut Project 2006).

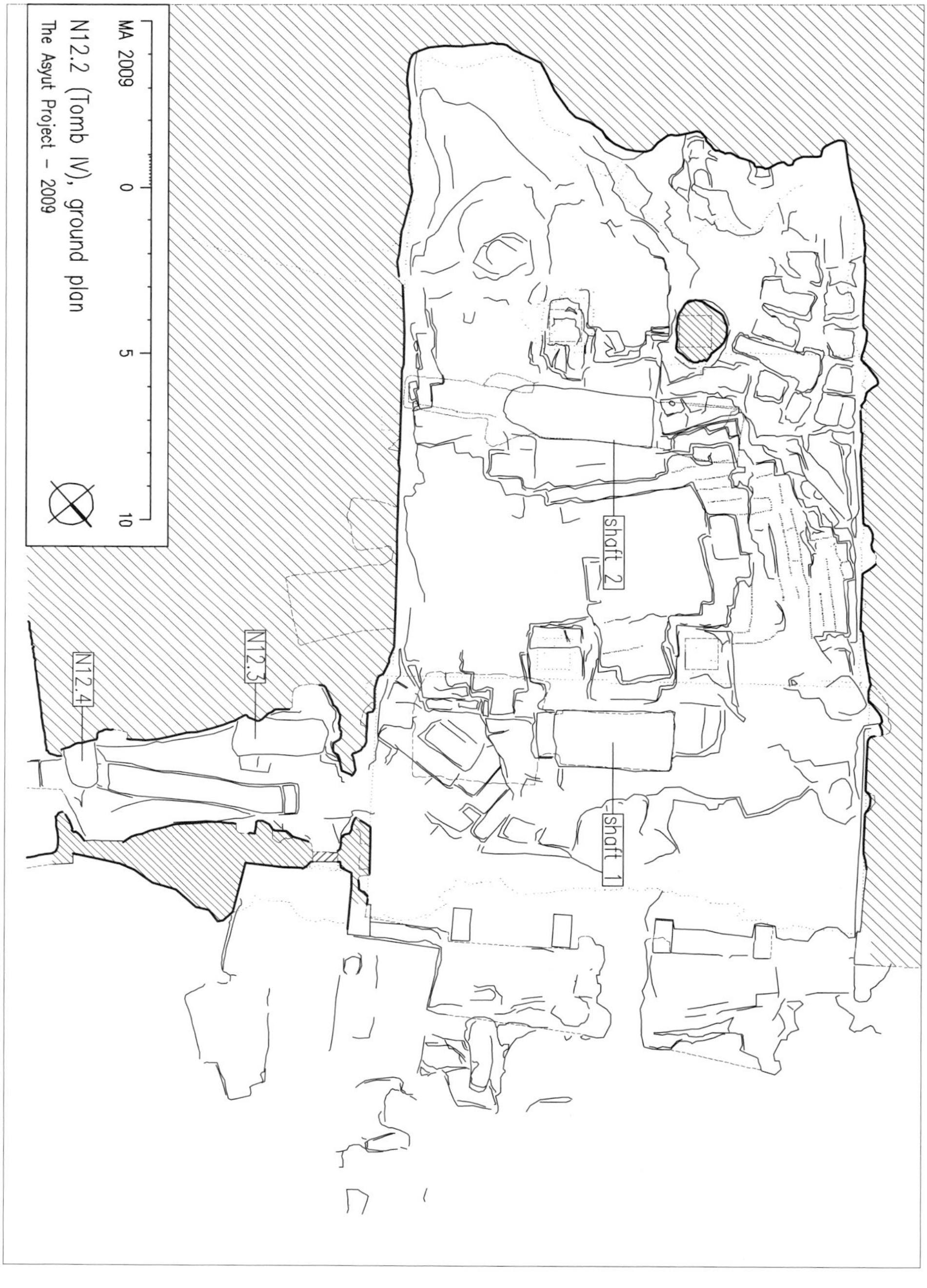

Pl. 26: Tomb N12.2 (Tomb IV), ground plan (© The Asyut Project; Maschke 2009).

Pl. 27a: Tomb N12.2 (Tomb IV), view from entrance area (© Kahl 2006).

Pl. 27b: Tomb N12.2 (Tomb IV), northern wall (© Kahl 2006).

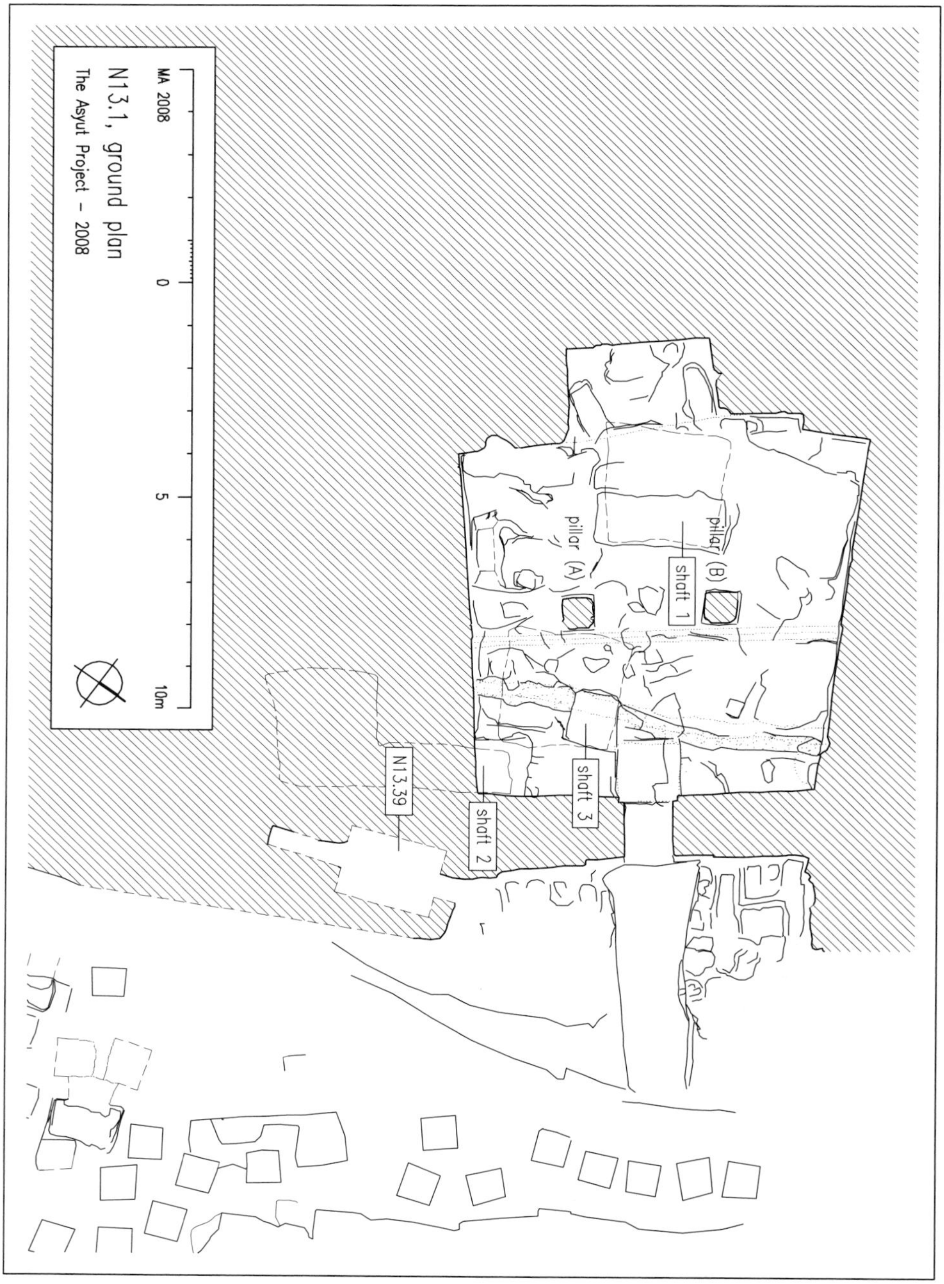

Pl. 28: Tomb N13.1, ground plan (© The Asyut Project; Maschke 2008).

Pl. 29a: Tomb N13.1, entrance (© Kahl 2006).

Pl. 29b: Tomb N13.1, view from the entrance (© Barthel 2007).

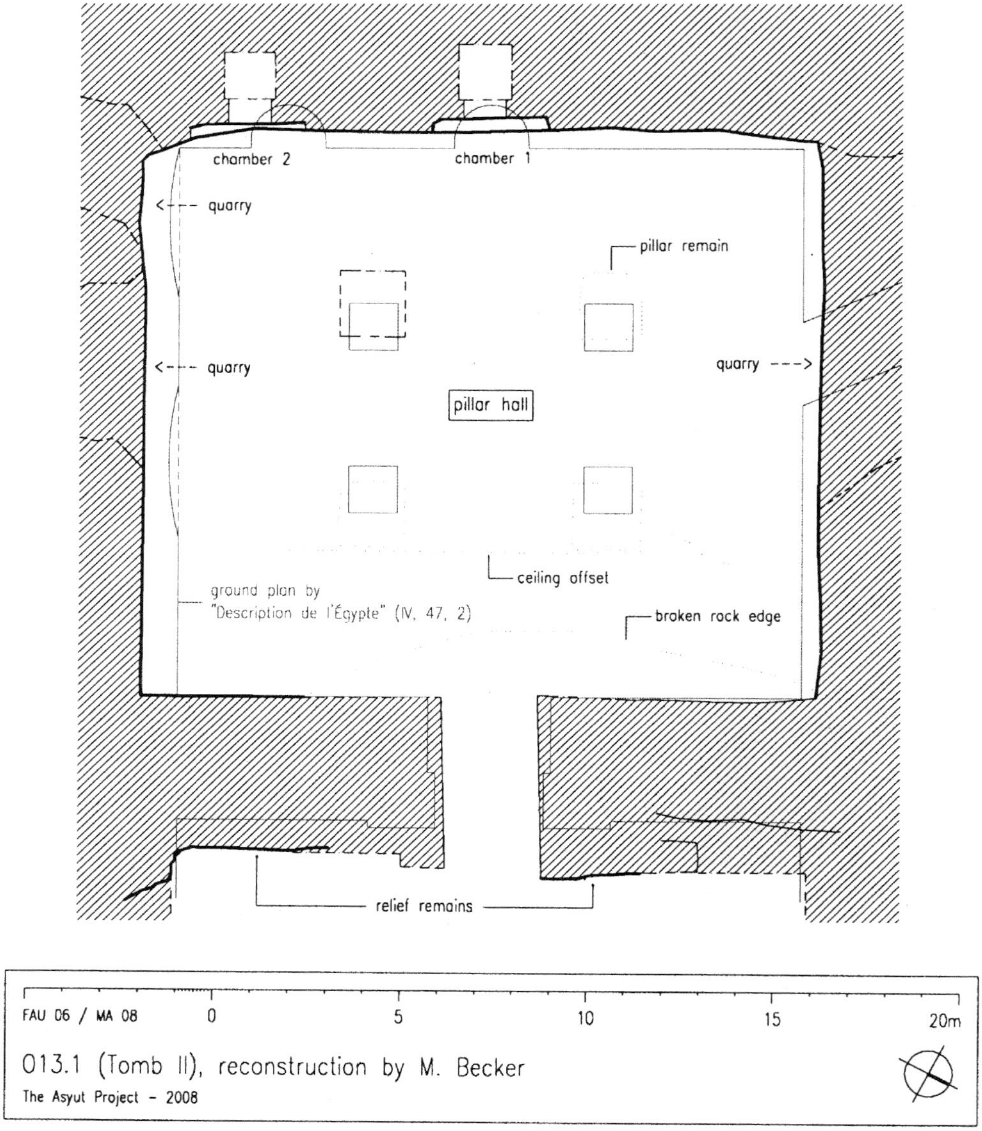

Pl. 30: Tomb O13.1 (Tomb II), ground plan 2008, with reconstruction (© The Asyut Project; Fauerbach/Maschke).

Pl. 31a: Tomb O13.1 (Tomb II), view from north-east (© Kahl 2003).

Pl. 31b: Tomb O13.1 (Tomb II), interior view from north (© Barthel 2010).

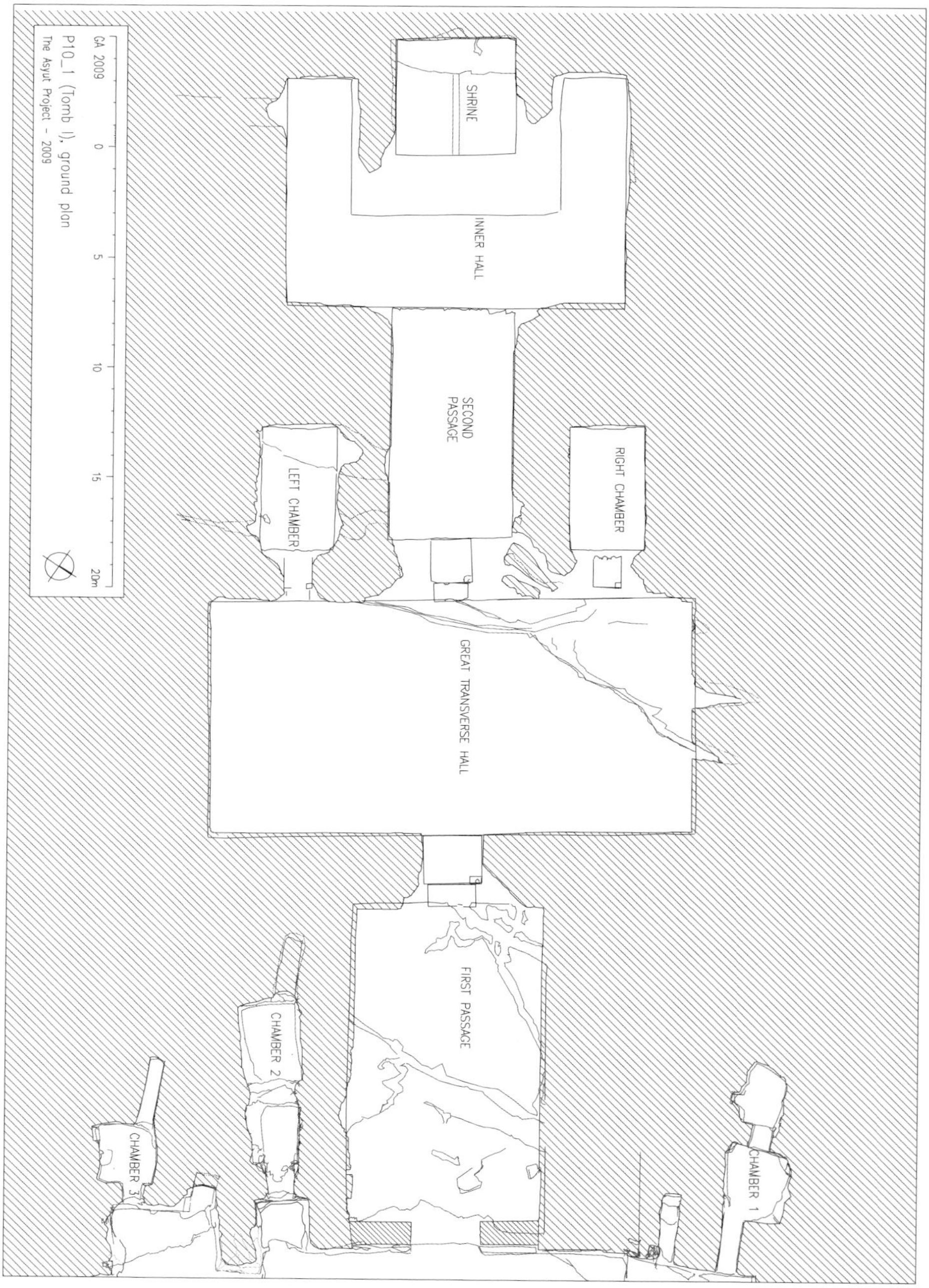

Pl. 32: Tomb P10.1 (Tomb I), ground plan (© The Asyut Project; Garbert 2009).

Pl. 33a: Tomb P10.1 (Tomb I), causeway to entrance (© Kahl 2006).

Pl. 33b: Tomb P10.1 (Tomb I), northern part of today's forecourt (© The Asyut Project).

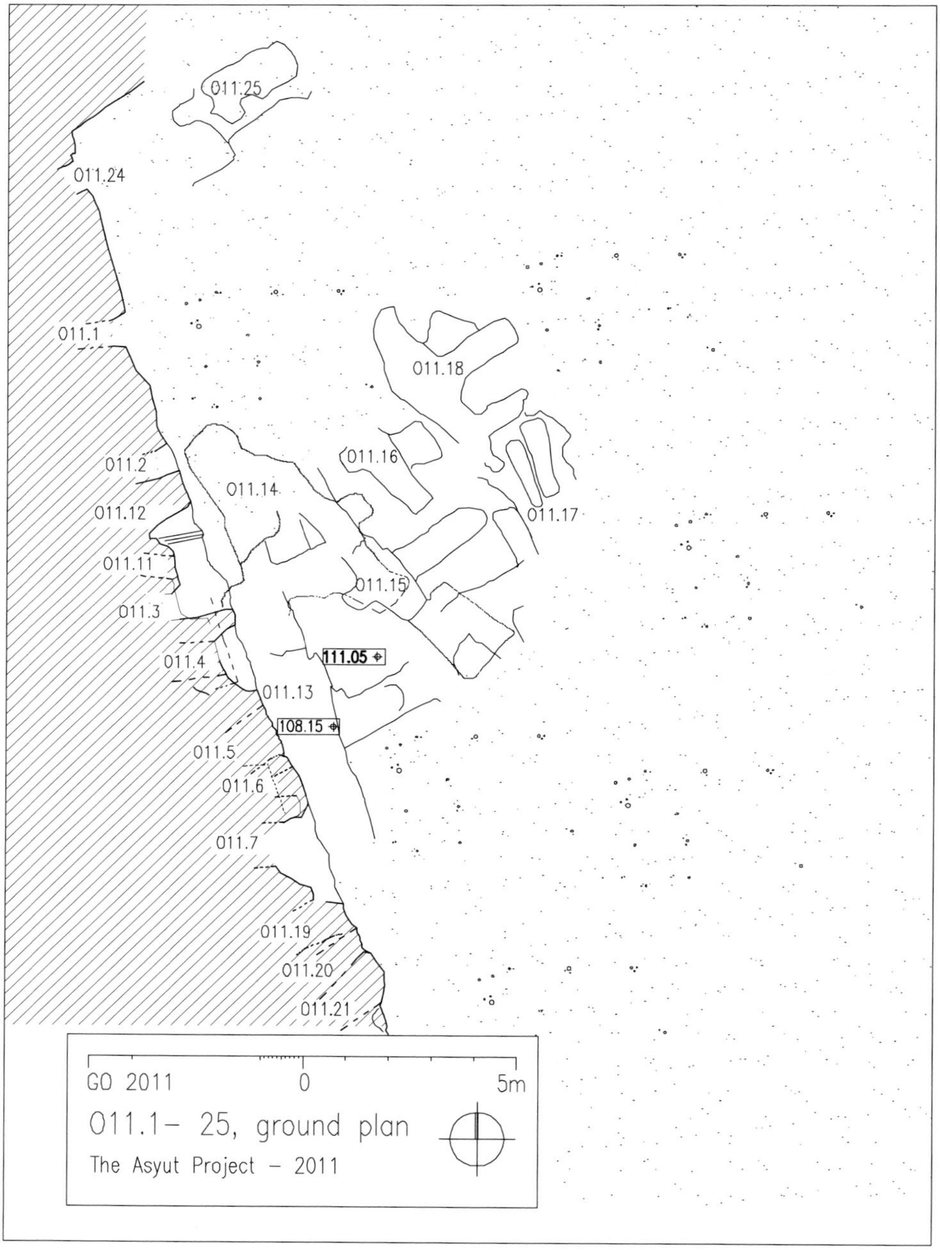

Pl. 34: O11.1-O11.25: Tomb of Dogs area, ground plan
(© The Asyut Project, Goerlich 2011).

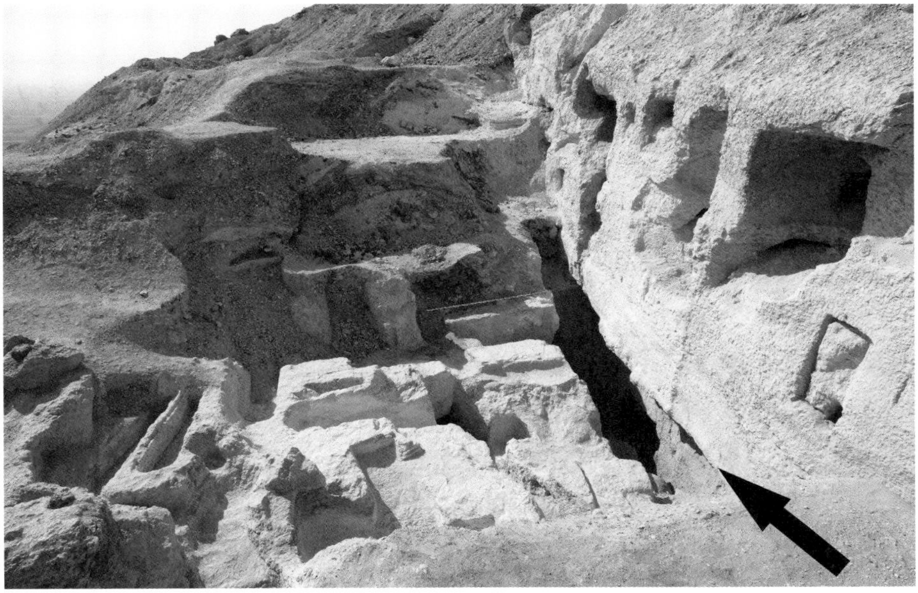

Pl. 35a: Tomb of Dogs area looking south, with entrance situation (© Kahl 2010).

Pl. 35b: O11.13: Tomb of Dogs, interior view (© Kahl 2010).

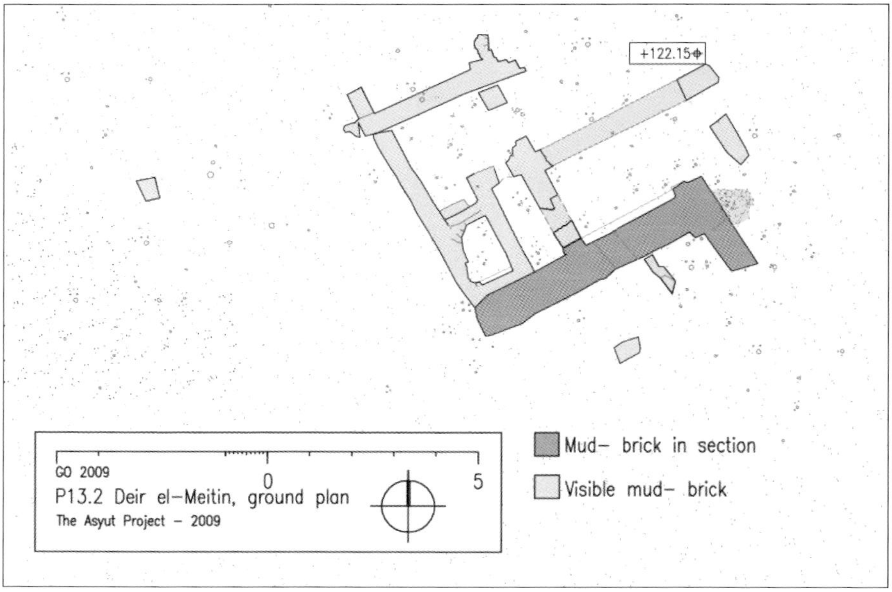

Pl. 36a: Monastery P13.2 (Deir el-Meitin), ground plan (© The Asyut Project; Goerlich 2009).

Pl. 36b: Monastery P13.2 (Deir el-Meitin) (©The Asyut Project; Sanhueza-Pino 2008).

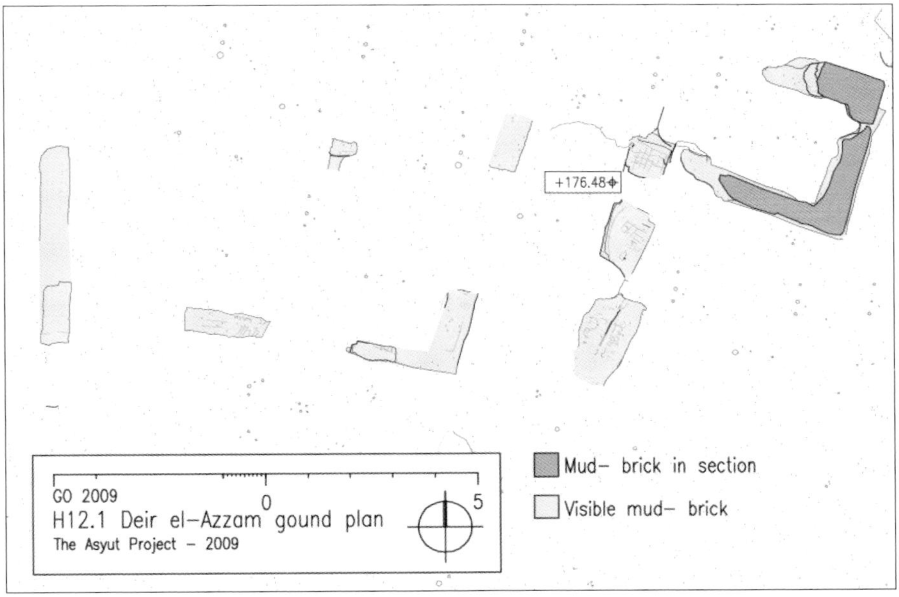

Pl. 37a: Monastery H12.1 (Deir el-Azzam), ground plan (© The Asyut Project; Goerlich 2009).

Pl. 37b: Monastery H12.1 (Deir el-Azzam) (© Kahl 2007).

Pl. 38a: Mausoleum of Sheikh Abu-Tug, view from north (© Barthel 2010).

Pl. 38b: Mausoleum of Sheikh Abu-Tug, interior (© Barthel 2010).